FORUM BOOKS

General Editor Martin E. Marty

New Testament Issues

edited by
Richard Batey

SCM PRESS LTD

LONDON

334 01138 8

© Richard Batey 1970

First British Edition 1970
published by SCM Press Ltd
56 Bloomsbury Street London WC1

Printed in Great Britain by
Richard Clay (The Chaucer Press), Ltd.,
Bungay, Suffolk

CONTENTS

PART THREE: THE WORLD OF PAUL

PART FOUR: THE WORLD OF JOHN

ABBREVIATIONS

AV	Authorized (King James) Version
HTR	*Harvard Theological Review*
HUCA	*Hebrew Union College Annual*
JBL	*Journal of Biblical Literature*
JBR	*Journal of Bible and Religion*
RSV	Revised Standard Version
RV	Revised Version
TWNT	*Theologisches Wörterbuch zum Neuen Testament* (English Translation *Theological Dictionary of the New Testament*)
ZNW	*Zeitschrift für die neutestamentliche Wissenschaft*
ZThK	*Zeitschrift für Theologie und Kirche*

The reader will notice that the authors represented in this volume vary in the conventions that they use to refer to the Bible and to other scholarly works. No effort has been made to impose a consistency which could conceivably be distasteful to an individual author.

FORUM BOOKS

The editors of this series recognize the need for books of a convenient size on religion and related topics. Laymen and clergymen, students and the interested general reader can use *Forum Books* for personal study, or as a basis for group discussion. At a time when religious institutions are experiencing dramatic change, when religious ideas are being debated with new intensity, and when religious elements in culture are being called into question, the books in the series gather together examples of important writings which reproduce both historical and contemporary reflections on these subjects. Each editor has taken pains to provide helpful background comment as a context for the readings, but for the most part the selections speak for themselves with clarity and force.

MARTIN E. MARTY, *General Editor*
Divinity School
University of Chicago

INTRODUCTION

ISSUES raised by the New Testament are interwoven in the fabric of Western history. Philosophers, artists, poets, and men of letters have all probed into the significance of its message. Reforms, counter reformations, persecutions, inquisitions, and wars have resulted from claims made about the authority and teachings of the New Testament. It should not be surprising that the present-day direction taken by New Testament scholars is determined by lively debates concerning the meaning and significance of these writings in their original setting and the present time.

The essays in this volume bring together thoughts of outstanding Jewish, Catholic, and Protestant scholars from both America and Europe. Since contemporary research on the New Testament presupposes the work of centuries of study, it may assist the reader to survey briefly the history of New Testament interpretation from the Reformation to the present. This survey will provide a context in which the following essays may be more readily read.

I. THE NEW TESTAMENT AND THE REFORMERS

The Protestant Reformation in the sixteenth century was predicated on the right of the believer to interpret Scripture. In the medieval Roman Catholic Church the authority of the Bible was not questioned. However, since the meaning of Scripture was frequently obscure, papal interpretation was necessary in order to set forth its true meaning and relate it to the traditions of the Church.

1. *Martin Luther*

Martin Luther's (1483–1546) efforts to reform the Church had at least three significant effects on the place of Scripture. (1) Luther's doctrine of *sola scriptura* emphasized the authority of the Bible over against the authority of the Church and ecclesiastical traditions. (2) He stressed the right of every man of faith to interpret Scripture for himself as the Holy Spirit guided him, denying the exclusive right of interpretation to the pope. (3) Luther also redefined the nature of the revelation contained in the Bible. (*a*) He believed that the Word of God was primarily revealed in the person Jesus. In Jesus the redeeming activity of God had been disclosed. (*b*) This redemptive act of God is the central norm of the message of the New Testament. (*c*) The Bible as a book contains the message of salvation and, therefore, conveys the Word of God to the one receiving it in faith.

Luther did not consider each page of the Bible equally inspired. The authority of various passages was dependent on the witness which it made to Christ as the means of justification by faith. Therefore, he could characterize the epistle to James as a "right strawy epistle". The interpretation of each passage by an individual should be in the light of the Bible's central message of justification by faith alone. In this way Luther was able to reject the papal claim to the exclusive right of interpretation and also to guard himself against the charge of subjectivism.

2. *Jean Calvin*

Jean Calvin (1509–1564), the younger reformer, brought to the Bible humanistic training as well as theological learning. He developed a more careful method of interpretation than did Luther, although similar to Luther's in many respects. Calvin also taught reliance on the testimony of the Holy Spirit confirming in the heart of the believer the truthfulness of the gospel message. The authority of the Scripture, therefore, was not based on an *a priori* acceptance but rather rested on the experience of encountering the Word of God through the biblical text. Calvin identified more closely than did Luther the work of the Spirit with the words of the text and stressed that neither should be separated from the other. Calvin's exegesis was consequently more literal – philological and grammatical – than was that of Luther, who readily interpreted passages in light of his focal theological conviction. Calvin's interpretation was influenced by his own conviction that the message of the Bible was a unity and, therefore, different passages which appeared to be contradictory should be understood in the context of the Bible as a whole. By this means contradictions could be reconciled and the discrepancies resolved. Calvin was more strict than Luther in his use of Scripture; since faith in Christ is attained through the Scripture, Calvin accepted the full inspiration of the literal words.

II. POST-REFORMATION DIRECTIONS

1. *Catholic Reformation*

At the Council of Trent, meeting originally in 1545 and continuing at irregular intervals during the following two decades, the Roman Catholic Church countered the growing Protestant movement by reaffirming its basic doctrines and initiating reforms within the Church. Among the numerous issues confronting the council was the authority of Scripture. (1) Alongside the Scripture the council maintained the authority of unwritten traditions which it held were dictated by Christ or the Holy Spirit to the apostles and preserved within the Church. (2) The canon, or acceptable books of the Bible, adopted was that contained in the Latin Vulgate. This included the fourteen books of the Old Testament Apocrypha which the reformers had rejected because they were not a part of the Hebrew Bible. (3) The right was denied any individual to interpret the Bible, that is to wrest the sacred Scripture to his own senses. The mother Church alone judged the true meaning of the Holy Scripture. Some significant results of the Council of Trent were to clarify and sharpen the issues separating the Roman Catholics and the Reformers on the authority of the Bible, the extent of the canon, and the right of interpretation.

2. *Protestant Orthodoxy*

With the growth of Protestant Orthodoxy late in the sixteenth century the character of the Protestant movement and the interpretation of the New Testament underwent a major transformation. The experience of faith and trust in God's grace, the ground of Reformation theology, gave way to an emphasis on right belief. Faith came to mean assent to correct propositional truths, i.e. orthodox teaching. This period, characterized as Protestant scholasticism because of similarities with medieval scholasticism, was dominated by a rational approach to the Christian faith which spawned numerous controversies concerning the content of sound doctrine. The Bible was no longer considered a witness to revelation, but the very words on its pages were identified with the Word of God. The whole Bible dictated by God to the original writers should be believed. The presence of the Holy Spirit that the early reformers had maintained was operative through the Bible enlightening the interpreter, was believed to be restricted to the original authors of the sacred Scriptures. This shift was influenced in part by threats of subjective interpretations from sectarian groups that claimed direct assess to God through the Spirit apart from the Bible. The norm of biblical interpretation became orthodox theology and the approach was predominantly rational. Miracle stories were accepted as literal records of historical fact which guaranteed the truthfulness of the Bible's teaching.

III. Seventeenth- and Eighteenth-century Rationalism

1. *Seventeenth-century Rationalism*

In the seventeenth century René Descartes (1596–1650) in his *Discourse on Method* prepared the way for the rise of rational philosophy. This philosophical trend initially seemed to offer little difficulty for orthodoxy which also held reason in high esteem. But, faith in an infallible Bible gradually became transformed into faith in human reason. Instead of reason being in the service of theology – rationalizing biblical teaching, interpreting the sacred Scripture, and proving the truthfulness of its message – reason became an independent authority by which the Bible was judged. This new direction in biblical interpretation may be observed in the writing of three representatives of this period – Baruch Spinoza (1632–1677), Thomas Hobbes (1588–1679), and John Locke (1632–1704). The trust in reason did not result in an immediate rejection of biblical teaching, because at first it did not appear incompatible with the rational mind.

2. *The Enlightenment*

With the Enlightenment in the eighteenth century confidence in reason and science continued to grow. Reason became increasingly critical of the authority of Church, Bible, and traditions. Voltaire's (1694–1778) invective against the Church, "Ecrasez l'infame" ("crush the infamous thing"), expressed a growing spirit of the time. Dogmatism, intolerance, and religious wars stimulated the desire for a religion acceptable to any reasonable man. Deism satisfied this desire among many of the intelligentsia. All claims for special revelation were abandoned because God no longer played an active role in the Newtonian mechanical world. The Bible then was read as a record of the religious thought of an ancient time.

IV. NINETEENTH-CENTURY BIBLICAL CRITICISM

1. *Biblical Criticism*

The nineteenth century brought with it the serious application to the Bible of the methods of literary or historical criticism. Literary criticism had developed with the study of classical literature during the Renaissance. Late in the eighteenth century J. S. Semler had done the spadework for later biblical criticism by seeing the implications of various viewpoints and contradictions in the Bible. Biblical criticism investigates the biblical literature at two levels. Lower criticism or textual criticism is concerned to recover as nearly as possible the text of the original documents by a careful comparison of extant manuscripts. By this collation of manuscripts errors in copying and interpolations by pious scribes are deleted. This method of study had been conscientiously applied to the Bible since the Reformation. Higher critics build on the work of textual critics. They are concerned with recovering the historical situation disclosed by the content of the document itself. The authorship, place and date of composition, recipients, purpose, sources – oral or written, canonical or non-canonical – which influenced the writer, and the theological perspective guiding his treatment of his subject fall within the purview of higher criticism.

An example of the results of higher criticism may be seen in the source criticism of the first three gospels, Matthew, Mark, and Luke. These Synoptic Gospels, so named because of the similarity of their presentation, have been painstakingly compared and the consensus reached that Mark was one of the sources used by both Matthew and Luke. Further, the close similarity between Matthew and Luke in sections which are paralleled by Mark has led scholars to postulate another source from which Matthew and Luke drew. This source, called "Q" from the German word for "source" (*Quelle*), contains approximately 250 verses that deal primarily with the teachings of Jesus. To these two sources (Mark and "Q") the authors of Matthew and Luke added their own peculiar material, M and L respectively. This discovery by the process of literary analysis has had profound effect on the interpretation of the Gospels and understanding the life of Jesus. With the acceptance of biblical criticism, the belief in the infallibility of the Bible held by Protestant scholastics was rejected and Scripture was subjected to the same type of literary analysis as classical literature.

2. Life of Jesus Research

The nineteenth century also was characterized by extensive research into the Life of Jesus. The history of this *Leben-Jesu-Forschung* is given excellent treatment in the definitive work of Albert Schweitzer *The Quest of the Historical Jesus* (1906 German, 1901 English). A few examples of the lives of Jesus written in this period will help to set the stage for contemporary debates on the life of Jesus.

(*a*) H. E. G. Paulus (1761–1851) in his *Life of Jesus* published in 1828 attempted to give a consistently rational treatment of his subject. Paulus' thoroughgoing rationalism was due in part to his reaction against the spiritualism that his father had forced on the family. His father believed that his deceased wife communicated with him from the dead; this necromancy was the cause of no little embarrassment to his son. Paulus in his treatment of the gospels reduced the narratives to logical categories. The miracles, that to the Orthodox Protestants had been proofs of divine activity, were explained in naturalistic terms. For example, the virgin birth was the result of a trick played on Mary and the resurrection was due to Jesus' regaining consciousness after being in a deep coma. Paulus did not deny the activity of God in these events but sought to rationalize them by reference to natural causes. He tried to recover the historical or objective facts behind the Gospels and manifested little sympathy for the religious significance of the language of poetry, legend, and myth.

(*b*) Friedrich Schleiermacher (1768–1834), a contemporary of Paulus, made a profound contribution to the biblical research of the nineteenth century, but his importance is more in the area of theology than historical criticism. Schleiermacher's *Life of Jesus* based primarily on the Fourth Gospel was published posthumously in 1864, thirty-two years after he had ceased to lecture on this course. The Jesus which he described was not a historical person but rather the Christ of his theological system. Schleiermacher received his early training among the Moravian pietists and grew to appreciate the subjective quality of religious experience. Religion for Schleiermacher was not founded on belief in an infallible Bible or orthodox doctrine; rather, religion was based on the feeling of absolute dependence – the immediate apprehension of the Infinite by the finite. The Bible, just as any other religious literature, is a record of this experience and therefore subject to human errors and contradictions. The truth of the Christian faith is grounded in the experience of the presence of God in Jesus Christ, i.e. the faith in the incarnation which historical research can neither prove nor destroy. Schleiermacher was also influenced by his association with Georg Wilhelm Friedrich Hegel (1770–1831) and his dualistic distinction between the realm of values, the noumenal, and the objective scientific realm, the phenomenal. The Christ of faith belonged in the former realm and the research of biblical critics in the latter. Perhaps the most significant effect which Schleiermacher had on biblical interpretation was to make biblical criticism acceptable to many churchmen.

(c) David Friedrich Strauss (1808–1874) also fell under the spell of Hegelian philosophy and saw in his own two-volume work *Life of Jesus* (1835) a working out of the Hegelian dialectic of progress by thesis, antithesis, and synthesis. The thesis had been Orthodox Protestantism's literal acceptance of the stories about Jesus with miracles viewed as supernatural history. The antithesis had been provided by the purely rational approach to the Gospels that rejected all accounts not subject to a rational recovery of objective facts. Strauss brought to his study an appreciation of and fondness for the nature of religious myth. Myth is the expression of religious ideas in historical narratives. The myths and legends concerning Jesus in the gospels are true expressions of genuine religious ideas even if they do not correspond to any historical person. The emergence of the Christ idea, which the early Christians fabricated primarily from the messianic hopes of the Old Testament, is the eternal reality of God-manhood. That concept historical research cannot annul. But, this reality has been articulated in the Gospels in mythic form – a form that must be understood as legitimate religious expressions and not reduced to dust-dry rationalism.

(d) With Bruno Bauer (1809–1882) the direction taken by Strauss reached its most radical conclusion. For Bauer the presentation of Jesus in the gospels revealed literary developments rather than historical fact. For example, the comparison of the totally dissimilar birth narratives in Matthew and Luke demonstrated that they were the literary creations of the authors rather than a trustworthy factual account. Further critical comparisons of the Gospels led him to believe that their portrayal of Jesus was the result of the myth creating community of faith quite remote from historical fact. Driven by his skeptical spirit and antagonism toward orthodox theology, Bauer in 1850–1851 published a two-volume work in which he denied that there ever had been a historical Jesus.

(e) Ernst Renan (1823–1892) introduced French Catholicism to the biblical criticism that had been flourishing in Germany. His *Life of Jesus* (1863), written in romantic and picturesque style, was more a work of literature than the result of serious scholarship. But, it was the first life for the Catholic world and touched off such a charge of reaction that the book went through twenty-three editions during Renan's lifetime. His *Life of Jesus* also popularized many of the issues and problems that had previously intrigued only the scholar. The work was conceived while he was on a trip to the Holy Land and dictated to his sister in Syria. Jesus is pictured as the amiable carpenter of Galilee moving against the background of seas of golden grain, sky blue waters, distant mountain peaks, and verdant fields dotted with wild flowers. This sentimental and artificial treatment of the Gospels betrayed Renan as one who thought too much of aesthetics and not enough of ethics.

(f) The nineteenth-century Liberal lives of Jesus reached their classical statement in Adolf Harnack's (1851–1930) book *What is Christianity?*, which appeared in 1900. The Berlin professor rejected the idea of miracles, demons, and an imminent end of the world as expendable aspects of the gospel's content. The truly valid and permanent character of Jesus' life was his ethical teaching. Harnack summarizes the leading features of Jesus' teaching about the Kingdom of God, that is, the rule of God in the heart of the individual, under three headings: (1) the Kingdom of God and its coming; (2) God the Father and the infinite value of the human soul; (3) the higher righteousness and the commandment of love.

3. *The Tübingen School*

Ferdinand Christian Baur (1792–1860) was one of the most important New Testament critics of the nineteenth century and professor of historical theology at the University of Tübingen from 1826 until his death. F. C. Baur, as also his student D. F. Strauss, was greatly impressed with Hegel's dialectical theory of history and imposed this theory on the theology of the New Testament. The thesis, Baur thought, was legalistic Jewish Christianity held by Peter and the leaders of the Jerusalem church; the antithesis was Paul's gospel of justification by faith apart from the Law; the synthesis was achieved at the end of the Apostolic Age in catholic Christianity. So great was F. C. Baur's influence that those subscribing to his scheme of reconstructing the history of the early church have been labeled the "Tübingen school".

V. TWENTIETH-CENTURY NEW TESTAMENT RESEARCH

1. *Albert Schweitzer*

Scarcely had Harnack affirmed the enduring quality of Jesus' ethical teaching before Albert Schweitzer at the age of thirty-three produced a volume which sounded the death-knell of the Liberal lives of Jesus. In *The Quest of the Historical Jesus* (1906) he summarized the research of a century and shocked the world of New Testament scholarship by stripping Jesus of the nineteenth-century garb in which Liberal research had arrayed him. Schweitzer cogently presented his case that Jesus was and remained a stranger to the twentieth century. He breathed the apocalyptic air of the first century and shared with the apocalyptists the confidence that the world would soon reach its end-time. The ethic of Jesus, therefore, was calculated to last only for a brief interim before the end came. It was a radical ethic born from an apocalyptic hope which was never realized. It was an ethic virtually irrelevant for modern man.

2. *Karl Barth: Kerygmatic Interpretation*

The bombshell exploded by Schweitzer among New Testament interpreters was soon followed by the First World War. Harnack's and Liberalism's confidence in progressively realizing the kingdom of God on earth and optimism in the attainment of the brotherhood of all mankind was deeply shaken. The times called for a new theological outlook and a renewed study of the New Testament's message. The Swiss theologian Karl Barth (1886–1968) supplied in part the need by stressing the power and relevance of the biblical message, the kerygma, for a broken world. In *The Epistle to the Romans* (1919) Barth threw down the challenge to listen to the New Testament again in its own idiom. No longer should the New Testament scholar stand over the shoulder of the biblical writers, like a high school teacher correcting his pupil's notebook. Rather the converse should be the case; the scholar must have his own concept of truth informed by the proclamation of the early church. Barth did not reject biblical criticism, but did not wish to let it control the Word of God encountered in the message of the New Testament.

3. *Comparative Religions Approach*

The challenge to take seriously the theology of the New Testament was taken up and a century of biblical criticism was redirected into a more appreciative concern with the development of the faith of the first Christians. Scholars intensified their investigations of the New Testament in the wider context of its non-Christian milieu. The comparative religions approach (*Religionsgeschichte*) had begun in the nineteenth century but achieved widespread acclaim through the work of men like Wilhelm Bousset, *Kyrios Christos* (1916) – recently reprinted – and his contemporary, Richard Reitzenstein. This fruitful research continues through the painstaking comparisons of the New Testament with the Dead Sea Scrolls from the Jewish sect at Qumran and also the newly discovered Coptic Gnostic library from Nag Hammadi in Egypt.

4. *Form Criticism*

Another type of research attempts to gain insights into the period of oral transmission prior to the writing of the gospels. It is concerned with the forms which developed through word-of-mouth preservation of the kerygma; hence its name Form Criticism (*Formgeschichte*). Each individual unit or short paragraph which circulated independently before becoming committed to writing has a history of its own. The form, style, and content yield to the trained observer hints of this history and the influence derived from the situation of the early church, *Sitz im Leben*, where it developed. It may prove an instructive study to attempt to establish streams of tradition (*Traditionsgeschichte*) that developed during the formative pre-literary period of the gospels and also the theological motives influencing their development (*Redaktionstheologie*).

5. *Rudolf Bultmann: Demythologizing*

Though Rudolf Bultmann (1884–   ) was one of the founders of the Form Critical approach to the gospels, his essay on "New Testament and Mythology" published during the Second World War has thrust him to the center of the debates on New Testament interpretation. He has maintained this central position due to the provocative nature of his program of demythologizing (*Entmythologisierung*) the message of the early church – this in spite of his retirement in 1951 from his professorship at the University of Marburg. Bultmann maintains that the meaning of the kerygma is contained in those mythical categories common to the first century concept of a three-storied universe, with heaven above, hell and demonic powers beneath, and man in the middle influenced from both directions. Though myth speaks of the world and transcendent reality in seemingly objective terms, its real purpose is not to present a scientific picture of the world but to set forth man's understanding of himself in the world and those transcendent powers which influence his life. Myth should neither be taken literally nor rejected as superstition; myth should be interpreted existentially, i.e. anthropologically and not cosmologically. The primary consideration should be: "Is the understanding of existence proclaimed in the kerygma true?" Bultmann accepts the analysis of existence spelt out by the distinguished existential philosopher Martin Heidegger (*Being and Time*) and attempts through Heidegger's categories of existence to express the self-understanding of the early Christian community. This method of demythologizing seeks to preserve the existential meaning of the New Testament which must be received in faith while removing the mythic categories unintelligible to modern scientific man. While Bultmann has been critical of the nineteenth-century quest for the historical Jesus, because its rational treatment superimposed a somewhat objective system of truth on the kerygma, he does not deny the validity of the historical–critical approach to the gospels. A small kernel of objective historical data can be recovered, but this kernel is theological husk; objective historical data cannot verify the shortest sentence of the kerygma – "Jesus Christ". Therefore, Bultmann bases his interpretation primarily on the kerygma virtually independent of factual information concerning Jesus' life. It is sufficient merely to affirm the *dass*, the fact that Jesus was a historical person.

6. *Ernst Käsemann: New Question of the Historical Jesus*

The question of the historical Jesus was again raised by Ernst Käsemann, a former student of Bultmann. Though thoroughly oriented in Bultmannian thought, Käsemann in a lecture delivered in 1953 criticized Bultmann for divorcing the kerygma from the necessity for historical interest in Jesus of Nazareth. To separate the Christ of faith presented in the kerygma from the earthly Jesus can only lead to moralism or mysticism and open the way for the revival of the ancient heresy of docetism, which completely denied the humanity of Jesus. The solution to the danger of Bultmann's position cannot be found by simply searching out again the bare facts of the life of Jesus. It must be sought through the recognition that the kerygma is not anonymous but depends on the message of Jesus – a message which has been blended with the preaching of the early church. The concern with the historical Jesus is legitimate and the danger of docetism can be avoided by investigating the blending and tension between the teaching of Jesus and the preaching of the early church. This new direction has been followed through with diverse responses under the somewhat misleading title "the new quest for the historical Jesus". The best example of the fruit of this approach is to be found in Günther Bornkamm's *Jesus of Nazareth* (1956 German, 1960 English).

VI. CONTEMPORARY NEW TESTAMENT ISSUES

The men who have done most to stimulate the study of the New Testament have done so not so much through the answers they have given as through the questions they have asked. The issues, arising both from the contemporary culture as well as from the ancient documents, capture scholars' interest and direct the course of their research. The essays contained in this volume, while selected from men of divergent religious traditions and different nations, reflect some basic and similar concerns about the New Testament and its meaning. It is through recognizing these central issues that the reader will be best prepared.

What is the nature of religious language? Can the words and symbols used to express the religious experience of men in the first century find corresponding words and symbols in an age when man has left his footprints on the moon? More specifically, are the mythic expressions of the early church to be accepted literally, rejected entirely, or restated in terms intelligible to modern man? Is human existence basically the same for all men and the self-understanding of one age relevant for another time and place? Conversely, can man articulate his ultimate concerns or his awareness of God in language other than the symbolic or mythic?

What is the relation between faith and fact? Is factual knowledge of Jesus of Nazareth necessary for believing in the Christ of faith, or can the man of faith be indifferent toward historical research into the life of Jesus? Are the New Testament writings capable of yielding factual information about Jesus? If so, how much? What effect did the faith in the resurrection have on the nature of their writings? Does it matter whether Jesus really said something which has been attributed to him by the gospels?

What was life like in the early church? How did the first Christians gain their identity and derive their self-understanding? What relationship did they feel they sustained with the historical Jesus and the risen Lord? What similarities and tensions existed between various Christians in their theologies? Is there a unity amid this diversity? Is it desirable to seek out this unity or is it better to emphasize the diversity within the New Testament church? What comparisons and contrasts may be drawn between the early church and its cultural milieu? How much do the oral forms which have been preserved in their extant writings reveal about the situation in the pre-literary development? What lost documents may be detected in their writings? What literary dependency may be observed within the books of the New Testament?

There are other important issues dealt with by these scholars but these must suffice to open the way for the reader. These essays have been selected primarily with the non-technical but serious reader in mind. The faint-hearted should be aware that he will here encounter the work of leading New Testament scholars. But, to the strong of heart these essays are an invitation to grapple with the significant New Testament issues for today.

I

THE CHALLENGE OF NEW TESTAMENT THEOLOGY TODAY

Norman Perrin

*Norman Perrin is Associate Professor of New Testament at the
Divinity School of The University of Chicago, receiving the D.Theol.
degree from the University of Göttingen, Germany. His books include*
Redaction Criticism (*1969*), The Challenge of Bultmann (*1968*),
Rediscovering the Teaching of Jesus (*1968*), *and* The Kingdom of
God in the Teaching of Jesus (*1963*). *The present article presents an
appropriate introduction and analysis of the focal concerns pre-
occupying New Testament research during the mid-sixties; it originally
appeared in* Criterion (*Spring, 1965*) *and is reprinted by permission.*

THIS paper is an attempt to present to the theological community of
the University of Chicago Divinity School the challenge of the
current discussion in New Testament theology[1] as I see it. It is
concerned with New Testament *theology* because it is the theological
aspect of New Testament studies, rather than the more technical
aspects, which challenges the theological community at large, and it
is concerned with New Testament theology *as I see it* because I can
only present a challenge to you that I personally have felt, and feel.

The challenge of New Testament theology today is very largely the

challenge of one man: Rudolf Bultmann. It is he who has raised the
questions with which we are wrestling, and his answers to these
questions are the starting points for debates which have begun in
Germany and reverberated around the world. In particular he has
raised the two central questions in New Testament theology, to a
discussion of which New Testament theologians challenge their
colleagues in other theological disciplines: the problem of the
historical Jesus and the question of demythologizing. As the discussion has developed, these have become related to one another as
two different aspects of the same ultimate question, but for the sake
of convenience we will approach them separately.

THE PROBLEM OF THE HISTORICAL JESUS

The starting point here is Martin Kähler's challenge to the liberal
Leben-Jesu-Forschung which flourished in Germany in the nineteenth century and in America in the first half of the twentieth. The
characteristics of this movement are too well known to need elaboration here: the conviction that a life of Jesus could and should be
written on the basis of material recoverable from the synoptic
gospels and freely supplemented by insights derived from other
historical figures by analogy, a life of Jesus which usually turned out
to be a portrait of the author or of the author's ideals; the claim that
the historical Jesus was the concern of faith and not the dogmatic
Christ of the church and the gospels, and so on. Kähler's challenge
to this movement is to be found in his lecture "The so-called historical
Jesus and the historic, biblical Christ", first published in 1892.[2] It
consists of three points:

1. The argument that there is a valid distinction between the
historical Jesus and the Christ of the gospels: it is the distinction
between the historical Jesus and the historic Christ, i.e. between the
Jesus of history and the risen Lord in his fulfillment and his significance for later generations.
2. The claim that the historic Christ is the only object of Christian
faith and not, repeat not, the historical Jesus.
3. The recognition of the fact that the gospels are not and cannot
be sources for a life of Jesus. They do not contain the necessary

material, e.g. they have no account of his personal development, and attempts to supply this material by analogy are inappropriate to the subject and catastrophic in their consequences. The gospels are products of early Christian preaching, the purpose of which is to proclaim the historic biblical Christ, or as Kähler liked to put it, the risen Christ in his fulfillment.

The subsequent discussion in Germany was in large part determined by the catastrophe of the First World War and its aftermath, which changed everything on the German theological scene. It completely destroyed liberalism with its interest in the historical Jesus and left the ground clear for the renaissance of Reformation theology spearheaded by Karl Barth. When, therefore, Bultmann took up the question in the 1920s he was writing in a different world, a world in which the effective death of liberalism and its *Leben-Jesu-Forschung* was recognized, in which a concept of faith quite different from the assumptions of liberal theology was accepted, and a world in which form criticism and existentialism were new and growing influences.

Bultmann's position can be summarized by beginning with the three points he takes over from Kähler and develops further himself:[3]

1. There is a distinction between historical Jesus and historic Christ; it is the distinction between the one who proclaimed the kingdom of God as the imminently to be expected eschatological act of God and the one who is himself proclaimed as the eschatological act of God. This is Bultmann's famous distinction between the Proclaimer and the Proclaimed. It should be noted that it includes three elements, all of which are very important to Bultmann:

(*a*) The distinction between historical Jesus and historic Christ, derived from Martin Kähler.

(*b*) The introduction of a reference to the eschatological act of God, proclaimed by Jesus in terms of the kingdom of God and by the early church in terms of the cross and resurrection of Christ. So far as the message of Jesus is concerned this comes from the "*konsequente Eschatologie*" of Johannes Weiss and Albert Schweitzer which Bultmann has taken up and demythologized; so far as the message of the early church is concerned it is Bultmann's own interpretation, largely derived from an exegesis of Paul and John.

(c) The emphasis upon the fact that in the message of Jesus this eschatological act of God is still future, albeit imminent and even now beginning to break in, whereas in the kerygma of the early church it is already past, although available ever anew as God manifests himself as eschatological event in the kerygma. So Bultmann always maintains that salvation is only a promise in the message of Jesus but a present reality through the kerygma of the church. This again, so far as the message of Jesus is concerned, is derived from "*konsequente Eschatologie*" and it has been furiously debated for the last half century, as I have shown elsewhere.[4]

2. The object of Christian faith is the historic Christ, the Christ of the kerygma and not the historical Jesus. This insight, derived from Kähler and developed by Bultmann, owes much to the revival of Reformation theology in Germany after the First World War to which I have already referred. It is also a point at which it becomes clear that Bultmann is both a Lutheran and an existentialist. As a Lutheran he sees the ultimate context of faith as the Word of God, i.e. for him the kerygma of the early church; and he sees faith as necessarily independent of any factors external to this context. As an existentialist he sees the ultimate moment as a moment of decision in the context of confrontation. Put these things together and we have faith arising by decision as the individual is confronted by the Christ present in the kerygma. Everything else finds its place in reference to this central aspect of Bultmann's theology. This moment of faith is the consummation to which all else is subsidiary and upon which all else is dependent. Appropriately enough the finest discussion of Bultmann's theology to be found in any language, by the German-speaking Roman Catholic Gotthold Hasenhüttl, is entitled simply *Der Glaubensvollzug* – "Faith: the consummation."[5]

Faith arises by decision out of confrontation with the Christ of the kerygma, the Christ present in the kerygma.

The presence of Christ in the kerygma is for Bultmann the meaning of the resurrection. He says that the resurrection is Christ risen in the kerygma and that Easter faith is faith in the Christ present in the kerygma. The presence of Christ in the kerygma is the eschatological act of God and confrontation with this Christ is the eschatological event.

The Christ present in the kerygma is necessarily distinct from the historical Jesus, above all in what we may call his effectiveness. The historical Jesus did not demand faith in himself but at the most in his word, especially in his word of proclamation of the imminence of the kingdom of God. Moreover, he did not offer salvation but only promised it for the future. The kerygma, however, does demand faith in the Christ present in it and it offers salvation now to those who believe on him. Again, the historical Jesus proclaimed the future eschatological event, whereas the kerygmatic Christ is the eschatological event as he confronts the man addressed by the kerygma. The historical Jesus proclaimed a message that was the last word of God before the End; the kerygmatic Christ is the word of God and the End.

Lastly on this point we come to the Reformation principle "by faith alone" as it was restated by Kähler, maintained by Bultmann and as it was generally acceptable in the Germany in which liberal theology was dead and Reformation theology in revival: faith as such is necessarily independent of historical facts, even historical facts about Jesus. In practice today's assured historical facts tend to become tomorrow's abandoned historians' hypotheses, and in principle a faith built upon historical fact would not be faith at all but a work. Further, faith is faith in the eschatological act of God in Jesus Christ, but that God has acted in Jesus Christ is not a fact of past history open to historical verification; this is shown by the way in which the New Testament describes the figure and work of Christ in mythological and not historical terms.

3. The gospels are not and cannot be sources for a life of Jesus; they are products and embodiments of the preaching of the early church. This third point of Kähler's is taken up and developed by Bultmann, to whom indeed it is very important. Form criticism reinforced Kähler's point by showing how very far and in what remarkable ways the gospels are dependent upon the preaching and kerygma of the early church. Bultmann is a leading form critic and he has shown convincingly that the gospel form was created to give literary form to the kerygma of the early church and that the gospel material has been shaped by, and was to a large extent created for, the use made of it in the kerygma.[6]

As a theologian Bultmann has taken seriously the consequences of his work as a New Testament critic. Indeed one of the most attractive things about his work is the ruthless honesty with which, as a theologian, he accepts the consequences of his work as a critical scholar. His critical studies convinced him that the gospels as such are necessarily concerned with only one historical fact: the "thatness" of Jesus and his cross. That there was a Jesus and that he was crucified is the necessary historical presupposition for the kerygma. But beyond this the synoptic gospels themselves seem to be uninterested in the historical element as such, since they freely overlay the historical with the mythical; much of the material they present is an historicization of myth, and they make absolutely no attempt to distinguish the historical as such from the mythical. They are a unique conbination of historical report and kerygmatic christology, the purpose of which is, however, through and through, proclamation and not historical reporting. This is even more clearly true of Paul and John, both of whom require no more than the "that" of the life of Jesus and his crucifixion for their proclamation. So the nature and purpose of the gospels as this is revealed by critical scholarship support Bultmann's understanding of the significance of the historical Jesus for Christian faith.

In addition to the three aspects developed from Kähler there is one further element in Bultmann's thinking that needs to be considered at this point: the significance of the historical Jesus for an individual's self-understanding, or understanding of existence.

Here let me pause to say that the term is self-understanding and not self-consciousness, a point which becomes significant in the post-Bultmannian debate. By self-understanding Bultmann means the understanding which the self comes to concerning the nature of its historical existence. In his *History and Eschatology*, originally written in English,[7] he often uses the phrase in close connection with the untranslatable German word *Weltanschauung*, and we are to understand it as referring to a person looking at the existence which is his and reaching an understanding of it in all its historicity. The actual word in German is *Existenzverständnis*; James M. Robinson has properly urged that we use the English "understanding of existence" to express it.[8] The problem is to grasp that we mean understanding of the self's own existence (what else is possible for an existentialist?), but at the same time we do not mean the subjective *self*-understanding where the emphasis is upon the self rather than the self's existence. The distinction might be expressed as a distinction between the self's understanding of its existence and the conscious decisions, deeds, and words to which this understanding leads and in which it may be expressed.

Bultmann espouses an existentialist understanding of historiography whereby the individual enters into dialogue with the past and is challenged by an understanding of existence (self-understanding) from the past which becomes significant to him in the historicity of his own existence. So, in the case of the historical Jesus, an understanding of existence (self-understanding, not self-consciousness) is revealed in his teaching which challenges us in terms of our understanding of our own existence. Hence Bultmann writes a Jesus book, *Jesus and the Word*, from this perspective.

Three things must, however, be said at this point:

(*a*) As the subject of this existentialist historiography Jesus is not unique. A similar study, with similar consequences in terms of a possible challenge to our understanding of existence, could be carried out in connection with any figure from the past for whom we have sources: Socrates the philosopher, or even Attila the Hun, as well as Jesus the Christ.

(*b*) This historiographical challenge to our self-understanding is not for Bultmann the challenge of faith, not even though the challenge of faith could be, and is, expressed by him in similar existentialistic terminology. He himself stresses that the Jesus of history is not kerygmatic and that his book *Jesus and the Word* is not kerygma,[9] because the essential aspect of the kerygma is that Christ is present in it as eschatological event, and Christ is not so present in existentialist historiographical studies of the historical Jesus. If he were then they would cease to be existentialist historiographical studies and become kerygma.

(*c*) This type of study of Jesus is to be sharply distinguished from the liberal Quest. In the liberal Quest attempts were made to reach and to understand the psychology and personality of Jesus (i.e. his self-consciousness) – an endeavor that was both impossible (no sources) and illegitimate (use of analogy) – whereas in the Bultmann study the concern is with the understanding of existence (self-understanding) revealed in the teaching of Jesus.

This position of Bultmann's on the question of the historical Jesus and his significance for faith has been attacked from three standpoints. One might say: from right, left and center.

The attack from the right has turned on the conviction that the historical nature of the Christian faith, or the meaning of the Incarnation, necessitates more emphasis upon the actual historical events *circa* A.D. 30 than Bultmann will allow. In this camp we find all kinds of strange comrades in arms united in their conviction that the historical events of the ministry of Jesus, in addition to the cross, are necessary to the Christian faith. We can find the whole gamut of possibilities ranging from the extreme conservative, who insists on the factual historicity of everything from the Virgin Birth to the Resurrection, to the old-fashioned liberal for whom only the Jesus reconstructed by historical study can be of significance to faith. Of all the possible names here I will mention only that of my own teacher, the moderately conservative Joachim Jeremias, who deserves to be heard on this point because he has done more than any other single scholar to add to our knowledge of the historical Jesus. He has published a booklet on the question which I have translated and which the Fortress Press has published.[10] In this he argues that the proclamation is not itself revelation, but it leads to revelation. Thus the historical Jesus is the necessary and only presupposition of the kerygma (a play on Bultmann's famous opening sentence of his *Theology of the New Testament*), since only the Son of Man and his word, by which Jeremias means the historical Jesus and his teaching, can give authority to the proclamation. This is a major issue in the contemporary debate: Does Bultmann's view do less than justice to the historical nature of the Christian faith? Does it do violence to the Incarnation? Is the historical Jesus as such the necessary ultimate concern to whom the kerygma points?

The attack from the left has taken the opposite position, namely that Bultmann is inconsistent in his views in that he properly sees Christian faith as a transition from inauthentic to authentic existence (more on this under "Demythologizing" below) and then illogically maintains a necessary link with the historical Jesus in this process. Surely he should recognize the fact that all he is really saying is that there are those for whom this is true. But there are those for whom the transition can be made in other ways. There is, in particular, the existentialist philosopher Karl Jaspers who debated this issue with Bultmann,[11] maintaining that the link with the historical Jesus introduces an objective factor into an existential moment where it has no place. Jaspers' views are actually in one respect reminiscent of liberalism of the Harnack variety in that he sees Jesus as an example, an example of the kind of existential relationship to the transcendent which the philosopher seeks for himself. It must be admitted that Jaspers appears to have the better of his immediate argument with Bultmann, Bultmann's final reply having been a three-sentence letter refusing to commit himself further at that time. But he returned to the discussion later, in a quite different context, and then it became obvious that he regarded himself as committed by the New Testament itself to a neccessary link with the historical Jesus. For he could only reiterate his major point, that the Christian faith as such is committed to the paradoxical assertion that an historical event within time, Jesus and his cross, is the eschatological event, and then support it by exegesis of New Testament texts, especially Paul and John. Thus we come to the unbridgeable gap between the New Testament theologian and the theistic existentialist, and we find that it is an old issue returning in a new form: Is the historical Jesus necessarily anything more than an example that we seek to imitate in his worship of the Father (Harnack) or in his breakthrough to true existential self-understanding (Jaspers)?

The attack from the center is not really an attack at all but a re-raising of the question of the historical Jesus from within the circle of Bultmann's own pupils. It is convenient but somewhat misleading to speak of the "new quest of the historical Jesus"[12] insofar as this implies a homogeneous group moving in a definite direction. The only elements of homogeneity in this group are the fact that they all began by accepting Bultmann's general position and that they all nonetheless agreed that he had not settled the question of the historical Jesus. From that point they take off on their own and any two or three of them in agreement today will almost certainly not be in agreement tomorrow. Also Bultmann's position turns out to be stronger than it first appears; a number of "new questers" have ended up back in the fold with the master, and more will probably do so.

The most important member of this group is, in my view, still the man who first raised the question: Ernst Käsemann, whose 1953 essay is now available in English.[13] Three points from this essay have proven to be of real significance. In the first place, Käsemann sounded a warning about the danger of a position in which there was no real and material continuity between the historical Jesus and the keryg-

B

matic Christ: the danger of falling into docetism or of having faith degenerate into a mere mysticism or moralism. This kind of thing had, of course, been said often enough by opponents of Bultmann from the right, but now it was being said by a member of the "Bultmann school" – a fact which gave it great weight. Even so, in itself, such a warning might not have been regarded as too significant – except by Bultmann's opponents! – had it not been for the fact that Käsemann supported it by observing that the synoptic gospel tradition is in fact more concerned with the historical Jesus than Bultmann had allowed. This was really important because Bultmann's strength had always been that his position is supported by his understanding and exegesis of the New Testament. But his exegesis is really determined by what he learns from Paul and John. Käsemann raised the question of the synoptic tradition, pointing out that the synoptic tradition is not uniform in its own understanding of the relationship between past fact and present faith. The gospels are in agreement that the "once" of Jesus' life history has become the "once for all" of revelation, the *chronos* of Jesus having become the *kairos* of faith. But the relationship between the now of the kerygma and the then of the historical Jesus is a problem for which they find no solution, or rather it is a problem for which they find their several different solutions. So Käsemann is able to claim that the problem of the historical Jesus is a problem which the New Testament itself bequeaths to us, and the complexity of the New Testament tradition on this point must warn us that it is by no means easy to do justice to both the "now" and the "then". Thirdly, Käsemann investigated our actual knowledge of the historical Jesus and showed convincingly that we know enough about his teaching to be able to say that the messiahship explicit in the kerygma is already implicit in the teaching of Jesus. Thus we stumble across a real element of continuity; for all the discontinuity between the historical Jesus and the kerygmatic Christ there is real continuity between the preaching of Jesus and the preaching about him. This seemed to Käsemann to offer real hope as a line of approach to the problem bequeathed to us by the New Testament and not satisfactorily solved by Bultmann.

At this point Käsemann's article ends and it is easy to see why it created the furor that it did; it raises questions and suggests lines of approach without really offering any solution of its own. Certainly it marked the beginning of all kinds of intensive work and interesting developments. The question of the historical Jesus had been raised in its modern form.

Every suggestion that Käsemann made has been intensively followed up. The theology of the synoptic tradition, and of the differing strata in that tradition, has become a major field for investigation. Some of the work done here can only be called brilliant.[14] The question of the parallels between the message of Jesus and the message about him has been explored from every conceivable angle, even from the perspective of Qumran[15] – the Dead Sea Scrolls had to be brought into the act somehow!

It is in this exploration of the parallels between the message of Jesus and the message about him that the most characteristic work of the "post-Bultmannians" has been done. They have attempted, and are attempting, to explore the relevance of the historical Jesus for the Christian faith from this point of departure. Probably the best known examples here are the work of James M. Robinson[16] on the one hand and Ernst Fuchs[17] and Gerhard Ebeling[18] on the other. Robinson accepted the parallels pointed out by Käsemann, Günther Bornkamm and others and added to them some of his own derived from a study of the kingdom of God sayings of Jesus. Then, in addition, he took the existentialist modern historiography which seeks to mediate an encounter with the past at the level of self-understanding and approached the historical Jesus and his message in this way. Now, you see, we have two sets of parallels: between the historical Jesus and the kerygmatic Christ at the level of meaning of the message of and about the one and the other, and the encounters mediated by modern historiography with the one and kerygmatic proclamation with the other. The encounter with the historical Jesus then becomes significant for faith, not because it replaces or makes unnecessary the encounter with the kerygmatic Christ, but because it serves to correct, supplement, and give content to the faith which arises here and only here.

May I say in passing that although I would want to express the matter in a somewhat different, and perhaps less ambitious, manner this seems to me to be a most valid and promising approach to the question.

Fuchs and Ebeling are the post-Bultmannians who have travelled farthest along the road of the "new quest". Indeed they have gone so far that they are no longer to be contained in these categories and must now be reckoned as having achieved a new and distinctive theological position, a position which is generally designated the "New Hermeneutic".[19] We will consider them together since the differences between them are insignificant in the immediate context of our discussion.

They begin by exploring the concept of "faith" as the parallel between the historical Jesus and the kerygmatic Christ. They argue that Jesus himself reached a decision in the context of a confrontation with God in which he decides for the love and forgiveness of God and accepts the consequences of suffering (Fuchs) and by reason of which he may properly be designated the witness of faith (Ebeling). Indeed, it may be said that faith is manifested in Jesus or, as they put it, faith comes to word or becomes a word-event in him (Ebeling), faith comes to language or becomes a language-event in him (Fuchs). Similarly, faith becomes a word or language event for the believer in the kerygma as the believer echoes the decision first made by Jesus (Fuchs). Since faith is the constant, the purpose of exegesis is to find a way in which faith may come to word or language in the New Testament texts for the believer.

I appreciate the fact that this bald summary is only a caricature of this most recent development, but I hope it is sufficient to show that we do indeed have here a new theological position. By pushing the Lutheran emphasis upon faith to an extreme Fuchs and Ebeling have arrived at a point at which faith is practically personified. By taking the Lutheran emphasis upon the Word to a similar extreme they have achieved a concept of faith coming into being or being manifested in "word" or "language", and so have made a new use of the parallel between the message of Jesus and the message about Jesus. By being prepared to think of decisions which Jesus himself made and in which the believer imitates him, they have reached a point at which they are restating a position which Schleiermacher and Harnack would surely have recognized despite the difference in conceptualization.

Bultmann has reacted very sharply against this development which he accuses of psychologizing about Jesus in the manner of an already discredited liberalism.[20] In the light of Bultmann's criticism Ebeling carefully restated his position,[21] making the following points:

1. It is not a case of psychologizing about Jesus but of recognizing that a person is necessarily involved in his word, that the message

necessarily involves the messenger, that a message challenging to faith necessarily involves a witnessing to faith on the part of the messenger.

2. Bultmann himself speaks of the Proclaimer becoming the Proclaimed. In the new terminology Ebeling is using, this is expressed as the witness to faith becoming the ground of faith.

3. The kerygma as such is kerygma by act of God, but it needs historical knowledge for its proper interpretation. Since it identifies kerygmatic Christ and historical Jesus, knowledge of the historical Jesus may properly be used to interpret the kerygma.

It is clear that we are only at the beginning of what promises to be a most lively discussion. I will say something more about the 'new hermeneutic" under the heading "Demythologizing".

THE QUESTION OF DEMYTHOLOGIZING[22]

The question of the historical Jesus and the question of demythologizing are ultimately two different aspects of the same question; since I have discussed the first in such detail as is possible in one paper I can be briefer in connection with the second. Demythologizing is an attempt to break through to what is essential in the New Testament message and then to find a way of expressing it that will be meaningful to modern man. It is based upon two assumptions: (1) that the message of the New Testament is expressed in terms that are meaningless to mid-twentieth century technological man, and (2) that nonetheless the New Testament message is descriptive of a reality that is meaningful to that man, indeed essential to his true being as man.

The New Testament is expressed in terms of a three-story view of the universe, of a world dominated by spirits good and evil: in other words, in terms of myth.[23] Further, the New Testament speaks of what it considers the ultimate realities of life equally in terms of myth: death as a punishment for sin, guilt as expiated by the death of a sinless man, a resurrection which releases a living supernatural power through the sacraments, and so on. But modern man does not think in these terms and therefore the message becomes meaningless to him. This is a false scandalon; offended by the terms in which it is expressed, modern man does not come face to face with the challenge of the message itself. Or, the other possibility, he sacrifices his intellect and understanding in order to accept the mythology and so he comes to a false kind of faith, and he comes to it as less than a whole man.

Facing this challenge Bultmann sought to express the reality of the Christian gospel in terms of a modern existentialist understanding of man. He argued that man is indeed fallen in that as man he has a possibility of authentic existence which in fact he does not achieve. What for him is a possibility in principle is not a possibility in fact. The one thing that can transform the possibility in principle to a possibility in fact is the act of God. True existence, the full realization of man's possibilities as man, is only available in faith; existence in faith is the only authentic existence.

The act of God which makes faith a possibility is the eschatological act of God in the kerygma of the church. This is for Bultmann a combination of the historical cross of Jesus and the mythical resurrection; but as proclaimed by the church it becomes truly historic as God addresses man through it with the offer and challenge of authentic existence.

Three things about Bultmann's theology need to be stressed at this point:[24]

1. For Bultmann the believer and the object of belief belong inextricably together. Revelation and faith, word and hearing, encounter and understanding belong together and must be held together because they live only in their relationship to one another. There can be no meaning for one without the other. Consequently we can never speak of God without at the same time speaking of man. Revelation of God has to be consummated in encounter with man; without this it is not truly revelation. So whenever we speak of revelation or salvation event we must at the same time be speaking of man who is called to hear and to believe.

2. There is in Bultmann's proposal for demythologizing a deliberate existentializing and personalizing of eschatology. The eschaton is God's freeing word addressed to man in the proclamation of the church. This proclamation is the proclamation of the cross and resurrection as the eschatological act of God, and this eschatological act is realized for me as I find myself addressed by God through the proclamation of the church. It is, so to speak, personalized for me as

it becomes God's eschatological act for me in my eschatological moment.

. 3. The key to understanding Bultmann's position is perhaps the idea of paradoxical identity. There is a paradoxical identity of proclamation and saving event as the saving event becomes the saving event for me in the proclamation. There is the paradoxical identity, above all, of eschatology and history in the cross which is at one and the same time eschatological and historical event. This is the absolutely necessary paradox, the one essential historical aspect of the eschatological event being the "thatness" of Christ and his cross.

As with the question of the historical Jesus there is a right, left and center reaction to Bultmann's demythologizing proposal, and the same people tend to be arrayed on the same sides in the discussion of the two questions. On the right there are the many theologians who claim that Bultmann has done less than justice to the objective element in the salvation process, that in his anxiety to speak meaningfully to man he has ceased to speak meaningfully of God. The best known name here is that of Karl Barth,[25] who argues that Bultmann has not done justice to the Christ event as significant in itself apart altogether from man's appropriation of that significance. He has failed to do justice to the fact that Christ was crucified and resurrected in the past and that faith is the appropriation of the benefits of that past historical event. For Bultmann it is as though the crucifixion and resurrection first take place in the attitude and experience of the believer. In his attempt to avoid a one-sided objectivism Bultmann has fallen into an equally one-sided subjectivism.

Of the critics from the left the best known names are probably Karl Jaspers in Europe[26] and Schubert Ogden in America.[27] These claim that Bultmann is wrong in seeing in the Christ event the only possibility for authentic existence. Here he is inconsistent, they claim, in that, having properly rid himself of mythology and having properly interpreted reality existentially, he has illogically retained one element of myth: the cross and resurrection of Jesus as eschatological act of God and as essential to authentic existence. If the possibility of authentic existence is a possibility offered to man by God, and Jaspers and Ogden would both agree that it is, then it must be seen as offered in many ways and not only through the one event. As we have already seen, Jaspers would view Jesus as an example to be imitated. Ogden, on the other hand, claims that the unconditioned gift and demand of God's love is the ground of man's possibility of authentic existence and that this is decisively manifested in Jesus. It is decisively manifested in Jesus but we may not say that it is manifested nowhere else; we must recognize that it is addressed to men in every aspect and event of their lives. Where Jaspers sees Jesus as the example of authentic existence to be imitated, Ogden sees the event of encounter with Jesus as only one possible way of encountering the gift and demand of God's love wherein lies the possibility of authentic existence, even if it is the most important way.

Unfortunately I have no time to discuss possible replies to these reactions from the right and the left but must turn immediately to the center, where we have many developments with again the most far-reaching being the "New Hermeneutic" of Fuchs and Ebeling.[28] They pick up the emphasis upon demythologizing as an existentialist interpretation of the New Testament, but they come to it in light of their emphasis upon faith's concern with the historical Jesus and not exclusively with the kerygma, as is the case with Bultmann. For them, as we noted earlier, faith comes to word or language in Jesus for those who heard his message and for subsequent generations in the church's message about him. This is the continuity of proclamation and the continuity of faith coming to word or language in proclamation for the believer. So far as we are concerned, the primary source in which we hear the word being proclaimed is the New Testament; thus the New Testament is to be interpreted in such a manner as to facilitate the coming of faith to word or language for us through its words. A true existentialist interpretation of the New Testament is one through which faith comes to be word or language event for us, and the hermeneutic by means of which this is to be achieved is the New Hermeneutic.

Here we have a new and interesting development in which hermeneutic has in effect taken the place of kerygma, and in which a concern for an existentialist interpretation of the kerygma has been modified by a concern for the historical Jesus until it has become a concern for an existentialist interpretation of the New Testament – now seen not as a source book for knowledge of the historical Jesus, as in the older liberalism, but as a means whereby that faith which came to word or language in Jesus may come to be word or language event for us. James M. Robinson appropriately suggests that this position be designated "Neo-liberalism".

The New Hermeneutic is an appropriate place at which to call a halt to this all too brief and cursory review of some of the challenging issues of contemporary New Testament theology. For in a sense we have come full circle, from nineteenth century liberalism to the twentieth century neo-liberalisms of the New Hermeneutic.

In a brief conclusion, may I point to some of the issues raised by these developments in New Testament theology and challenging all theologians to discussion. I am deliberately omitting the detailed issues which concern only New Testament theologians as such.

In the first place we have the challenges that can be summed up under the rubric "Faith and History". What is the nature of faith and its relation to history, of history and its relation to faith? There can be no doubt that these are vital questions. It is very important that they should be taken up by theology as a whole, and that they should be taken up by theologians who are equipped to discuss them with emphases other than the Lutheran approach to faith and the existentialist approach to history which tend to be dominant among contemporary New Testament theologians. Personally I am inclined to think that these particular emphases will turn out to be dominant after all, not because of the historical accident that the leading New Testament theologians today tend to be Lutherans and existentialists, but because they will prove to be the categories most appropriate to the problems – and I say that as a liberal Baptist, but perhaps the discussion will prove me wrong!

Secondly, we have the problems that can be included in the category "Man and God", if you will forgive the obvious naïveté of such a rubric. How should a man think of himself and his existence? How can he think of God? How may he think of Christ in relation to human existence on the one hand and God on the other? These are, of course, perennial theological problems, but they surely have new force and vigor as a consequence of the intensive discussion going on in New Testament theology and the variety of positions there represented. It is in connection with this group of questions that I believe the American theological situation will prove to have a particular contribution to make, for in American theology we have a much more radical scepticism about what my colleague Mr. Gilkey calls "the possibility of God language" than is the case in the pre-

dominantly German-oriented New Testament theology, and we also
have over here a concern for the realities of human existence which
demand expression in categories other than the existentialist. Both
of these factors need to find expression in the discussion. Lastly we
have the group of questions which may be summed up under the
heading "The Word of God". We have seen how New Testament
theology has been exploring the manifold issues raised here: the word
of God as medium of revelation or the context of the salvation event;
the kerygma of the church as the word of God; the word of Jesus and
the word about Jesus; and, most recently, faith as word or language
event and the hermeneutical task as the central theological task. It
is, I think, clear that one thing urgently needed is further discussion
of these issues, perhaps particularly those raised by the "new
hermeneutic", on the basis of an ontology and an epistemology other
than the existentialist. An assault on the "new hermeneutic" from
the standpoint of a linguistic analytical philosophy would be a real
contribution to our discussion. Another thing urgently needed at this
point is a discussion of New Testament hermeneutics in general from
the standpoint of the findings of general literary criticism. It is, after
all, not only in the field of New Testament studies that we face the
problem of myth and the question of a present understanding of
a text from the distant past; general literary critics have been wrestling
with these problems every bit as intensively as have Bultmann and
his followers and it is high time that their findings came to word in
our discussion. This is perhaps particularly a task for the English
language discussion for the simple reason that literary criticism flour-
ishes much more strongly today in Britain and America than it does
in Germany. Here in Chicago we might feel a particular responsibility
for this aspect of the discussion since we have an emphasis upon
theology and literature in our Divinity School and a number of most
eminent literary critics working and teaching in the Humanities
division of the University.

NOTES

1. Throughout the paper the expression "New Testament theology" will be
used as are such expressions as "systematic theology" or "constructive theology"
to denote an aspect of theological study and discussion.

2. Martin Kähler, *The So-Called Historical Jesus and the Historic, Biblical Christ*, ed. and trans. by Carl E. Braaten (Philadelphia, Fortress Press, 1964).

3. Rudolf Bultmann, *Jesus and the Word* (New York, Scribners, 1958); *Theology of the New Testament*, Vol. I (New York, Scribners, 1951); *Primitive Christianity* (New York, Meridian Books, 1956); "The Primitive Christian Kerygma and the Historical Jesus", *The Historical Jesus and the Kerygmatic Christ*, ed. by Carl E. Braaten and Roy A. Harrisville (New York, Abingdon, 1964).

4. Norman Perrin, *The Kingdom of God in the Teaching of Jesus* (Philadelphia, Westminster Press, 1963).

5. Gotthold Hasenhüttl, *Der Glaubensvollzug* (Essen, Ludgerus-Verlag Hubert Wingen KG, 1963).

6. Rudolf Bultmann, *History of the Synoptic Tradition*, trans. by John Marsh (New York, Harper, 1963); *Form Criticism*, trans. by F. C. Grant (New York, Harper, 1962).

7. Rudolf Bultmann, *History and Eschatology*, Gifford Lectures, 1955 (New York, Harper, 1957) (American edition sometimes titled *The Presence of Eternity*).

8. James M. Robinson, "The New Hermeneutic at Work", *Interpretation*, Vol. 18 (1964), pp. 347–359, esp. p. 358.

9. Rudolf Bultmann, *Kerygma and Myth*, ed. by H. W. Bartsch (New York, Harper, 1961), p. 117.

10. Joachim Jeremias, *The Problem of the Historical Jesus* (Philadelphia, Fortress Press, 1964).

11. Karl Jaspers and Rudolf Bultmann, *Myth and Christianity* (New York, Noonday Press, 1958). Bultmann's later rejoinder is his essay, "Das Befremdliche des christlichen Glaubens", *Zeitschrift für Theologie und Kirche*, Vol. 55 (1958), pp. 185–200.

12. The phrase was coined by James M. Robinson as the title of a book in which he presented and interpreted the discussion to English language readers: *A New Quest of the Historical Jesus*, "Studies in Biblical Theology", No. 25 (Naperville, Allenson, 1959).

13. Ernst Käsemann, "The Problem of the Historical Jesus", *Essays on New Testament Themes*, "Studies in Biblical Theology", No. 41 (Naperville, Allenson, 1964).

14. Particularly interesting here is the work of Günther Bornkamm and his pupils in Heidelberg: G. Bornkamm, G. Barth, H. J. Held, *Tradition and Interpretation in Matthew* (Philadelphia, Westminster, 1963); H. E. Tödt, *The Son of Man in the Synoptic Tradition* (London, SCM Press, 1965); F. Hahn, *Christologische Hoheitstitel* (Göttingen, Vandenhoeck and Ruprecht, 1963). Käsemann himself has done significant work here also, particularly "Sätze Heiligen Rechtes im Neuen Testament", *New Testament Studies*, Vol. 1 (1954–1955), pp. 248–260; "Die Anfänge christlicher Theologie", *Zeitschrift für Theologie und Kirche*, Vol. 57 (1960), pp. 162–185; "Zum Thema der urchristlichen Apokalyptic", *ZThK*, Vol. 59 (1962), pp. 257–284.

15. Herbert Braun, "The Significance of Qumran for the Problem of the Historical Jesus", *The Historical Jesus and the Kerygmatic Christ*, ed. by Carl E. Braaten and Roy A. Harrisville (New York, Abingdon, 1964), pp. 69–78.

16. James M. Robinson, *A New Quest of the Historical Jesus*, "Studies in Biblical Theology", No. 25 (Naperville, Allenson, 1959); "The Formal Structure of Jesus' Message", *Current Issues in New Testament Interpretation*, ed. by W. Klasson and G. F. Snyder (New York, Harper, 1962), pp. 91–110; "The Recent Debate on the New Quest", *Journal of Bible and Religion*, Vol. 30 (1962), pp. 198–208.

17. Ernst Fuchs, *Studies of the Historical Jesus*, "Studies in Biblical Theology", No. 42 (Naperville, Allenson, 1964).

18. Gerhard Ebeling, *The Nature of Faith*, trans. by Ronald G. Smith (London, Collins, 1961); *Word and Faith*, trans. by James W. Leitch (London, SCM Press, 1963); *Theologie und Verkündigung* (Tübingen, J. C. B. Mohr, 1962).

19. *The New Hermeneutic*, "New Frontiers in Theology", Vol. 2, ed. by John Cobb and James M. Robinson (New York, Harper, 1964).

20. In his essay "The Primitive Christian Kerygma and the Historical Jesus", *The Historical Jesus and the Kerygmatic Christ*, ed. by C. E. Braaten and R. A. Harrisville (New York, Abingdon, 1964), esp. p. 33.

21. In his *Theologie und Verkündigung*, pp. 19–82; 119–125.

22. A brief selection from the more important literature on this question is as follows: *Kerygma and Myth*, ed. by H. W. Bartsch (New York, Harper, 1961); *Kerygma and Myth*, Vol. 2, ed. by H. W. Bartsch (London, SPCK, 1962); *Kerygma and History*, ed. by C. E. Braaten and R. A. Harrisville (New York, Abingdon, 1962); G. Bornkamm, "Die Theologie Rudolf Bultmanns in der neueren Diskussion", *Theologische Rundschau*, Vol. 29 (1963–1964), pp. 33–141.

23. We are now following Bultmann's original essay, "New Testament and Mythology", *Kerygma and Myth*, ed. by H. W. Bartsch (New York, Harper, 1961), pp. 1–44.

24. Cf. G. Bornkamm, "Die Theologie Rudolf Bultmanns . . .", *Theologische Rundschau*, Vol. 29, esp. pp. 124–141.

25. Karl Barth, "Rudolf Bultmann – An Attempt to Understand Him", *Kerygma and Myth*, Vol. 2, ed. by H. W. Bartsch (London, SPCK, 1962), pp. 83–132.

26. Karl Jaspers and R. Bultmann, *Myth and Christianity* (New York, Noonday Press, 1958). Cf. also H. W. Bartsch, "Bultmann and Jaspers", in *Kerygma and Myth*, Vol. 2, ed. by H. W. Bartsch (London, SPCK, 1962), pp. 195–215.

27. Schubert Ogden, *Christ Without Myth* (New York, Jarper, 1961).

28. The works of Fuchs, n. 17 above, Ebeling, n. 18, Cobb and Robinson (eds.) n. 19; also the reviews by James M. Robinson, "Neo-Liberalism", *Interpretation*, Vol. 15 (1961), pp. 484–491; "The New Hermeneutic at Work", *Interpretation*, Vol. 18 (1964), pp. 347–359.

2

ON THE PROBLEM OF
DEMYTHOLOGIZING

Rudolf Bultmann

Rudolf Bultmann is Professor Emeritus of Theology at the University of Marburg. Born on August 8, 1884, and retiring from his professorship in 1951, Bultmann has remained at the center of debates on interpreting the New Testament, due largely to his program of demythologizing the New Testament. Some of Bultmann's principal publications available in English are: The History of the Synoptic Tradition (*7th edn., 1963*), Theology of the New Testament, *I and II* (*1951, 1955*), Jesus and the Word (*2nd edn., 1958*), Jesus Christ and Mythology (*1958*). *The essay reprinted here by permission appeared in English in* The Journal of Religion (*April 1962*); *it was originally published in* Il Problema della Demitizzazione (*1961*).

I

By "DEMYTHOLOGIZING" I understand a hermeneutical procedure that inquires about the reality referred to by mythological statements or texts. This presupposes that myth indeed speaks of a reality, although in an inadequate way. It also presupposes a specific understanding of reality.

"Reality" can be understood in a double sense. We commonly

understand it to refer to the reality of the world as represented in objectifying vision. This is the reality in which man finds himself, in which he orients himself by standing over against it, and with whose continuum of happenings he reckons in order to master it and thereby to secure his life. This way of looking at reality is fully developed in natural science and in the technology it makes possible.

As such, it of necessity demythologizes because it excludes the working of supernatural powers about which myth speaks – whether it be the working of powers that initiate and sustain natural processes or the working of powers that interrupt such processes. A thorough-going natural science has no need of the "God hypothesis" (Laplace) because it understands the forces that govern natural processes to be immanent within them. Likewise, it eliminates the idea of miracle as an event that interrupts the causal continuum of the world process.

As with all the other phenomena in the world, man can also subject himself to objectifying vision insofar as he appears within the world. He then stands over against himself and makes himself an object. In so doing, he reduces his true and distinctive reality to the reality of the world. This happens, for example, in an "explanatory" psychology (as distinct from an "understanding" psychology in Dilthey's sense) and in sociology.

This way of looking at reality can also become determinative in historical science and in fact does so in a positivistic historicism. Here the historian stands over against history as an object that he observes as subject and thus places himself as a spectator outside of the historical process as it takes its course in time.

Today, we have more and more come to recognize that there is no such stance because the act of perceiving a historical process is itself a historical act. The distance required for a neutral observation of an object is impossible. The apparently objective picture of historical processes is always conditioned by the individuality of the observer, who is himself historical and can never be a spectator who stands outside of historical time.

I cannot go into the question here of whether there is an analogous understanding of the subject–object relation also in modern natural science, which has recognized that what is observed is already formed or in some way modified by the observer. The exact extent of this analogy between modern historical and natural science would require special investigation. The point here is simply that, in the modern understanding of history, reality is understood in a different way than in the way of objectifying vision, namely, as the reality of man whose existence is historical.

Distinctively human being is different in principle from the being of nature as perceived through objectifying vision. We are accustomed today to refer to specifically human being as "existence", by which we mean not mere actuality in the sense in which plants and animals also "exist" but the mode of being that is distinctively human.

Unlike the beings of nature, man is not placed in the causal continuum of natural processes but must himself take over his being and is responsible for it. This means that human life is history; through concrete decisions in the present it leads into a future in which man chooses himself. These decisions are made in accordance with the way he understands his existence or in keeping with what he sees to be the fulfilment of his life.

History is the field of human decisions. It is understood when it is seen as such, that is, when one recognizes that what is at work in it is the possibilities of human self-understanding – possibilities that are also the possibilities of self-understanding in the present and that can only be perceived in unity with present self-understanding. I refer to this kind of interpretation of history as "existentialist interpretation", because, motivated by the existential question of the interpreter, it inquires as to the understanding of existence concretely at work in a given history.

Since all men in fact come out of a past in which possibilities of self-understanding are already determinative, that is, are offered or called in question, decision is also always a decision with respect to the past – indeed, finally with respect to a man's own particular past and his future.

To be sure, this decision does not need to be made consciously and, in most cases, it is unconscious. In fact, it can even appear as a failure to decide, which is actually an unconscious decision for the past, a fallenness into bondage to the past. This means, however, that man can exist either authentically or inauthentically; and just this possibilitity of being authentic or inauthentic belongs to historicity, or to the specifically human reality.

If authentic human being is an existence in which man takes over himself and is responsible for himself, then authentic existence includes openness for the future or the freedom that becomes an event in the concrete present. Hence man's reality as historical is never complete or finished like that of the animal, which is always what is wholly and completely. His reality, rather, is his history; that is, it constantly stands before him so that one can say the reality in which he stands is a being of the future.

In the history of mankind, it becomes clear that the historical meaning of an event can be understood only from the standpoint of its future. The future belongs to the very essence of the event. Therefore, only from the vantage point of the end of history is the meaning of a historical occurrence finally understandable. Since, however, such a vantage point is not possible for man, a philosophy that endeavors to understand the meaning of history is likewise impossible. One may speak of the meaning of history only in the sense of the meaning of the moment, which is meaningful as the moment of decision.

All decisions, however, are made in concrete situations, and even the decisionless existence of an inauthentic human life always takes place in such situations. If, then, the science of history seeks to make clear the possibilities of self-understanding that appear in human decisions, it also has to present the concrete situations of past history. These situations are accessible, however, only to an objectifying view of the past. Although such a view can hardly grasp the historical meaning of an act or an event, it nevertheless can and must seek to know the simple facts of acts and events and, in *this* sense, to establish "how it really happened". Furthermore, although the continuum of human actions is not determined by causal necessity, it still is connected by the sequence of cause and effect. No event, no act of the will, no decision is without a cause. Precisely a free decision is based on reasons if it is not to be blind caprice. Hence it is possible at any time to look back and to understand the course of history as a closed causal continuum, and, in fact, this is the way an objectifying view of history has to regard it.

The question now is whether an existentialist interpretation of history and an objectifying presentation of it are mutually contradictory, or, in other terms, whether the reality seen in the one case stands in contradiction with that seen in the other, so that one must speak of two realms of reality or even of a double truth. This clearly would be a wrong inference; for there is in fact only *one* reality and only *one* truth about the same phenomenon.

The *one* reality, however, can be seen under a double aspect in accordance with man's double possibility of authentic or inauthentic existence. In inauthentic existence man understands himself in terms of the world that stands at his disposal, whereas in authentic existence he understands himself in terms of the future of which he cannot dispose. Correspondingly, he can regard the history of the past in an objectifying way, or else as personal address, insofar as in it he perceives the possibilities of human existence and is summoned to responsible choice.

The relation of these two modes of self-understanding must be characterized as "dialectical", insofar as in actual fact the one is never given without the other. The man whose authentic life is realized in his decisions is also a being with a body. Responsible decisions take place only in concrete situations in which one's bodily life is also at stake. The decision in which a man chooses himself, his authentic existence, is always simultaneously the decision for a possibility of life in the body. Likewise, the responsibility for one's self is always simultaneously a responsibility for the world and its history. For the sake of his responsibility, man has need of an objectifying view of the world in which he is placed, which is the "work-world" that stands at his disposal. But precisely herein is also the temptation of regarding this "work-world" as the true reality, of losing his authentic existence and attempting to secure his life by disposing of what stands at his disposal.

Therefore, it is quite clear that an existentialist interpretation of history has need of an objectifying view of the historical past. Although such a view is quite unable to grasp the historical meaning of an act or an event, existentialist interpretation is equally unable to dispense with establishing facts as reliably as it possibly can. Nietzsche's anti-positivistic statement that there are no facts, but only interpretations, is open to misunderstanding. If one means by "fact" a historical fact in the full sense, inclusive of its meaning and its significance in the continuum of historical occurrences, then the statement is correct. In this sense, a fact is always an "interpretation", a picture drawn by the historian who is personally involved in it. But an interpretation clearly is not a creature of fantasy but the means whereby something is interpreted; and this something to be interpreted is the "facts" that (within whatever limits) are accessible to the historian's objectifying view.

II

If this may be assumed as valid, then it is possible to solve the problem of demythologizing with reference to the science of history. Does history, like natural science, of necessity demythologize? Yes and no.

History necessarily demythologizes to the extent that it views the historical process in an objectifying way and thus understands it as a closed continuum of effects. The historian cannot proceed otherwise if he wants to achieve reliable knowledge of some particular fact – for example, if he wants to determine whether some traditional account is really a valid testimony to a certain fact of the past. Thus he cannot allow that the continuum of historical happenings is rent by the interference of supernatural powers; nor can he acknowledge any miracles in the sense of events whose causes do not lie within history itself. Unlike the biblical writings, historical science cannot speak of an act of God that intervenes in the historical process. The only thing it can perceive as a historical phenomenon is faith in God's act, but not God himself. Whether such faith corresponds with reality it cannot know, since a reality that lies beyond the reality visible to an objectifying view is for it invisible. For it, all talk must be regarded as mythology that claims to speak of the activity of transcendent powers as something that can be observed and established in the world accessible to an objectifying view and also used, say, as an argument to support certain truths. Likewise mythological for it is all talk of transcendent spheres, such as heaven and hell, that are spatially tacked on to the visible world.

Even so, there is a difference in principle from the position of natural science in relation to such mythological speaking: Whereas natural science eliminates myth, historical science has to interpret it. The historian must raise the question of the meaning of mythology, which lies before him as a historical phenomenon.

This question as to the meaning of mythological speaking may be answered quite simply. Myth intends to speak of a reality that lies beyond what can be objectified, observed, and controlled, and that is of decisive significance for human existence. It is the reality that means for man salvation or damnation, grace or wrath, and that demands of him respect and obedience.

I can disregard here the etiological myths that seek to explain striking natural phenomena or appearances. They are significant in the present context only insofar as they permit us to understand mythological thinking as something that arises out of astonishment, fright, and questioning and that thinks in terms of the connection of cause and effect. Such thinking can be characterized as a form of primitive science, and many researchers in fact seek to reduce it to just such terms.

This primitive scientific and thus also objectifying thinking is peculiar to all mythology. But there is also a difference in principle. It must be asked, namely, whether or to what extent the intention of myth is simply to speak of the world so as to explain it or whether it intends to speak of the reality of man himself, and thus of his existence. In the present context, myth is involved to the extent that what is expressed in it is a certain understanding of human existence.

But what understanding of existence? It is an understanding in which man finds himself in a world filled with riddles and mysteries and in which he experiences a destiny likewise enigmatic and mysterious. He is compelled to realize that he is not lord of his life, and he becomes aware that the world and human life have their ground and limit in a transcendent power (or powers) that lie beyond whatever he can calculate and control.

Mythological thinking, however, naïvely objectifies the beyond as though it were something within the world. Against its own real intention it represents the transcendent as distant in space and as only quantitatively superior in its power to man's own capacities. By contrast, demythologizing seeks to give full weight to myth's real intention to speak of man's authentic reality.

But is there a limit to demythologizing? It is often said that neither religion nor the Christian faith could dispense with mythological speaking. But why not? Such speaking does indeed provide images and symbols for religious poetry, and for cultic and liturgical language, in which pious devotion may sense a certain amount of meaning. But the decisive thing is that these images and symbols conceal a meaning which it is the task of philosophical and theological reflection to make clear. Furthermore, this meaning cannot be re-expressed in mythological language, for if it is, then the meaning of this language also must be interpreted – and so on *ad infinitum*.

The claim that myth is indispensable, however, implies that there are myths that cannot be existentially interpreted. And this means that, in certain cases at least, it is necessary to speak of the transcendent, or of deity, in objectifying terms, since mythology is an objectifying way of speaking.

Can this be correct? Everything turns on the question of whether speaking about God's action is of necessity mythological or whether it, too, can and must be interpreted existentially.

Since God is not an objectively demonstrable fact within the world, his action can be spoken of only if at the same time we speak of our own existence which is affected by his action. One may call this way of speaking of God's action "analogical". In this way, one may express that being affected by God has its origin solely in God himself and that man is merely a passive recipient.

But, even so, it must be maintained that being affected by God's action can be spoken of only as an existential event that cannot be objectively established or proved.

Every such existential encounter, of course, takes place in a concrete situation, and it is easy or, so to say, natural for the one encountered by God to refer this situation also to God's action. This is perfectly legitimate, provided only that the origin in God's will is not confused with the causality accessible to an objectifying view. Here to speak of a "miracle" – although not, of course, as an event that interrupts the causal continuum of the world process – is fully justified.

Just as faith speaks of miracle, so also must it speak of God's action in the sense of his rule as Creator and Lord in nature and history. For if man knows himself in his existence to be called into life and supported by God's almighty power, he also knows that the nature and history within which his life takes place are ruled by God's action. But this knowledge can only be expressed as a confession and never as a general truth, like a theory in natural science or in the philosophy of history. Otherwise God's action is objectified into a process within the world. The statement that God is Creator and Lord has its legitimate basis only in man's existential self-understanding.

This means, however, that the statement contains a "paradox". It asserts the paradoxical identity of an occurrence within the world with the action of the God who stands beyond the world. Indeed, faith asserts that it sees an act of God in an event or in processes that are at the same time, for an objectifying view, demonstrable processes within the continuum of natural and historical occurrences. Thus, for faith, the action of God is a miracle in which the natural continuum of worldly occurrences is, as it were, transcended.

The peculiar thing about the Christian faith, however, is that it sees in a certain historical event, which, as such, is objectively demonstrable, an utterly unique act of God. This is the appearance of Jesus Christ, who is seen to be the revelation of God that calls every man to faith. The paradox of this claim is expressed most sharply in the Johannine statement that "the Word became flesh".

Clearly, this paradox is of a different kind from the other one that claims that God's action is everywhere and at all times indirectly identical with the world process. The Christ-occurrence is the eschatological occurrence through which God has put an end to the world and its history. Therefore, this paradox is the claim that a historical event is at the same time the eschatological event.

The question now, however, is whether this event can be understood as an event that takes place in one's own unique existence or whether, in relation to the person summoned to faith, it remains an object over against a subject in the manner of worldly reality. In the latter case, it would be an event of the past that is re-presented through the objectifying view of the historian, or, in other words, is "remembered". If, on the other hand, it is to be understood as an event that affects me in my own unique existence, it has to be or become present in some other sense.

But just this is involved in its meaning as an eschatological event. Precisely as such, it cannot be or become an event of the past, since historical events can never have the meaning of $\dot{\epsilon}\phi'\ddot{\alpha}\pi\alpha\xi$ (once for all). Yet just this belongs to the nature of the Christ-event as an eschatological event.

Therefore, unlike other historical events, it cannot be made present through "remembrance". Rather, it becomes present in the proclamation (or the kerygma), which has its origin in the event itself and without which the event is not at all what it is. This means that the proclamation itself is eschatological occurrence. In it, as personal address, the event of Jesus Christ becomes concretely present – present as an event that affects me in my own unique existence.

The bearer of the proclamation is the church, and here the paradox is repeated. For under one aspect the church is a phenomenon that can be disposed of by an objectifying view, while in its real nature it is an eschatological phenomenon – or better, an eschatological event that constantly occurs in the concrete moment.

I therefore agree with Enrico Castelli "that the 'kerygma' calls for the being of the event [as much as mystery]; and the eventual historical analysis of the event does not encroach on the revelation because it is the revelation of the message and of the event [i.e. of the history] at the same time".

3

PROLEGOMENA TO A COMMENTARY ON MARK

Samuel Sandmel

Samual Sandmel is Distinguished Service Professor at the Hebrew Union College – Jewish Institute of Religion, Cincinnati. He holds the Ph.D. from Yale University; in 1962 he served as president of the Society of Biblical Literature. Sandmel's publications include: A Jewish Understanding of the New Testament (*1956*), The Genius of Paul (*1958*), We Jews and Jesus (*1965*), The First Christian Century in Judaism and Christianity (*1969*). *His article was originally published in* The Journal of Bible and Religion (*October 1963*) *and is reprinted with permission.*

IN MY *Genius of Paul: A Study in History* I set forth some opinions and tentative suggestions about the Gospel According to Mark, and these brought a flattering invitation from the editor of *JBR* to expand and develop them.

These opinions, for whatever they are worth, derive in greatest part from whatever academic and strictly scholarly inclinations I have, yet also from my being a teacher. I teach "an introduction to the New Testament", a course prescribed in our curriculum for rabbinic students. The course has several purposes, and among them that of leading the students to a beginning appreciation of the religion and the Scripture of our Christian neighbors and friends. The friendly interpreter and the pedant are often blended harmoniously in one single person, but at times they are not. For me to try to portray affirmatively what seem to me to be Christian attitudes toward the Gospels cannot always preclude the assessment which the pedant in me must make of the Gospels. Accordingly, there are junctures at which I am impelled to say something of this kind, that while the Gospels have come over the centuries to mean "X" to Christians, in my judgment, when they were written they meant "Y".

I

About a year ago I was with a close and warm friend whom I had not seen for several years. As the talk veered to his future writing and mine, I mentioned my intention to write a commentary on Mark. In the friendliest possible indignation, he said, "What the devil do you have to say that hasn't been said a hundred times already?" There is, of course, a large sense in which he is right, for much that appears in a commentary simply repeats, out of requirements of completeness, what is the common property of commentaries. The area in which to say something new is hence limited. This is as true for me, a Jew, as for any other scholar.

That commentary on Mark, should I get around to write it, ought to reflect solid learning and not simply the curiosity that its author is Jewish. I was taught New Testament not by Jewish teachers but by Protestants. A book I wrote, *A Jewish Understanding of the New Testament*, evoked a frequent comment that it could have been written by a Protestant; this was sometimes said in praise, and sometimes in lament. My commentary on Mark, then, will reflect not as much my being Jewish as my being whatever I chance to be. A Reform Jew, I suppose my relationship to the long Jewish past is kindred to that of an extreme Christian modernist to the Christian past. Hence, there is a sense in which my approach to Tanak or rabbinic literature is kindred to my approach to the New Testament; these ancient writings call for answering the questions, when was this written, where, by whom, and for what purpose. In externals the method would be the same.

But beyond the externals of method, there is the subtle yet real question of one's relationship, of one's feeling toward the document he is studying. I feel, for example, a sense of deep and direct relationship to such books as Job, Amos, and Jeremiah. Toward Chronicles I feel a much lesser kinship. This difference is the result of how I chance to respond to some particular context. Toward rabbinic literature my relationship involves ambivalences, for there is much I respect and admire, and some that I do not; basically my attitude is, or I think it is, that this literature represents, worthily, an age and a genre now happily past. Yet I would be untruthful if I did not say that along with my personal rejection of the ancient rabbinic Judaism as authoritative, or even normative, for me, there still abides in me some affirmative sense of relationship to it.

Respecting the New Testament and me, this question of relatedness or unrelatedness often baffles me. This is probably the case because of fluctuations, themselves the product of changing moods. Thus, when I read an old-fashioned liberal like Frederick C. Grant, I have a feeling of affirmative relationship both to his scholarship and to what he studies, but when I read the newer scholars, especially the neo-Orthodox, I sense in me a negative relationship to both. Any approach I would have to Mark or some other New Testament book, would consciously or unconsciously derive some part of its substance from this matter of relatedness.

I think I am aware of my tending, mostly but not entirely, to some scale of values. Thus, I have a much, much higher regard for Paul than for any of the canonical evangelists (*the evangelists*, *not Jesus*). Yet my feeling for Paul is close to my feeling for Philo; they were both men of great gifts, and they evoke my ungrudging admiration, but never my assent. On the other hand, there is much in the Gospels which evokes both admiration and assent, with the end result that I feel a relatedness to portions of the Gospels which I chance to admire less than Paul, and less relatedness to Paul, even though I admire him more.

Mark fascinates me in the same way that a first class enigma can fascinate. I feel no affirmative kinship with its author, nor with his presentation of Jesus. It is Matthew's Jesus somewhat, and Luke's much more, to whom my relatedness exists. But the contents and the form of Mark intrigue as a puzzle might, and as an essay might not. I think that I have seen, or at least glimpsed, in Mark things which others seem to me not to have seen. Perhaps I have seen correctly, perhaps I have not. But if there is something which I have seen and others have not, this is due not to better eyesight on my part, but to the accident of the angle of vision. And it is to express as clearly as I can this matter of the angle of vision that I have felt the need of the foregoing.

Those readers acquainted with my book, *The Hebrew Scriptures*, will know that in one important matter I swim against what seems to be the current today, namely, I am not an affirmer of the history encased in Scriptural writings. I am not the thorough-going sceptic that many nineteenth-century German scholars were, nor, like certain present-day journalists who popularize archaeology, the thorough-going affirmer. Rather, my conscious assumption is that ancient writers were not modern historians. They were not trained in research, and were not habitués of archives, and, moreover, history in Ranke's definition was never their intention. Hence, to try to meet Scriptural authors on our modern plane of historical reliability is to be inevitably working on the wrong level, and must result in our minds never truly meeting theirs. If the historical statements they make chance to be reliable, this is only coincidental.

These quasi-historical writings are, of course, theological. This statement, correct as it is, tends also to become a cliché and to sanction an avoidance of clarification. If it were to be stated more precisely, the judgment would run along these lines, that the ancient writer had a theological viewpoint, itself a composite of multiple items, and when he wrote, it was in reflection of, or in exposition of, or in advocacy of this complex of multiple items. The ancient writer may have been a poor or an expert craftsman; but his possession of craftsmanship or his lack of it is far less significant than that he had a viewpoint, and that his viewpoint affected what he wrote.

I stress this because it is in opposition to the opinions, implicit or explicit, of what needs to be denominated as the "tape-recorder" theory of ancient writers. In such a theory, the writer's heart and mind are supposedly of no import whatsoever, for the writer only recorded, and without change, what he heard or read. This theory is implicit in some versions of the "folk-memory" hypothesis, and is explicit in an important work in form-criticism, Dibelius, *From Tradition to Gospel*. Here are Dibelius' words: "A community of unlettered people which expects the end of the world today or tomorrow has neither the ability nor the inclination to produce books; thus we should expect not the production of real literature from the Christian community of the first two or three decades."[1]

My own opinion is exactly the reverse. No man ever picked up a pen without having some purpose in writing.

Indeed, there have been to my mind three deficits in form criticism. First, the method is unreliable, for it builds up a suppositious case about the universals in the growth of folk literature (and hence the classifications into types) and then proceeds to try to make Gospel materials fit the pre-conceived patterns – and subjectivity has nowhere been more rampant in scholarship than in New Testament form criticism. Second, the inference of form criticism is that the content of a Gospel under study is the *altered* form of inherited material, so that back of a pericope used by a Mark or a Luke there must always, *always* lie a source or sources. Ergo, an evangelist never created material, he only copied it. The key word here is my word always; this is not to deny that writers used sources, but only that when scholarship spends its energy on ferreting out sources virtually to the exclusion from study of how these sources were used, or whether any source at all underlay a pericope, the Gospel under study comes to be distorted. To many workers in the field, form criticism is distasteful because in attributing this or that to the faith of the early church, it left very little to Jesus himself. Though Henry Cadbury in "Between Jesus and the Gospels" (*HTR*, XVI, 81–92), thought Bultmann, *Geschichte der synoptischen Tradition*, excessively sceptical, I must comment that form criticism strikes me as a desperate effort to find a basis and a method for salvaging historical reliability in the Gospels. Cadbury stresses this point. The "negative" results of form criticism seem to be adjudged too harshly by those who fail to discern that it was actually intended to come up, impregnably, with some items which would be positive, this in an era when Gospel study revolving about historicity was largely negative. The bent of form criticism was to suggest that one could strip off layers of the onion and get back to the pristine vegetable; instead, when once the theory was applied, one stripped and stripped and there was practically no onion left. Form criticism, then, was a valiant effort to find a basis to affirm history; the conviction that the "history" is at best coincidental leads me to believe that form criticism is a wrong method the results of which, whether they are negative or positive, are inevitably wrong. Such a view does not, of course, deny that accurate bits of history are in the Gospels; it denies that form criticism or any other method hitherto devised can enable the modern scholar to separate the historical from the unhistorical, if the scholar once concedes that unhistorical materials are to be found in the Gospels. The greatest distortion in form criticism is that it unduly elevated the problem of historicity. The theory of the priority of Mark predisposed this Gospel in particular to the distortion; and while scholars from time to time have stressed that Mark is as theological as the others, even John, I suspect that a poll-taker would find a considerable number of votes for Mark, theological as it is, as yet the *most* historical.

The third deficit in form criticism is that it directed scholarship to the study of pericopes, to the Harmony or Synopsis, and as a consequence the appraisal of Gospels, each as a totality, virtually ceased. If there was still lip service to the mathematical theorem that the whole is the sum of its parts, form criticism acted as an obstacle to the adding up of the parts so as to assess the whole. We have had in recent decades few essays or books that treat the total Mark in its own terms; essays, many good and some bad, have dealt with special theories (e.g. Mark and liturgy), but apart from Enslin's "Twixt the Dusk and The Daylight" (*JBL*, LXXV, 19–26), I can recall little recent writing that deals searchingly with Mark in Mark's own terms.

The question of historicity in Mark, like that of historicity in Genesis, is at most a sub-topic in any full treatment of the writing. The question must not arise too early and thereby obstruct an understanding and appraisal of Mark. Indeed, historicity should be placed as the final sub-topic; it must not be allowed to elbow its way to the head of the topics.

II

It is a truism that first there were writings and only after that was there a canon. There exist a good many books, Jewish as well as Christian, which assess the ancient writings exclusively through the spectacles of canonicity. Some pious works even attribute to the unknown canonizers measures of inspiration exceeding that allotted to the writers. New Testament scholarship, possibly under an influence such as that of Irenaeus, who wrote eloquently (*Against*

Heresies, 3.11.8) as to why there were four and only four Gospels, seems to me to treat Mark without regard to its having had some pre-canonical existence.

The assumption seems almost universal today that each Gospel, on being written, promptly gained assent from those who then read it. The theory of the priority of Mark would imply, so it is to be inferred, that Matthew approved of Mark, as did Luke, but each had some more to tell. The possibility that Matthew and Luke disapproved of Mark, and had good reasons for doing so, remains largely unexplored. Ernest Colwell, in *John Defends the Gospel*, proposes that John wanted to supplant the Synoptics, but his seems to me a somewhat lone voice. I myself went beyond Colwell in a paper, "Genealogies and Myths and the Writing of Gospels" (*HUCA*, XXVII, 1956, 201–211). It is there suggested that Matthew wrote because he disapproved of Mark, and Luke, because he disapproved of Mark and Matthew; and the judgment is expressed that all four were disapproved of in a work designed as an appropriate and approvable form of Gospel composition, namely the Epistle to the Hebrews. In that paper, I tried to raise the question, in the light of hellenistic conventions, of what were the facts involved in the writing of a Gospel, and how did a Gospel sound to different levels of readers, especially in its pre-canonical days. When the Pastorals denounced genealogies and Jewish myths – recall that the Pastorals are regarded as among the latest of New Testament writings – is the allusion to material now found in Talmud and Midrash? Or is it, in the supposedly latest of New Testament writings, to intra-Christian concerns, such as the discordant genealogies in Matthew and Luke? And why does Hebrews use (about Melchizedek, though the author means the Christ) the phrase "without father, without mother, and without genealogy"?

In short, modern interpreters do not raise the question, what is Mark like that Matthew and Luke reject him, but handle the so-called "synoptic problem" as though Matthew and Luke were benign supplementers who had more data than Mark. Those who study pericopes necessarily note tiny items involving rejection; hence the convenient summaries in the commentaries of "*Abweichungen*". But the really insistent question is, what is Mark as a totality? Indeed, the process of comprehending a Gospel, since we have multiple Gospels, seems to me to require the following: The first step is the reading of the totality, with no attention to the pericope parallels; next, one studies the pericopes, for the differences in a pericope common to two or more Gospels will disclose for us, as dye does for the microscope, things we might otherwise miss; thereafter, however, one must return to the Gospel as a totality.

Having myself done this with tolerable thoroughness, I find, at least to my own satisfaction, that Mark in many treatments is explained incorrectly because Matthew and Luke (and John) are read with him.

I will here confine myself, in illustration, to three topics.

The first is the role of the disciples. I allege that Mark regards them as villains. (Pious interpreters sometimes phrase this in the form that Mark is "rather hard" on the disciples.) The disciples do not understand who and what Jesus is, do not understand what he says, cannot follow through on his wishes and instructions, and at the crucial moment abandon him. Chief among the villainous disciples, as Mark would have it, is Peter. Not only does Mark portray Jesus as saying to him, "Get thee behind me, Satan," but at the climax Peter three times denies him. Pharisees and Sadducees and chief priests (how much ink has been spilled on the plural priests!) are hostile and opaque; they are the enemies. But the disciples are worse, for they are an epitome of disloyalty. The only man who really comes out well (the women do) is the *goy*, the Roman centurion who can see what the Jews, disciples as well as opponents, have missed, that Jesus was truly the "son of God".

Mark's treatment of the disciples is not some minor thread. Indeed, it is a major motif which almost vies for attention with Jesus himself. It is a large part of the warp and woof of Mark. Not only do Matthew and Luke omit or soften in details Mark's black portrayal of the disciples (and Luke introduces a theory of an unlimited number of disciples, but only twelve "apostles"), but the villainy of the disciples recedes in Matthew and Luke to mere stray bits. (Luke 22:32 portrays Jesus as saying to Peter, "When you have turned, shepherd my flock.")

Is this unsavory role of the disciples historical? If so, did Paul know nothing of it? Is it conceivable that he would have abstained in Galatians from throwing into the teeth of Peter-Cephas some recollection of Peter's triple denial? I do not think it is historical; by chance I also do not think that Peter-Cephas-Simon are historically one person; they are at least two.

Mark is not correctly interpreted unless the interpreter is prepared to receive what Mark is saying in Mark's terms. When the interpreter introduces into Mark the favorable attitude to the disciples characteristic of Matthew and Luke, he is distorting Mark.

The second item is the phrase Son of Man. Here is a locution which has claimed the attention of countless writers, both the strictly academic and also the pious. The greatest barrier to its comprehension probably lies in the circumstance that Mark employs it as Jesus' term for himself. Yet the student must press on and inquire what the term meant to Mark, or to put it differently, what Mark meant by the term. I have published in a Festschrift to Abba Hillel Silver, *In Time of Harvest*, a paper called "Son of Man in Mark", which was given before the SBLE in a somewhat different form in December 1959. I used the previous researches, principally Lietzmann, as the point of departure, namely, that the phrase is borrowed from Daniel and that only with Mark does it become a title. In proceeding, however, I diverged – to an extent, unprecedented even for me! – from antecedent scholarship and declared that Son of Man is a *literary device* in Mark. I reviewed the other titles (Messiah, Lord, King, Son of God) for Jesus, and concluded that none of these was consistent with Mark's needs and purposes. I defined these latter as requiring a sufficiently mystifying effect so as to make it possible for the reader of Mark to understand Mark's Jesus, while simultaneously Mark's characters, principally the disciples, can fail to understand him. None of the other possible titles can serve this double and contradictory purpose of clarity and mystification, for so specific are these titles that the disciples could scarcely credibly misunderstand and misconceive who and what Jesus is. But Son of Man does serve in this way. I went on to suggest that as a literary work Mark has a kinship with "disguise" dramas in which the writer and the audience share information which key characters lack.

This treatment of Son of Man moves considerably beyond the implication of Mark's portrayal of the disciples, for the Gospel, to my mind, is not simply a partisan tendentious writing, as the "anti-disciples" motif would imply, but is, actually, a studied and artful creation. The simplicity of Mark's style, as a consequence, is misleading; interpreters who have stressed the unornate character of his writing have failed to grasp that involved sentences and orotundity result not from skill so much as from pretentiousness, and that in Greek, as in English, it is more difficult to write simply than to write complicatedly. While I would not attribute to Mark the great felicity which I think characterizes Luke, I regard Mark as an inordinately skilful writer.

I fail to grasp the bases on which some have characterized Mark as a Gospel of little profundity, as if it had only one dimension, that of surface. To my mind Mark is replete with nuances and overtones, carefully put there by the author. Whoever wrote Mark was neither simple writer, nor a simpleton, but an artful writer usually in full control of his pen. He slipped a few times. With the Syro-Phoenician woman, it is infelicitous that Mark has her, rather than Jesus, say the tolerant thing. He should have credited Malachi as well as Isaiah for his opening quotation. And he should have given more care to the passage "It was two days before the festival . . ."

I say "more care", for to my mind, and this is my third item, Mark is a rewritten Gospel, not a brand-new creation. Some form of theory of an Ur-Mark seems to me a necessity, even though I cannot pretend to be able to reconstruct it. The oft-cited words of Papias that Mark was Peter's interpreter writing down Peter's reminiscences cannot be applied to the canonical Mark. They might conceivably apply to an "Ur-Mark", if only we could find that hypothetical document.

If there was indeed an "Ur-Mark", and if the canonical Mark is an artfully rewritten tract against Jewish Christianity, then Mark has a long and complicated literary history. It does not seem to me reasonable that "Ur-Mark" was a polemic against Jewish Christianity. If the Passion Narrative was the first portion to have been set down in writing, it could conceivably have been anti-Jewish, or, more precisely, anti-Pharisaic, not so much out of animus as out of an effort to increase the pathos of the writing, for hellenistic writers tended to use pathos. But the point of this guess-work about the literary history of Mark is to underline a conviction: the conviction that the canonical Mark bristles with problems many of which are beyond solution, but many of which, hitherto unsolved, tend toward solution, when they are looked at from a completely new angle of vision. For example, the ending, *ephobounto gar*, previously viewed as abrupt and possibly truncated, can now emerge as the exactly needed last sentence, for it brilliantly passes a scornful judgment on the scorned disciples. That Mark closes without a Resurrection appearance would no longer be a surprise, for how could an artful author depict Jesus as appearing to the disloyal and the deniers? The words "Tell his disciples and Peter that he is going before you to Galilee" (16:7), now take on a new sense, for they are not so much the promise they are usually thought to be, but are instead a prime rebuke, meant to be understood as conveying contempt. (Luke and John allocate the Resurrection appearance to Jerusalem.) The date of the crucifixion in "Ur-Mark" was what John gives (neither "Ur-Mark" nor John knew the exact date, for the association with Passover is theological, not historical), and the shift into Passover night is tendentious, and reflective of the author's slip. The Quarto-Deciman controversy in the early church gains a little illumination from such a recognition, for we see the more clearly that the historic controversies were not just abstract viewpoints, but reflect vibrant people earnestly and forcefully in conflict. Not impossibly Mark's dating of the crucifixion is an end result, a literary creation emerging from Christians who, still in some proximity to Jews, felt that the occasion must have been on Passover, and not the night before – an end result, rather than the source for the dating.

Moreover, if interpretation is able to get over the hurdle of questions of historicity, then the inutility of certain historical questions is manifest. Sober scholarship need not agitate itself with inquiries into the birth, growth, and development of Jesus' messianic consciousness. A Gospel, in my view, is a tract dealing with the human career of a being conceived of as divine; it is not a tract dealing with a human. The questions about whether or not Jesus in his lifetime claimed to be the Messiah – and related questions deriving from Wrede's brilliant but wrong assessment of the "secret"[2] – need not detain serious scholarship.

Lastly, at least here, we can view in perspective the contours of the new quest for the historical Jesus, and perhaps discern how empty of real significance is much of the writing which seems to me to have turned the respectable word Kerygma into a mere slogan. It is as easy, and methodologically as sound, to recover the historical Abraham the patriarch from the fancies of Philo, Josephus, and the rabbis as to recover the historical Jesus from the Kerygma. The Jesus of the nineteenth-century scholarship which Schweitzer surveyed never existed. The new quest can at best turn up a twentieth-century Jesus who never existed.

C

What is it that is being sought? A man, superbly gifted, but still only a man? Or is it a man who was more than a man? The new questers ought to try to understand that the most they can come up with, through historical research, is only a man. My judgment is that the quest cannot succeed. But if it by chance should succeed, will it be the desired success, or will it be, paradoxically, that success that is indistinguishable from failure?

No one who takes Mark seriously can make the claim that he has learned to know the Jesus of history. That there was such a Jesus I firmly believe. We cannot get to know him, unless new documents should turn up.

We cannot get to know Jesus the man. It is Gospels we can know, not Jesus. Mark can be known, and a better knowledge of Mark can in turn lead to a better knowledge of Matthew, Luke, and John. The first step is to know Mark.

A commentary on Mark is very much on my mind. Two other projects precede it on my agenda. Meanwhile, there is the teaching that one does, and there are administrative obligations which consume time. Some day, *deo volente*, I will get to my commentary on Mark.

NOTES

1. See *Die Formgeschichte des Evangeliums* (Tübingen, 1919), pp. 4–5.
2. The real clue to the "secrecy" is the need to emphasize the disciples' blindness.

4

CONCERNING JESUS OF NAZARETH

Francis W. Beare

Francis W. Beare is Professor Emeritus of New Testament at Trinity College, University of Toronto. He served as president of the Society of Biblical Literature during 1969. "Concerning Jesus of Nazareth" deals with the state of the tradition in the Gospel according to St. Matthew and was published in the Journal of Biblical Literature *(June 1968). This essay is reprinted with the editor's approval. Beare's most significant publications include:* The Earliest Records of Jesus *(1962),* A Commentary on the Epistle to the Philippians *(2nd edn., 1969),* The First Epistle of Peter *(3rd edn., 1969), and the introductions and exegesis for Ephesians and Colossians in* The Interpreter's Bible, *Vols. X and XI (1953, 1955).*

THE GOSPEL according to St. Matthew was composed and published late in the first century, that is to say, nearly seventy years after the death of Jesus of Nazareth. This dating is widely, though by no means unanimously, accepted by the NT scholars of our time. On this basis, we are dealing with a document which presents the tradition in a form which it had assumed two generations or more after the end of the public ministry of Jesus. This paper has the very modest purpose of summing up the conclusions that may be drawn about the state of the tradition at that stage of its history, with some attempt to distinguish between what the evangelist received and what he himself contributed in presenting it to his readers. Given the limitations of time, a good deal of what I say will of necessity be little more than an arbitrary statement of my own conclusions; I do not claim that they represent a consensus of scholarship.

We may begin with the observation that the totality of the tradition available to any one evangelist was defective, even before he reduced the stock in his notebooks by selection in accordance with his estimate of what was necessary and relevant to his purpose in writing. The original nucleus of the tradition concerning Jesus was given in the personal recollections of eyewitnesses, as these were communicated by the immediate disciples of Jesus and a relatively large number of other people who had seen him and heard him speak during the brief period of his ministry. Jesus left nothing in writing, and gave no charge to his followers to prepare a written record of his sayings or of his deeds. They were commissioned to preach, not to write, and the substance of their recollections was in fact not committed to writing in any degree for a number of years; the greater part of those recollections were never committed to writing at all. All the gospels put together contain only a small proportion of the things that Jesus said and did, or even of what was remembered in the communities at the time that they were written. Like the others, the Gospel according to St. Matthew represents a selection made by him, in keeping with his own conception of what was relevant and necessary for the times, from a considerably wider range of materials which were even then available in the oral traditions of his community and such written sources as had come into his hands. This in turn would represent a stock considerably diminished from that which would have been available shortly after the crucifixion – say on the first Christian Pentecost – if there had been any desire at that time to prepare a complete record for the archives of the nascent society of believers. We have to recognize, then, that we are dealing in this gospel – the same thing is true if we take all the gospels together – with a record based on a diminished stock of materials. Much of what would have been available two generations earlier had already been lost simply because it ceased to be repeated by the preachers and teachers; and much of what was still extant was not incorporated into his work by this evangelist or by any or all of them. "There were many other things which Jesus did [and said]"; "Jesus did many other signs in the presence of his disciples which are not written in this book."[1] The words are just as applicable to the Gospel of Matthew as to the Gospel of John. We are dealing with a document that is incomplete, fragmentary, deficient.

But if the tradition had been diminished by the loss of stories and sayings which had once been remembered, we can hardly fail to see that it had been enlarged by the admission of both sayings and incidents which derived from other sources. This principle would not be so generally accepted as the first, but it is really inconceivable – contrary to all that we know of the transmission of other traditions – that the story of Jesus should remain immune to the tendency to transfer to it tales that had been told earlier in relation to others, and sayings which were first uttered by other lips. The question is not whether this type of contamination has taken place, but how far it extends. Few of us, I take it, would go along with the notion that the incidents of the gospel story were transferred in the mass from folktales of Heracles, or from a pattern-making Life of Pythagoras, or from OT stories of wonder-working prophets, or from haggadic midrashim on the life of Moses. But there are elements of our gospels, and of the Gospel according to St. Matthew in particular, which appear to find their most reasonable explanation along these lines; and we may without undue boldness conjecture that such elements were much more widespread in the oral tradition – that they were to some extent screened out by the writers.

A special – perhaps unique – type of addition to the store of genuine reminiscences of Jesus is to be found in the transfer to the story of the public ministry of events which were originally conceived as activities of the risen Jesus, and of sayings which first took shape as utterances of the risen Jesus. The transfiguration, even the messianic confession which precedes it, the epiphany-type story of the call of the first disciples as it is recounted by Luke – these and other incidents which are set within the framework of the public ministry may have originated as stories of appearances of the risen Jesus, "visions and revelations of the Lord". With much less hesitation, we can affirm that a number of sayings in all the gospels, and in all the sources which they employ, so clearly presuppose a post-resurrection situation that they can hardly have originated except as sayings of the risen Jesus. "Where two or three are gathered together in my name, there am I in the midst of them" – these words, for instance, clearly presuppose a Jesus who is no longer limited by space and time; and this saying is by no means unique in this respect. The early church, of course, had no motive for making a distinction between sayings of the historical Jesus and sayings of the risen Lord. They were far from attaching any lesser authority to the latter.

Another factor of great importance in the history of the tradition is the effect of the transference of the gospel from Jewish to gentile soil, and from a Palestinian environment to the hellenistic life of the Roman empire – mainly to its eastern provinces, and to the Levantine populations of Rome and other western cities – within the first generation. The fact that all our gospels are written in Greek is evidence enough of the sweeping sociological change that had taken place; and this is confirmed for a still earlier period by the astonishing assumption of St. Paul in his letter to the Romans – which cannot possibly be dated later than 58 – that the church is predominantly gentile, and that he must now plead with gentile Christians to recognize that God has still a place for Jews in the Christian community and in the economy of salvation. This means that the tradition in its manifold elements had to be translated into Greek, and that the transmission took place to a large extent in Greek, before it was committed to writing. We cannot rule out the possibility – indeed we should accept this as a probability rather than a possibility – that some of it was committed to writing in Aramaic, even though we reject the theory of an Aramaic proto-Matthew which is still cherished in a diluted form by virtually all Roman Catholic scholars. (Naturally, we reject still more brusquely the theory of the late C. C. Torrey that all our gospels are translations of Aramaic originals.) A fair amount of material in the synoptics looks like the literal translation of an Aramaic source, either written or oral, and in some cases, for instance, in the case of the parable of the sower in St. Mark, the evangelist probably had before him an Aramaic collection, or a literal translation of a collection originally set down in Aramaic. Nonetheless, there can be no doubt that by the later years of the first century, and probably by the seventies, if not still earlier, the transmission of the tradition was made chiefly by men who spoke Greek, and knew the tradition only in its Greek dress. Now anyone who has had experience in translation is aware of the fact that any translation involves some measure of refraction, even of distortion, of the original, no matter how competent the translator may be, and it would be absurd to suppose that the translation of stories about Jesus and sayings of Jesus was restricted to men of undoubted competence. Translation into Greek and transmission in Greek add a further element of modification in the substance of the original tradition.

In the case of the Gospel according to St. Matthew we have the peculiar feature, difficult to assess, that it came out of a bilingual society, in which both Greek and Aramaic were used fairly freely. Since the gospel was composed in Greek, and its principal written source (the Gospel according to St. Mark) was a Greek document, it is probable that the author and his readers used Greek as their principal medium of intercourse, and that the oral tradition known to them circulated mainly in Greek; but it is likely that some elements of it were currently available to them in Aramaic – partly, it may be, in writing, and partly oral. All this is based upon the assumption that the gospel itself is the product of the Antioch region or, if you prefer Kilpatrick's suggestion, the Phoenician coast. But in any case, there was nothing sacrosanct for them – and there need not be for us – about Aramaic traditions; and we have no reason to suppose that if they had parallel fragments of tradition available in both Greek and Aramaic, they would be inclined to subordinate the understanding of the Greek form to its Aramaic partner. "Aramaic" is not a synonym for "authentic", even though it seems to be taken in that sense by some of our colleagues. To some degree, for Matthew as well as for the other evangelists, the sense of the tradition as he received it was affected by its rendering into and its transmission for some time in Greek.

Joachim Jeremias discounts the distorting effect of translation, largely because he is confident of his ability to recover the original sense by retranslating into Aramaic, even though he admits that "every intelligent person will realize the tentative nature of such retranslations".[2] But he has analyzed very comprehensively the many other factors which have entered into the transmission of the parables. He calls them "principles [or 'laws'] of transformation". His work is so familiar to all of us that I need only list his ten "laws of transformation".[3]

(i) Translation into Greek
(ii) Representational changes (substitution of hellenistic practices

and furnishings for Palestinian; this is not particularly applicable to Matthew, where we see rather a tendency to recast hellenized materials into a Palestinian shape)

(iii) Embellishment

(iv) Influence of the OT and of folk story themes

(v) The change of audience (especially from opponents to disciples; this is most marked in Matthew)

(vi) A shift of emphasis to the hortatory, especially from the eschatological

(vii) The influence of the church's situation; subdivided under (a) the delay of the parousia, (b) the missionary situation, and (c) regulations for the leadership of the church

(viii) Allegorization (particularly marked in Matthew)

(ix) Collection and conflation (this too is done more frequently and consistently by Matthew than by the others)

(x) Changes of setting, which "often produced a change in the meaning"; the supplying of introductions and generalizing conclusions.

All of these "laws of transformation" have been operative in the oral tradition and also in the editorial work of the evangelists. But it is important to keep in mind that similar tendencies have had an equally penetrating effect upon the non-parabolic elements of the tradition, though they have not been traced out in the same systematic way. Let me add that I no longer believe that the process can be successfully reversed, as Jeremias claims and attempts to do. Nor am I at all confident that "a return to the living voice of Jesus" or a recovery of "the original tones of the utterances of Jesus" would be so great a gain as Jeremias imagines. After all, it is perhaps easier for us to come into an effective *rapport* with Jesus through the medium of the refracted tradition of the gospels, which grew out of prolonged and varied efforts to make him comprehensible to another age and to a different culture, than through an exact verbatim report of his original sayings, in his native Aramaic, in the precise form and context in which they were first delivered.

We have now to take note of the fact that for its narrative, the Gospel according to St. Matthew makes astonishingly little use of the traditions which were in circulation in its immediate environment. We take it that it was composed and published for a Christian community of Syria not too far removed from Antioch on the Orontes. Let us recall, then, that Antioch had been evangelized something like sixty years earlier, in the course of the persecution that arose around Stephen, by fugitives from Jerusalem, who presumably carried with them some account of Jesus. It had been visited by several leading members of the mother church in Jerusalem – notably Barnabas, Peter, and the prophets Judas and Silas ("leading men among the brethren").[4] Thus it had every opportunity of receiving a reliable store of information about Jesus very early in its history, and from the fountainhead – the mother church itself and even from the very Prince of the Apostles. If Matthew did not write in Antioch itself, the store of tradition of the great Syrian metropolis was available to him. In view of this, it is truly astounding to observe that Matthew derives the narrative structure of his gospel, not from the tradition independently preserved in his own church, but from the Gospel according to St. Mark, which had been published at Rome (as is generally supposed) some thirty or forty years earlier. This would be almost equally astonishing if we accepted a date in the seventies for Matthew – perhaps even more so, in that the Antiochene traditions would be that much closer to their origins.

It is hardly necessary to review even in broad lines the extent of the dependence of Matthew upon Mark, for its narrative. It extends to the whole of his gospel, apart from the cycle of nativity stories, but is perhaps most striking in the structure of the passion narrative. Now it is very hard to imagine that the churches of western Syria had to wait until a copy of Mark came into their hands to learn of the baptism of Jesus by John, or of the call of his first disciples, or of his controversies with scribes and Pharisees, and of all the other anecdotes which make up the Markan narrative; but it is beyond all the bounds of the credible that they should not have had their own account of the passion. If there is one area of agreement among scholars, it is in the recognition that the passion narrative took shape as a coherent, consecutive account of events far earlier and far more consistently than the rest of the gospel material. It is utterly inconceivable that the church of St. Matthew should have had to wait upon the publication of Mark to learn of this part of the story of Jesus. Yet even in this area, Matthew takes over for his own use the story as it was set down by Mark; and such changes as he makes do not in any instance contribute one single new fact, except the naming of Caiaphas. Some of his additions appear indeed to come from the local traditions of Jerusalem, but they are not any the more authentic for that – they are popular tales, legend, and that sort of thing. They do not enable us to fill in or to correct the Markan narrative in the slightest degree.

The Gospel according to St. Matthew is from one point of view a revised and enlarged edition of Mark; but it is abundantly evident that the main purpose of his revision is not to give a more complete account of events in the life of Jesus, but to give a more adequate record of the *teachings* of the Lord, beginning with the sermon on the mount, which owes nothing whatever to Mark. He retains the basic framework of Mark, and virtually the whole of its narrative material in detail; but upon it he has superimposed a new framework, which is not narrative at all, but consists of a number of collections of sayings of Jesus, arranged in the form of connected discourses, and it is precisely in this *arrangement* of the discourse material that he has made his own principal contribution. We are left with the impression that Matthew is not greatly interested in the story for its own sake, but only – or primarily – as a series of demonstrations of how ancient prophecies were fulfilled in the life of the Messiah. "All this took place to fulfill what the Lord had spoken by the prophets."

In addition to the narrative, for which he is the only significant source, Mark has also supplied Matthew with a certain amount of discourse material (sayings of Jesus), but in this area he is no longer the principal source; and where Markan discourse material is used by Matthew, it is almost always combined with more abundant materials drawn from other sources. The outstanding feature of Matthew is the five great collections of sayings, organized into the form of continuous discourses of Jesus, and terminated by a kind of rubric which at the same time serves as the formula of transition to the next section of narrative. These five major discourses are (i) the sermon on the mount, chs. 5 to 7; (ii) the mission charge, ch. 10; (iii) the book of parables, ch. 13; (iv) the manual of discipline, or church order, ch. 18; and (v) the discourse on the last things, chs. 23–25. The fifth discourse may equally well be treated as a double collection, if we prefer to look upon the discourse against the scribes and Pharisees (ch. 24) as a separate collection of sayings (as is done, for instance, by J. Schmid); but as it culminates in the pronouncement of judgment upon Israel, it seems better to take it as the first section of the wider discourse on the last things.

Besides these five collections, which constitute the basic framework of the book, Matthew includes four much briefer groups of sayings, which we may add to our list, to wit: (vi) a discourse on demon possession (Beelzebul), 12:25–45; (vii) a discourse on the way of the cross, 16:21–28; (viii) a discourse on the dangers of wealth and the rewards of discipleship, 19:23–30; and (ix) a second collection of parables, 21:28–22:14.

Of all these, only the sermon on the mount is wholly lacking in Mark. For the mission charge, Mark provides – at most – parts of 14 verses out of the 42. All but four of these are transferred from a different context, and even these four appear to be conflated with an independent parallel source. The book of parables is built around the smaller parable collection of Mark 4, with the omission of one parable and the addition of four others, together with a certain amount of nonparabolic sayings-material. The manual of discipline is in part a radical rewriting of the amorphous concatenation of sayings in Mark 9:33–48, with notable additions from other sources, including two important parables. The discourse on the last things falls into three parts. The first part, directed against the scribes and Pharisees, includes only two Markan verses (out of a total of thirty-eight), and these are recast to form one of the seven woes. The second part is drawn largely from the Markan apocalypse (Mark 13), with some omissions and some brief supplements; and the third part – the whole of ch. 25 – is in its entirety non-Markan. The four shorter collections give much the same picture. The discourse on demon possession has a partial parallel in Mark 3:23–30, but there is no close similarity in wording except for one verse, and there are eleven verses which have no parallel in Mark at all. The discourse on the way of the cross is taken directly from Mark, with changes that suggest editorial rewriting, rather than the use of any independent source. The discourse on the dangers of wealth is drawn directly, and almost word for word, from Mark, except for a single verse; and, as in Mark, it is attached to the incident of the rich man who refused to give up his wealth in order to follow Jesus. The second collection of parables includes only one that is taken from Mark, and that one (the parable of the wicked tenant farmers) is significantly pointed by additions and revisions which are probably to be attributed to the editorial work of the evangelist, rather than to the use of another source.

By far the greater part of the discourse material in Matthew is not derived from Mark, and it is in this great and important area, if anywhere, that we must look for traces of the traditions which had been preserved in his own church – that is to say, substantially, the early traditions received by Antioch from Jerusalem, even to some extent from Peter himself – in the form which they had assumed as a result of some decades of transmission by word of mouth. This is not to say, of course, that everything non-Markan in the Matthean sayings material is drawn from the stores of his own region. If he drew practically the whole of his narrative material from a document published a generation earlier in another region, there is no immediate reason for supposing that he would not draw upon another document, or other documents, from other areas, for some or all of the sayings which he attributes to Jesus. But we may at least say that if his own church did possess some store of traditions, and attached some value to them – and especially if, as we have suggested, some of them stemmed from the emissaries of the primitive church in Jerusalem and even from St. Peter in person – then it is in the sayings collections that we must look for traces of them. It would be quite unreasonably skeptical, indeed, not to recognize it as a probability that the sayings do contain a fair proportion of materials transmitted in the churches of the Antioch region, and at least a core of sayings that go back to the tradition originally received from responsible and representative leaders of the Jerusalem church.

But perhaps the most remarkable feature of this gospel is the attribution to Jesus of sayings which have been composed by the evangelist himself. Some of his materials are not derived from any tradition, written or oral, faithful or distorted, but from his own mind and pen. We may cite as our most conspicuous example the interpretation of the parable of the wheat and the tares ("darnel", if you like; I never hear the word "darnel" or the word "tares" except in connection with this parable). It is generally recognized that the interpretation of the parable of the sower in Mark is not the work of Jesus, but the deposit of an early midrash which was framed in the Palestinian church; and Matthew takes this over with little change. But no one supposes that Mark himself composed that interpretation; he found it attached to the parable in his source and simply reproduced it. But Matthew did not find his interpretation of the parable of the wheat and the tares in any source; he composed it himself. He even went so far as to introduce extraneous elements into the very parable in order to pave the way for the allegorizing interpretation which he had in mind. After bringing forward no less than thirty-seven examples of "the linguistic characteristics of the Evangelist Matthew" which are to be found in the eight verses of this "Interpretation", J. Jeremias states that "it is impossible to avoid the conclusion that the interpretation of the Parable of the Tares is the work of Matthew himself".[5] He adds that "this conclusion is confirmed by the Gospel of Thomas which has preserved the parable but not the allegorizing interpretation".

Again, the sayings of Jesus as they are presented to us by Matthew are marked by an exceptionally high amount of *gemara*, by which – to use the words of Professor W. D. Davies – "these *radical* words [of Jesus] begin to take on a *regulatory* character, that is, they became used as guides for the actual business of living, the *point d'appui* for an incipient Christian casuistry".[6] Professor Davies adduces evidence for the same kind of practical adaptation in Mark and in "Q", but indicates that it is much more frequent in "M" – that is, in the material peculiar to Matthew. [He evidently thinks of "M" as a single written source, but for our purposes it makes no difference whether we take this position or look upon it as the deposit of many sources employed by Matthew – or even, in part, composed by him.] For example, in the sermon on the mount, he speaks of the passage 5:22b–24[7] as "a kind of gemaric addition, explanatory of v. 21, 22a",[8] and suggests that a former member of the Dead Sea sect may have formulated some of it: "the kind of *gemara* we find in v. 22b would come very naturally to a person brought up in or influenced by the Dead Sea Sect".[9] From among his many other examples, we may select for mention his treatment of Matt. 19:10–12 (the bizarre supplement to the saying which defines remarriage after divorce as adultery).

These words form a bit of Christian *gemara* – an explanatory addition or comment. They cannot be said to arise naturally out of the content of xix. 2–9. . . . Pertinent to our purpose is the attempt made in Matthew to come to terms with the actuality of marriage: the material from M in xix. 10–12 reflects the same kind of concern, to make the ethic of Jesus practicable, as we find in Paul. Radicalism is tempered to the generality.[10]

It is true that Davies raises the question – in apparent seriousness – of whether such *gemara* goes back to Jesus himself. But he notes nonetheless that Paul still distinguishes carefully between what he has as a "word of the Lord" and what he gives as his own opinion, for which he thinks that he has the Spirit of God (I Cor. 7:12, 25, 40), whereas in the gospels, and with particular frequency in Matthew, similar regulatory applications of the absolute demands of Jesus are ascribed to Jesus directly. I do not think we need hesitate to attribute all this *gemara* to the apostolic church, in its efforts to find guidance for its own living in the teachings of Jesus; and the greater frequency with which it occurs in Matthew is most naturally understood if we regard the evangelist himself as the framer of the regulatory adaptation, at least in a fair proportion of the cases. It makes little difference to the main point – whether it were he or those who worked before him. The tradition as he presents it reflects this type of development.[11]

It would appear from all this that we cannot employ the Gospel according to St. Matthew directly as a source of historical knowledge concerning Jesus of Nazareth, either for the events of his life or for the substance of his teaching. The tradition, at the stage which it had reached when it came into his hands, had undergone manifold changes; and in his hands it was changed still more. At the heart of it there was the deposit of an early tradition which was passed on to his church or region from the original eyewitnesses and hearers of Jesus; but this deposit had been both diminished in the long process of oral tradition, and enlarged by the admission of new elements. In both respects, the evangelist has contributed to the reshaping of it. By his own selection, he has reduced the amount of accumulated tradition to that which he considered it necessary or desirable to transmit; and in the exercise of his own literary and religious gifts – the particular *charismata* of the Spirit which were given to him – he has introduced into it elements of his own composition. Above all, by his arrangement of his materials, by his supplying of new contexts for sayings and by his addition of comments by way of introductions and generalizing conclusions, he has, as it were, transposed it into a totally different key. He has transformed teaching directed to the Jewish people of Galilee and Jerusalem and their leaders into instructions laid down by the Messiah of Israel, now exalted to be the Lord of the universal church, for the direction of the community of believers. In the words of the late T. W. Manson:

We must realize that the five great discourses of Matthew, of which the Sermon on the Mount is the first, are not shorthand reports of actual addresses delivered by the Prophet of Nazareth on specified dates at specified places. They are systematic presentations of the mind of Christ on various matters of great moment to his Church.[12]

Thirty-three years ago, Professor R. H. Lightfoot closed his Bampton Lectures on *History and Interpretation in the Gospels* with the words:

It seems, then, that the form of the earthly no less than of the heavenly Christ is for the most part hidden from us. For all the inestimable value of the gospels, they yield us little more than a whisper of his voice; we trace in them but the outskirts of his ways.

This echo of the words of Job went for the most part unrecognized, and a storm of protest broke over the theological scene in England, where Wrede had never been taken seriously and form criticism had scarcely been noticed. In 1967, would the same words evoke indignation or would they pass unnoticed in a generation that talks nonsense about the Death of God?

NOTES

1. John 21:25, 20:30.
2. *The Parables of Jesus* (rev. ed., 1963), p. 25.
3. *Op. cit.*, pp. 113 f.
4. Acts 15:22.
5. *Op. cit.*, pp. 81–85.
6. *The Setting of the Sermon on the Mount*, p. 387 – in the section headed "*M* and Gemara", to which I am largely indebted for this paragraph.
7. This is the supplement to the first of the six antitheses; it runs: "Whoever insults his brother shall be liable to judgment, and whoever says 'You fool' shall be liable to the hell of fire." It is followed by the command to seek reconciliation with your brother before offering gifts at the altar of God.
8. *Op cit.*, p. 239.
9. *Ibid.*, p. 238.
10. *Ibid.*, pp. 393, 395.
11. Cf. the remarks of T. W. Manson, in the posthumous work, *Ethics and the Gospel*, ch. 6, "The Original Teaching of Jesus and the Ethics of the Early Church", pp. 92 ff. He speaks of the "standing temptation for the Christian community to become a 'saved Remnant' rather than a 'saving Remnant' . . . and so to make the words and deeds of Jesus the standard and pattern of their internal discipline rather than the inspiration of an apostolic mission". But he finds a good

side to this. "If the primitive Church tended to keep Jesus to itself, at least it did take him seriously. One of the ways it did so was by turning his teaching inward upon itself. . . . They saw themselves as the messianic community, and the words of Jesus their Master as full of instruction for them. They were prepared to take his sayings and apply them to their own case, and if in the process sayings which had originally been intended to serve other purposes were diverted, that did not seem to them to be a serious matter." It is not a very long step farther to attribute to Jesus sayings which express what the church now believed to be his mind and will in respect to emergent situations.

12. *Op. cit.*, p. 40.

5

THE INTERPRETER AND
THE PARABLES

The Centrality of the Kingdom

A. M. Hunter

Archibald M. Hunter is Professor of New Testament Exegesis at Aberdeen University, Scotland. He received the degree of D.Phil. from Oxford University and is author of The Message of the New Testament (*1944*), Introducing New Testament Theology (*1958*), Paul and His Predecessors (*1961*), *and* The Gospel According to John (*1965*). *His article was printed in* Interpretation (*January 1960*) *and is included in this volume with the editor's consent.*

THE IMPORTANCE of our subject may be gauged from the fact that no less than 35% of our Lord's teaching is in parable.[1] Moreover, no part of it, with the exception of The Lord's Prayer and The Beatitudes, is better known or loved. Not a day passes but we quote the parables, often unconsciously. We talk about "acting the Good Samaritan" or "passing by on the other side". Some of us "bear the burden and heat of the day"; others indulge in "riotous living". Some use their "talents" rightly; others "hide their lamp under a bushel"; and others leave things until "the eleventh hour". We "count the cost" or we "pay the last farthing". All these phrases – and how many more – come from the parables.

Yet verbal familiarity with them does not necessarily mean that we interpret them rightly, or that we do not often make them teach lessons they were never meant to teach. We may wax scornful, for example, of the early Fathers when we find Irenaeus identifying "the fatted calf" in The Prodigal Son with the Saviour himself or Augustine identifying "the innkeeper" in the Good Samaritan with the apostle Paul. But have we any right to criticize them if we find a warrant for *laissez faire* economics in The Labourers in the Vineyard or use The Tares as an argument against eugenics?

BASIC QUESTIONS

Interpretation, then, is going to be our major concern in these articles; but before we come to it, we must find answers to certain basic questions about the parables.

What Is a Parable?

In Sunday School we were taught to define it as "an earthly story with a heavenly meaning". For those beginning Bible study this can hardly be bettered; but it is not precise enough for the pundits. If we want to please them, we had better define it as a comparison drawn from nature or human life, and intended to illuminate some spiritual truth, on the assumption that what is valid in one sphere is valid also in the other.

Parable is a form of teaching. "Almost all teaching," Dean Inge has said, "consists in comparing the unknown with the known, the strange with the familiar."[2] It is a matter of everyday experience that you can hardly explain anything at all except by saying that it is *like* something else, something more familiar. So the Gospel parable often begins: "How shall we liken the kingdom of God?" or "The kingdom of God is like leaven . . . or a grain of mustard seed . . . or a dragnet." (Notice, by the way, that you cannot stop there: you must follow the parable to its end if you are to find the point of comparison. The kingdom is not like leaven but like what happens when you put leaven in a batch of meal.)

Combine, then, this mode of teaching by analogy with the Oriental's innate love of pictorial speech and every man's delight in a story, and you have most of the reasons why men took to using parable to communicate truth. But who made the first parable, and how many centuries it was before Christ, are questions, as Sir Thomas Browne would say, "above antiquarism".

The word itself, *parabole*, is of course Greek and means a comparison or analogy. Aristotle discusses it in his *Rhetoric*; but the antecedents of Christ's parable must be sought not in Hellas but in Israel, not in the Greek orators but in the Old Testament prophets and the Jewish Fathers; as doubtless it was in the synagogue that Jesus first heard men talking in parables. But observe: the Hebrew word, *mashal* (Aramaic: *mathla*), derived from a verb meaning "to be like", is a pretty wide label for any verbal image, from a figurative saying ("Like mother, like daughter", Ezek. 16:44) or a proverb ("Is Saul also among the prophets?" I Sam. 10:12), up to a proper parable (like Nathan's famous one about the ewe-lamb, II Sam. 12:1–7), an allegory (like Ezekiel's about the eagles and the vine, Ezek. 71:1–10), or even a long apocalyptic prediction (of which the "parables" of the Book of Enoch are examples). When therefore the men who made the Greek Old Testament chose *parabole* to translate *mashal*, it attracted to itself most of *mashal's* meanings. And this is why in the New Testament, which owes so much to Septuagint usage, proverbs like "Physician, heal thyself" are called "parables" equally with long stories like The Talents.

In germ, then, a parable is a figurative saying: sometimes a simile ("be wise as serpents", Matt. 10:16), sometimes a metaphor ("beware of the leaven of the Pharisees", Matt. 16:6). What we call parables are simply expansions of these. "All we like sheep have gone astray" (Isa. 53:6) is a simile. Expand it into a *picture* and you get a similitude like The Lost Sheep. Expand it into a *story* by using past tenses and you get a story-parable like The Prodigal Son. The difference between a similitude and a story-parable is this: whereas the similitude bases itself on some familiar truth or process (like putting a patch on a coat or leaven in meal), the story parable describes not what men commonly do but what one man did: "A sower went out to sow" (Matt. 13:3). "A man once gave a great banquet" (Lk. 14:16).

Most of the Gospel parables are either similitudes or story-parables. Though we must not distinguish too rigorously, parables are *not* allegories. What is the difference? In a proper allegory (like *The Pilgrim's Progress*) each detail of the story has its counterpart in the meaning; whereas in a parable, story and meaning meet, not at every point, but at *one* central point.

The other main point of difference to bear in mind is this. The true parable must be lifelike. By contrast, the allegory need not conform to the laws of lifelikeness, but may stray off into some "never-never land" where eagles can plant vines or stars become bulls. In a parable things are what they profess to be: loaves are loaves, stones are stones, lamps are lamps. But in an allegory it is not so. The room which the woman sweeps in The Lost Coin is a Galilean "but-and-ben". The room which the man sweeps in *The Pilgrim's Progress* is not a room but the "heart of a man never sanctified by the sweet grace of the Gospel."

How Many Parables Are There?

Counts have varied greatly, depending on how many of Christ's short figurative sayings one includes. A rough answer would be "fifty plus". My own estimate would be "about fifty-five". About twenty-five of these are similitudes. A further twenty-five are story parables. Four parables, which teach not by analogy but by direct example, are commonly called "Example Stories" (for example, The Good Samaritan). And one, The Last Judgment scene in Matthew 25, refuses to be classified.

Three features of Jesus' parables, which will concern us later, deserve brief mention here.

To begin with, Jesus' parables *obey the rules of popular story-telling*. Down the centuries men have found by experience that stories become more effective if you follow certain rough rules in telling them. "Repetition" in the "build-up" is a common one. Another is "the rule of contrast" whereby wisdom and folly, riches and poverty, etc., are set in contrast. Yet a third is "the rule of three" whereby the story has three characters ("An Englishman, an Irishman, and a Scotsman . . ."). A fourth is the rule of "end stress" whereby the spotlight falls on the last in the series, whether it is the youngest son or the final adventure.

Now look at the Gospels. Dives and Lazarus or The Wise and the Foolish Virgins illustrate the "rule of contrast". The three travelers in The Good Samaritan or the three excuse-makers in The Great

Banquet exemplify "the rule of three". The sending of "the only son" in The Wicked Vinedressers and the episode of the slothful servant who buried his talent are examples of the "rule of end stress"; and so on.

Second, the Gospel parable is something *extemporized* in living encounter with men rather than something lucubrated in study or cell. If the sonnet, for example, grows slowly in the soil of quiet – is essentially "emotion recollected in tranquility" – the parable is often improvised in the cut-and-thrust of conflict. For Jesus' parables, as we shall see, arise out of real situations and are often instruments of controversy in which he justifies his actions, confronts men with the will of God, or vindicates the gospel against its critics.

Third, every parable of Jesus was meant to evoke a response and to strike for a verdict. "What do you think?" he sometimes begins, and where the words are not found, the question is implied. There follows a true-to-life story or the description of a familiar happening; and the hearer is invited to transfer the judgment formed on the happening or the story to the urgent issues of the Kingdom of God, which is the theme of all his parables. "He that hath ears to hear, let him hear," he sometimes concludes. Which means: "This is more than just a pleasant story. Go and work it out for yourselves."

Why Did Jesus Use Parables?

The short answer is: to quicken understanding, by putting truth in a vivid and challenging way. And therefore, if the notorious verses in Mark 4:11 f. mean what, at first glance, they appear to mean – that Jesus deliberately used parables to *hide* God's truth from the masses and make them ripe for judgment – they cannot be words of Jesus. (My own view is that they are genuine words but that they do not belong here.)

For consider: Jesus knew himself to be God's Messenger to Israel at the supreme moment of her history, called to alert her to the great crisis, which was the inauguration of the Kingdom of God. If his "alarm signals" were to work, they could not afford to be unclear. As Paul put it, "if the trumpet gives an indistinct sound, who will get ready for battle?" (I Cor. 14:8). Accordingly, Jesus' parables, when first uttered, cannot have been dark riddles designed merely to mystify the multitudes.

Yet this conclusion must be held along with the recognition that the Gospel parable is not merely like an "illustration" in a sermon – a concrete example from life meant to make the truth plain as a pikestaff or sugar-coating on the theological pill to make it more palatable. The Gospel parable is meant to make people *think*. It appeals to the intelligence through the imagination. And sometimes, like the smoked glass we use during an eclipse – it *conceals* in order to reveal. Seen thus, the parable is not so much a *crutch* for limping intellects as a *spur* to spiritual perception.[3]

But if the parable is meant to quicken understanding, it requires that the hearer be in some kind of spiritual *rapport* with its teller, if he is to divine the heavenly truth behind the earthly story. A parable may miss its mark for one of two reasons: first, if the hearer lack the spiritual insight we have been describing; and, second, if the hearer understands but rejects the divine revelation the parable conveys.

One final remark. The parable, by its very nature, is hard to contradict. Demanding an opinion on its own human level, the parable finds an opening which makes the hearer lower his guard and leaves him defenceless. Then, before he is aware of it, the sword thrust is home – "Thou art the man!" Or, as P. G. Wodehouse makes one of his characters say: a parable is one of those stories in the Bible which sounds like a pleasant yarn and then suddenly pops up and leaves you flat! But if the parable is hard to contradict, how much also it can convey! What solemn warnings, what heart-searching accusations! Yes, but also what gentle and gracious assurances of God's mercy and God's love!

Where Did Jesus Get the Stuff of His Parables?

Not from some "never-never land" but from the real world all around him. Everybody knows how many images and illustrations he took from the book of *nature*. "The simplest sights we met," wrote Sir Edwin Arnold, after visiting Palestine,

> The simplest sights we met:
> The sower flinging seed on loam and rock;
> The darnel in the wheat; the mustard tree
> That hath its seed so little, and its boughs
> Wide-spreading; and the wandering sheep; and nets
> Shot in the wimpled waters – drawing forth
> Great fish and small – these, and a hundred such,
> Seen by us daily, never seen aright,
> Were pictures for him from the book of life,
> Teaching by parable.

(Sometimes today city-bred ministers, preaching to rural congregations, use pastoral illustrations, only to reveal their own ignorance and court the countryman's mockery. But the great Master of preaching makes no such mistakes. Your European – or American – farmer today, reading that the Sower cast his seed on the *un*plowed stubble, might suppose that Jesus had blundered. He would be wrong, for this is precisely what happens in Palestine, where sowing *precedes* plowing.[4])

Still larger in the parables bulks *the human scene* and the life of ordinary men and women in home or farm or market. The Leaven must go back to the time when Jesus watched "Mary his mother" hiding the yeast in "three measures of meal"; The Playing Children, to a Nazareth street where Jesus watched the lads and lassies playing "make believe" at weddings and at funerals. Other parables depict characters whom Jesus and his followers must have seen every day. Here, on the one hand, is a "gay Sadducee" clothed in purple and fine linen; or a rich farmer, building bigger granaries to house increasing crops. Here, on the other, is a farmer's man, who, having done a hard day's work in the field, must fall to and prepare his master's supper before he can get a "bite" for himself. But the list is endless. All are real folk; all act in character.

But the realism of the parables goes even further; for many of them – The Burglar, The Unjust Steward, The Hard-hearted Judge, The Ten Virgins – must have been based on real happenings to real people. The tale of The Wicked Vinedressers rings true of a Galilee that was cursed by absentee landlords and agrarian discontent. We may well hesitate to follow those who think that Jesus himself was the man who fell among thieves; but brigandage of that kind was common enough then on the twenty miles that lay between Jerusalem and Jericho.

We need say no more. The parables are not fables. They hold the mirror up to life.

Is the Tradition of the Parables Trustworthy?

The answer is: Yes, for various reasons. For one thing, in many parables the Palestinian background and the Aramaic idiom still traceable in the Greek, betoken the original.[5] For a second point, the parables reveal everywhere Jesus' own highly individual way of thinking – the daring faith in God, the picturesque outlook on man and nature, the occasional flash of humor, the swift little surprises of thought, etc. And, for a third and general consideration, it is worth observing that great parables are evidently so difficult to create, that it is hard to name another person in history with more than one or two good ones to his credit.

But if the tradition is to be trusted, this does not mean that no changes overtook the parables in the forty or fifty years which elapsed before they were committed to writing. Here we may learn much from the Form Critics. We are to think (they tell us) of the parables, in the period of the oral tradition, circulating singly or in pairs and taking a second lease on life as the early church impressed them into her service. For what did the early church use them chiefly? For preaching and teaching, exactly as we do today.

Thus the parables, in the earliest days, had *two* settings – their original setting in the life of Jesus, and their later one in the life of the early church. How did the church treat them? The Gospels supply the answer. Some they "re-audienced". The Lost Sheep, originally a parable of the redemptive joy of God addressed by Jesus to the Pharisees, became in Matthew 18 (the church chapter) a summons to pastoral concern for erring members. Others they "re-applied" to their own eschatological situation, "between the times". Thus The Ten Virgins, which had been on Christ's lips a rousing "Be prepared" to Israel in view of the impending crisis, became, in the church's use, a summons to be ready for Christ's Second Advent. Others again they "generalized", by adding a *logion* of Jesus which did not originally belong to the parable.[6] The saying, "He who humbles himself will be exalted," appended to the The Pharisee and the Publican, is one example of several. Finally, in three cases (The Tares, The Dragnet, and The Sower) the church added interpretations which read like early Christian expositions of these parables.

The recognition of these things should not shake our confidence in the tradition of the parables. It simply means that when we try to restore some of the parables to their original setting in the life of Jesus, we must make allowance for the church's usage. On the general question the verdict of Jeremias is to be accepted. "The student of the parables," he writes, "may be confident that he stands upon a particularly firm historical foundation. The parables are a fragment of the original rock of tradition."[7]

We are going to consider what light twentieth-century scholarship has to shed on the parables; but, before we come to it, we ought to have in our minds at least an outline of the history of exegesis.

THE HISTORY OF EXEGESIS

All down the centuries one question has dominated the discussion: How much of the parable is really significant? That is: Does a parable exist to make one point or many? To allegorize, or not to allegorize, that is the question.

As we listen to the answers given by the Fathers of the church, we may observe how deeply their interpretation of the parables has been affected by the doctrine of Scripture which they held and by their own particular theological emphasis.

From New Testament Times to the End of the Middle Ages

We may start by saying that from New Testament times to the Reformation, allegory supplied the chief key for the interpretation of the parables. Basically, allegory means the interpretation of a text in terms of something else, irrespective of what that something else may be. The method was Greek and older than Plato. Homer, whose works became a kind of Bible for the Greek races, was the first author to receive allegorical treatment. If the literal sense of Homer yielded an unworthy meaning (and the amours of the Olympian deities often shocked the morally sensitive), it became the custom to dig deep and discover some convenient and helpful "under meaning". So Homer was made, by the Stoics and others, to teach many things never dreamt of by the blind bard of Chios. But we need not dwell on this: for our purpose the important name is that of Philo, the Hellenist Jew of Alexandria who, in the first century B.C., used allegory to reconcile the faith of the Old Testament with Greek philosophy. With Philo allegory found a firm foothold in the Jewish exegetical tradition.

Paul uses it occasionally (witness the allegory of Sarah and Hagar in Galatians 4); but, except in Hebrews, allegory is not commonly employed by the New Testament writers. Yet the first attempts to apply it to the parables can be seen in the allegorical expositions of The Sower, The Tares, and The Dragnet. In the second century allegory became increasingly popular. The Gnostics, for example, poured their own wild fancies into the parables. Irenaeus and Tertullian, who refuted the Gnostics, themselves also used allegory and not always with restraint.

This is how Tertullian expounds The Prodigal Son: The elder son is the Jew; the younger, the Christian. The patrimony of which the latter claimed his share is that knowledge of God which a man has by his birthright. The citizen in the far country to whom he hired himself is the devil. The robe bestowed on the returning prodigal is that sonship from which Adam fell, as the feast is the Lord's Supper. But the biggest shock of all comes when we find him identifying the fatted calf with the Saviour.

What shall we say of this? *C'est pittoresque, mais ce n'est pas histoire.*

It was not in Carthage, however, but in Alexandria – Philo's city – that the allegorization of the parables was developed into a fine art, first by Clement and then by Origen. If any man deserves the name of *maestro* here, it is Origen, who held that Scripture might bear three senses – a literal, a moral, and a spiritual. And when he gets to work on the parables, his *expertise* almost takes our breath away.

Hear him, for example, expounding The Laborers in the Vineyard: Abel and Noah are the first laborers summoned to work; those called at the third hour are the patriarchs; the ninth hour men are the prophets; and the eleventh hour men, Christians. The penny paid them is salvation, and the man who hired them God.

Most of the trouble here is due to the love of allegory and an uncritical view of the Old Testament.

Now hear his exposition of The Good Samaritan: The man who fell among thieves is Adam. As Jerusalem signifies heaven, so Jericho, to which the traveler was bound, is the world. The robbers are man's enemies, the devil and his minions. The priest stands for the Law, the Levite for the prophets. The Good Samaritan is Christ himself; the beast, Christ's body; the inn is the church; the two pence the Father and the Son; and the Samaritan's "When I come again", Christ's Second Coming.

We might imagine that ingenuity could go no further; yet a hundred and fifty years later we find the great Augustine out-origening Origen. For now we learn that the binding up of the traveler's wounds signifies the restraint of sin, and the pouring in of oil, the comfort of hope. The Innkeeper, dropping his incognito, turns out to be the apostle Paul, and the "two pence" are the two commandments of love. With engaging frankness Augustine tells us that he enjoyed the exercise of ingenuity which this method affords, and adds that, as a preacher, he found it gripped his hearers' attention. How many preachers since have made like Augustinian confessions?

If you ask: Did none of the early Fathers realize that this was no proper way to treat the parables? the answer is: "the men of the rival school of Antioch did." Here the great names were those of Theodore of Mopsuestia and Chrysostom. Chrysostom, the prince of patristic exegetes, rejected Alexandrian allegory, insisting that all sound exegesis must start from the literal sense. We might sum up his view thus: "Always consider the parable as an organic whole, meant to make one point. Carry the judgment you have formed on the earthly story over into the spiritual sphere – be not over busy about the rest."

O si sic omnes!

It was the misfortune of history, however, that Alexandrian allegory prevailed over the good sense of Antioch, so that Origen's methods kept their vogue in the church for the next thousand years. In the Middle Ages dogmatic theology rather than exegesis was the main interest; and for their understanding of the parables the medieval exegetes relied for the most part on the Fathers. Indeed, they went one better than Origen. Where he found three senses in the sacred text, they found four.[8] From time to time voices were raised in protest against this wholesale discovery of spiritual meanings in scripture; but, where the parables were concerned, it was generally a case of "the allegorical mixture as before". Conrad Pepler has unearthed the sermon notes of a medieval English friar who preached to his congregation about 1150 on The Good Samaritan. But when we examine his exegesis, it is Origen and Augustine over again, with only minor variations. The medieval scholars liked to quote Augustine's dictum: "The scripture teaches nothing but the Catholic Faith." This is precisely what the friar makes the parable do, in an allegorizing line that runs back to Origen. And so it continued till the eve of the Reformation.

It is told of the Emperor Galerian that he once watched an archer ring twenty successive arrows at a target and failing with the lot.

"May I congratulate you," said the Emperor to the archer afterwards, "on your splendid talent for missing?" Would it be unfair to
say of the exegetes we have been discussing – with of course shining
exceptions like John Chrysostom – that, where the true meaning of
the parables was concerned, they showed a like talent for missing?

The Reformation and After

With the Reformation, Scripture, not the Pope, became the supreme authority. The Bible, through vernacular translations like
Luther's, was put within the reach of the humble believer. In theory,
at any rate, the time-honored interpretations of the Fathers were
rejected, and everyman, with the Holy Spirit's help, became his own
interpreter of Holy Writ. (In practice, this was not an unmixed
blessing; for now it became possible for everyman to make himself
a public nuisance with his private opinions.)

How did the parables fare at the Reformers' hands? As an interpreter, Luther's principles were much better than his own practice.
When we find him dismissing the allegorizing method as "monkey
tricks" (*Affenspiel*), saying hard things about Origen, and expressing
a strong preference for the literal sense of a passage, we are filled with
great expectations. In practice, however, Luther remained quite
hospitable to the allegories of the Fathers, and his own sermon on
The Good Samaritan shows as many "monkey tricks" as Origen's.
Nevertheless, if Luther did not rid himself of allegory, and if he
succeeds in finding justification by faith in passages where it would
not readily occur to most of us, he does bring to the exposition of
the parables his own grasp of evangelical truth and a sense of what is
vital, as his sermon on The Great Banquet, too long to quote here,
shows. Jülicher justly says of him that he combined the clear insights
of Chrysostom with the errors of Origen.

The other great Reformer, John Calvin, was the finest interpreter of
the parables since Chrysostom. The allegorizing of the Fathers he
pronounces "idle fooleries". "We ought," he says, "to have a deeper
reverence for scripture than to reckon ourselves at liberty to disguise
its natural meaning." And in his own comments on the parables he
goes, arrow-straight, for this "natural meaning", setting down the
central point in one clear sentence: as, for example, in his comment
on The Unjust Steward: "How silly it is to want to interpret each
detail!" he says. "Christ simply meant that the children of the world

are more diligent in their concern for their own fleeting interests than the sons of light for their eternal happiness."

Calvin is chiefly concerned to make each parable speak to the needs of his people, and naturally has no knowledge of modern critical methods; but for good sense and terse lucidity he deserves a place among the greatest expositors of the parables.

Alas, the new insights of the Reformers did not last very long. Their successors showed little of the freshness and acumen of Calvin; and in the seventeenth century a new era of scholasticism settled, like a depression, on the Protestant Church. The root of the trouble was that the inspiration of the Bible came to be equated with verbal inerrancy. During this time there arose on the Continent the "historico-prophetical" school of interpreters whose chief representatives were the German Cocceius (Koch) and the Dutchman Vitringa.[9] These men rightly saw that the parables of Jesus concerned the Kingdom of God; but they were resolved to find in each of them a part of that Kingdom's progressive development till the end of the world. And of course the parables were never meant to supply such a map of future history.

The Modern Period

In the seventeenth and eighteenth centuries the Bible had been largely a holy book to be kept in a glass case. But in the beginning of the nineteenth century, with the rise of biblical criticism, it was taken out of its glass case to be studied like any other book. How did this affect the study of the Gospels?

It meant of course a mortal blow to the doctrine of verbal inspiration; but it meant also a fresh, unfettered approach to all the problems connected with the life and ministry of Jesus, including the parables.

In the nineteenth century many books were written about the parables. We have space to mention only the three most important.

A hundred years ago the standard work on the subject was Archbishop Trench's *Notes on the Parables* (1841), a book sometimes still found on minister's shelves. A marvelous mine of learning it was too; but when we open it today, we cannot help feeling that the good archbishop is still in the Middle Ages and has learned nothing from Calvin. Fearful of the new criticism, he keeps harking back to the Fathers for his views, so that the inn (in The Good Samaritan) is still the church, the robe (in The Prodigal Son) is imputed righteousness, and the oil (in The Ten Virgins) is the Holy Spirit. He rightly says that the details in a parable are ancillary to the making of the main point; but in practice he tries to squeeze some spiritual meaning out of most of them, and is sometimes hard put to it to catch hares he should never have started running.

The first major book in English to harvest the fruits of the new criticism was A. B. Bruce's *The Parabolic Teaching of Christ* (1882). Allegorizing he repudiates. The numbers in Luke's three parables of the Lost (Chap. 15) are "natural, not mysterious". "The hundred sheep are the property of a shepherd of average wealth; the ten pieces of money are the pecuniary possession of a woman in humble life; the two sons signify a family just large enough to supply illustrations of the two contrasted characters." Discussing The Lost Coin, he observes that it would be easy to say that the house is the church; the woman, the Holy Spirit; the coin, man stamped with the image of God but lying in the dust of sin; the candle, the Word of God. But (he comments) how much better to feel the human pathos of the parable as a story from real life, and to make that pathos the one connecting link between the natural and the spiritual world? This is typical. Bruce's faults are those of a man of his time – he is a Liberal, and so tends to think of the Kingdom of God as a Divine Commonwealth and to talk of "the sweet reasonableness" of Jesus in a Renanesque way. But he brings a true breath of Galilee back into the parables. Of him his greatest pupil, James Denney, was to say: "He let me see Jesus."

The most famous book on the parables in this century came six years later from Germany: *Die Gleichnisreden Jesu* (Vol. I, 1888; Vol. II, 1899), by Adolf Jülicher. Jülicher sounded the death-knell of that allegorizing of the parables that had bedevilled interpretation through the centuries.

First, said Jülicher, the parables of Jesus are similitudes, not allegories. Accordingly, each of them has one *tertium comparationis* (point of likeness), not half a dozen.

Next, these similitudes Jesus employed to make his message plain and vivid to the multitudes. If Mark 4:11 f. says that he used parables to blind and befog his hearers, this is the early church speaking, not Jesus.

Therefore, in studying a parable, concentrate on the one central point of likeness, and consider the rest dramatic machinery necessary to the telling of the tale. What about allegorizing the details? What about killing a man!

So thoroughly did Jülicher do his work that for a time it seemed as if he had spoken the last word. Then gradually men began to see that, for all his great abilities, he had performed his task with too much Teutonic vigor and rigor. His book had two main faults.

To begin with, Jülicher took his idea of a parable from Aristotle when he should have sought its prototype in the rabbinical *mashal*. Now the rabbinical parables are not all pure similitudes; some have allegorical elements; a few are allegories. We cannot then declare *a priori* that Jesus' parables could not have contained allegorical elements.

Second: Jülicher said that a parable existed to make one point. But what kind of point? His answer was: a general moral truth. The point of The Talents, for example, was: "A reward is only earned by performance." Yet the Man who went about drawing these innocuous morals was eventually spiked to a cross. Would men have crucified a Galilean Tusitala who told charming stories to enforce prudential platitudes? Of course, they wouldn't! For all his merits, Jülicher had left the task of interpretation half done.

Nevertheless, he had cleared the way for the next and revolutionary advance which came thirty-six years later with C. H. Dodd's *Parables of the Kingdom* (1935). I should agree with Joachim Jeremias who, a dozen years later in his *Parables of Jesus* (1947), was to dot the i's and stroke the t's of Dodd's exposition, that it is unthinkable there should ever be any retreat from Dodd's essential insights. What then did Dodd and Jeremias do which Jülicher had not done? *They put the parables back into their true setting, which is the ministry of Jesus seen as the great eschatological act of God in which he visited and redeemed his people.*

This needs explanation.

In the thirty-odd years that followed Jülicher's *magnum opus* New Testament science made one very important advance. It discovered the true meaning of the Kingdom of God, which is the theme of all the parables.

The Kingdom, which means the rule or reign of God, is an eschatological concept. Eschatology means the doctrine of the End – the End conceived as God's age-long and final purpose destined to be realized in the future and to give meaning to the whole travail of history. Now, in Jewish thought, the reign of God is *the* great hope of the future. It is another name for the Good Time Coming, the Messianic Age. Thus, in reading the Gospels, we are to think of the Kingdom not as some moral disposition in the heart of man or some utopian society to be built by his efforts, but as the decisive intervention of the living God on the stage of human history for man's salvation. This is the first point. The second is this: The heart of Jesus' message was that this royal intervention of God was no longer a shining hope on the far horizon but a *fait accompli*. The Kingdom had arrived – was invading history. The living God was laying bare his arm for men's salvation. The "good news" is therefore not so much a program for human action as the proclamation of an *act* of God in Jesus Christ. This is what we know nowadays as "realized eschatology"; and though the word "realized" may not be the best one,[10] the theory makes sense of the Gospels and represents essential truth.

To this discovery was added in "the twenties" the work of the Form Critics. These scholars taught us that in the period of the oral tradition the parables circulate singly or in pairs and were used by the church for preaching and teaching purposes. This means that many of the parables, as they now stand in the Gospels, have been reapplied by the church to their own situation and needs. Once you recognize that the present settings of the parables are often those given them by the church, and that their original setting, when Jesus spoke them, was one of "realized eschatology", you begin to see them, along with the miracles, as part and parcel of Jesus' great proclamation that the Kingdom of God was breaking into history in his person and mission. Against this tremendous background the parables of Jesus become pregnant with meaning – weapons of war, if you like, in the campaign of the Kingdom of God against the Kingdom of the Devil, a campaign which culminated in the Cross.

NOTES

1. The amounts of parabolic teaching, *vis-à-vis* straight teaching, in the four Gospel sources are these: Mk. 16%; Q. 29%; M. 43%; L. 52%.

2. *The Gate of Life* (Longmans, Green & Company, London, 1935), p. 73.

3. Cf. T. W. Manson, *The Teaching of Jesus* (The University Press, Cambridge, 1931), p. 73.

4. Cf. Joachim Jeremias, *The Parables of Jesus* (SCM Press, London, 1954), p. 9.

5. For example, the parable of the Sower (Mark 4:3–9). "Here in Mark we may speak with confidence of a literal translation Greek version of Jesus." (Matthew Black, *An Aramaic Approach to the Gospels and Acts* [The Clarendon Press, Oxford, 1946], p. 45.)

6. For example, "To him that hath shall be given," etc.

7. *Op. cit.*, p. 9.

8. The new one was the "anagogical".

9. Bengel, author of the famous *Gnomon*, shared some of these views.

10. "Inaugurated" or "contemporized" might be less misleading.

THE LORD'S PRAYER IN MODERN RESEARCH

Joachim Jeremias

Joachim Jeremias is Professor of New Testament at Göttingen University, Germany. He holds the Ph.D. from the University of Leipzig. The essay which is reprinted by permission originally appeared in The Expository Times *(February 1960). Jeremias' principal works in English are:* Rediscovering the Parables *(1966),* The Eucharistic Words of Jesus *(1966),* The Central Message of the New Testament *(1965), and* Jerusalem in the Time of Jesus *(1969).*

I. THE LORD'S PRAYER IN THE ANCIENT CHURCH

DURING the time of Lent and Easter in the year A.D. 350 a Jerusalem presbyter, who in the next year was consecrated Bishop, Cyril of Jerusalem, held in the Church of the Holy Sepulchre his celebrated twenty-four catecheses, which have been treasured for us through the shorthand notes of one of his hearers.

From these notes we learn that at that time the Lord's Prayer was used in the Church Service. Cyril is the first to mention this use of the Lord's Prayer. He tells us that in Jerusalem the Lord's Prayer was prayed as the end of the Eucharistic prayers before the communion. This means that the Lord's Prayer was part of the Missa Fidelium in which only those who were baptized were allowed to participate. The late Professor T. W. Manson[1] has shown that this leads to the conclusion that the knowledge of the Lord's Prayer and the privilege to use it was reserved for the full members of the Church. As a matter of fact, the transmission of the Lord's Prayer was connected with baptism. The candidates for baptism learned the Lord's Prayer either shortly before or immediately after baptism. Sentence by sentence it was repeated to them with an explanation. Henceforth they prayed it daily and it formed a token of their identification as Christians. Such was the practice not only in Jerusalem but in the whole ancient Church.

The connection of the Lord's Prayer with baptism can be traced back to early times. In the beginning of the second century, we find a variant to Lk. 11:2 which reads: "Thy Holy Spirit come upon us and cleanse us." The heretic Marcion (about 140) had this instead of the first petition; his wording of the Lord's Prayer seems to have been as follows: "Father, Thy Holy Spirit come upon us and cleanse us. Thy kingdom come. Thy bread for the morrow give us day by day. And forgive us our sins for we also forgive everyone that is indebted to us. And allow us not to be led into temptation." Two minuscules (162, 700) and two late Church Fathers (Gregory of Nyssa † 394 and Maximus Confessor † 662) have the petition for the Holy Spirit instead of the second petition. It is quite improbable that the petition for the Holy Spirit should be the original text, its attestation is much too weak. From where, then, does this petition originate? We know that it was an old baptismal prayer and we may conclude that it was added to the Lord's Prayer when this was used at the baptismal ceremony. One may compare the Marcionite text quoted above which, in the petition for the bread, has "Thy bread". This, probably, is an allusion to the Eucharist; thus Marcion has both sacraments in view, the baptism in this first petition and the Eucharist, which followed baptism, in his "Thy bread".

But we must go one step still further back. The connection of the Lord's Prayer with baptism which we have found already in the first part of the second century can be traced back even into the first century. In an old document, *The Teaching of the Twelve Apostles* (*Didache*) which is dated by its most recent commentator, perhaps somewhat too confidently, as early as A.D. 50–70,[2] we find the following arrangement: chs. 1–6 the way of life and the way of death (which seems to have been the content of the instruction of the candidates for baptism), ch. 7 baptism, ch. 8 fasting and the Lord's Prayer, chs. 9–10 the Eucharist. Again, the Lord's Prayer as well as the Eucharist is seen to be reserved for those who have been baptized.

All this leads to a very important result which, again, T. W. Manson has pointed out most lucidly.[3] Whereas nowadays the Lord's Prayer is understood as a common property of all people, it was otherwise in the earliest times. As one of the most holy treasures of the Church, the Lord's Prayer, together with the Eucharist, was reserved for her full members. It was a privilege to be allowed to pray it. How great was the reverence and fear which surrounded it is best seen by an introductory formula found both in the liturgies of the East and in those of the West, ancient and modern: "*audemus dicere*", i.e. we make bold to say "Our Father". We should attempt to regain this reverence which says: I make bold to pray "Our Father". Perhaps, it may prove to be a modest help if we listen to what modern research has to tell us about the original meaning of the prayer which our Lord taught His disciples.

II. THE ORIGINAL WORDING

We find the Lord's Prayer twice in the New Testament: Mt 6:9–13 and Lk 11:2–4. Before trying to consider the original meaning of its petitions we must face the strange fact that the two Evangelists, St. Matthew and St. Luke, transmit it in slightly different wording. It is true that in the Authorized Version the differences are limited, the main divergence being that in Luke the doxology is absent, i.e. the concluding words: "For thine is the kingdom, and the power, and the glory, for ever." But as a matter of fact, the divergences are greater than this. Within the last hundred years, older texts have been found and in this last century New Testament scholarship, especially in Great Britain and Germany, and in the last decades also in the United States, has done admirable work in recovering the oldest text. The result of textual criticism in connection with the Lord's Prayer has been the following.

(*a*) St. Matthew has from the beginning the text which is familiar to us. Only originally the doxology was lacking; it was added very early – we find it already in the first century, as it is attested by the Didache. This does not mean, however, that our Lord meant that the Lord's Prayer should be used without a word of praise at the end. Only, in the very earliest time, the doxology was not fixed but its wording was left to the free formulation of those who prayed. Afterwards, when the Lord's Prayer began to be used more and more in the Service as a common prayer, it was felt necessary to establish a fixed formulation of the doxology.

(*b*) If we turn to St. Luke, we find that according to the oldest MSS, the text runs as follows:

> Father,
> Hallowed be Thy name,
> Thy kingdom come,
> Give us day by day our bread for the morrow
> And forgive us our sins, for we also forgive everyone that is indebted to us,
> And lead us not into temptation.

How came it that our Gospels give us different texts? It can be taken as a matter of course that the differences do not originate in the caprice of the particular evangelist; no author would have dared to make such alteration on his own. Here it may be helpful if we remind ourselves that St. Matthew as well as St. Luke gives us the Lord's Prayer as part of an instruction in prayer, the former as part of a Jewish-Christian instruction (Mt 6:5–15), the latter as part of a Gentile-Christian lesson (Lk 11:1–13) in prayer. From this we are in a position to understand that the differences are due to the different constituencies for which the two forms are intended. In other words, we are faced with the different liturgical wording of the Lord's Prayer in two different parts of the Church about the year A.D. 75. St. Matthew shows us the form in which the Jewish-Christian Church prayed the Lord's Prayer and St. Luke shows us that in which the Gentile-Christian Church prayed it in the eighth decade of the first century. But which form is the older one?

If we compare carefully the two texts, the chief divergence, which strikes us at once, is the difference in length. The Lucan form is shorter than that of St. Matthew at three places. Firstly, the invocation is shorter. St. Luke says only "Father", in Greek $\pi\acute{a}\tau\epsilon\rho$, in Aramaic, *abba*, whereas St. Matthew says, according to the pious and reverent form of Palestinian invocation, "Our father who art in heaven". Secondly, whereas St. Matthew and St. Luke agree in the two first petitions – the Thou-petitions ("Hallowed be thy name, thy Kingdom come"), there follows in St. Matthew a third Thou-petition: "Thy will be done in earth, as it is in heaven." Thirdly, in St. Matthew the last of the following We-petitions has an antithesis. St. Luke has only: "And lead us not into temptation", but St. Matthew adds: "but deliver us from evil".

Now, if we ask, which form is the original – the longer form of St. Matthew or the shorter form of St. Luke – the decisive observation is the following: the shorter form of St. Luke is completely contained in the longer form of St. Matthew. This makes it very probable that the form of St. Matthew is an expanded one. All liturgical texts have a tendency to expansion. Nobody would have dared to shorten a sacred text like the Lord's Prayer and to leave out two petitions if they had formed part of the original tradition. This result is confirmed by three supplementary observations. Firstly, we shall see that the simple *Abba* was a unique note in Jesus' own prayers and from St. Paul (Ro 8:15, Gal 4:6) we learn that this short address "*Abba* Father" was used by the oldest Christians. Thus we must conclude that this plain *Abba* was the original address. Secondly, the threefold expansion which we find in St. Matthew in comparison with St. Luke is always found towards the end of a section of the prayer – the first at the end of the address, the second at the end of the Thou-petitions, the third at the end of the We-petitions. This is exactly in accordance with what we find elsewhere in liturgical texts: they have a preference for expansions at the end. The third observation concerns the three We-petitions. The first two of them show a parallelism:

"The bread for to-morrow/give us to-day
 Do Thou forgive us/as we forgive."

But the third is shorter in St. Luke, apparently with intention:

"And lead us not into temptation."

Matthew offers here, too, a parallelism:

"And lead us not into temptation; but deliver us from evil."

This is also in accordance with what we find in liturgical texts: they have a tendency to give a symmetrical structure.

Thus, all these observations lead us in the same direction: The common substance of both texts, which is identical with its Lucan form, is the oldest text. The Gentile-Christian Church has handed down the Lord's Prayer without change, whereas the Jewish-Christian Church, which lived in a world of rich liturgical tradition, has enriched the Lord's Prayer liturgically.

Of course, we must be cautious with our conclusions. The possibility remains that Jesus Himself spoke the "Our Father" on different occasions in a slightly differing form, a shorter one and a longer one. But perhaps it would be safer to say that the shorter Lucan form is in all probability the oldest one, whereas St. Matthew gives us the earliest evidence that the Lord's Prayer was used liturgically in worship and service. In any case, the chief thing is, that both texts agree in the decisive contents.

There remains still a last remark concerning the original wording. If we compare the common substance of the two forms, we find several small divergences in the two We-petitions. The first We-petition: Matthew has: "Give us this day our bread for the morrow," Luke reads: "Give us day by day our bread for the morrow." The Lucan form is a generalized saying "day by day", and therefore he was obliged to use (only at this place in the Lord's Prayer) the present imperative δίδου (Matthew δός). Clearly Matthew's form is the more original. The second We-petition: Matthew has "our debts", Luke "our sins". The Aramaic word (*hobha*) originally meant debt and then had come to be used for sin. Matthew gives a literal translation using ὀφείλημα, which means debt but is not usual in Greek for sin. Luke has replaced this word by the usual Greek word for sin. Finally, Matthew has ἀφήκαμεν ("we have forgiven"), Luke has ἀφίομεν ("we forgive"). Matthew has the more difficult form, as the past tense (ἀφήκαμεν), erroneously, as we shall see, could be understood as if our forgiveness preceded God's forgiveness. In such cases the more difficult form is to be regarded as the more original. On the whole then we must conclude that whereas Luke has preserved the original form in respect of the length, Matthew has preserved the original form in respect of the common wording.

The important thing is that the differences between Matthew and Luke concerning the choice of the words must be regarded as so-called translation-variants, i.e. they give us evidence that an underlying Aramaic original was translated into Greek in different ways. This is an important help if we try to retranslate the Lord's Prayer into the mother-tongue.

I shall give a retranslation of the shorter form.[4] Even if we do not understand the single words, we may be able to note that our Lord used the solemn language of the prophets, as Burney has shown in his admirable book *The Poetry of Our Lord*. Especially, we should pay attention to three features of this solemn language – namely the parallelism, the two-beat-rhythm, and the rhyme. This, then, may be approximately the original wording:

> *Abba*
> *jithqaddaš šᵉmakh*   *tethe malkhuthakh*
> *laḥman dᵉlimḥar*   *habh lan joma dhen*
> *ušᵉbhoq lan ḥobhain*   *kᵉdišᵉbhaqnan lᵉḥajjabhain*
> *wᵉla taᵉelinnan lᵉnisjona.*

III. The Original Meaning

Having considered what can be said about the original wording, we are prepared to face the main question: What was, as far as we can judge, the original meaning?

It is holy ground on which we tread. St. Luke gives us the situation: the praying Lord and the disciples asking: "Lord, teach us to pray" (11:1).

> And he said unto them: When ye pray, say:
> Abba,
> Hallowed be Thy name,
> Thy kingdom come,
> Our bread for tomorrow/give us today
> And forgive us our debts/as we forgive our debtors
> And lead us not into temptation.

The structure of the Lord's Prayer is quite easy to follow:

(1) The address, (2) the two Thou-petitions in parallelism, (3) the two We-petitions, forming both, as we shall see, an antithesis, (4) the concluding request.

1. *The Address.* When we trace back the history of the invocation of God as father we are confronted with unexpected and even moving facts. It is surprising to see that in the ancient Orient, as early as the third and second millennium B.C., we find the deity addressed as father. In Sumerian prayers, long before the times of Moses and the

prophets, we find this title, and there already the word father does not merely refer to the deity as the procreator and as the powerful lord, but it has also quite another significance: "O God, whose forgiveness is like that of a kind father."

When we, secondly, turn to the Old Testament we find that God is only seldom addressed as father, in fact only on fourteen occasions, but all these are important. God is Israel's father, but now not mythologically as the procreator, but as He who elected, delivered, and saved His people by mighty deeds in history. God is Israel's father – but, this is the constant reproval of the prophets, Israel has not given Him the honour which a son should give to his father. "If then I be a father, where is mine honour? saith the Lord" (Mal 1:6). And Israel's answer to this reproval is the confession of sin and the cry: *Abhinu atta*, "Thou art our father". And God's reply is mercy beyond all understanding: "I taught Ephraim also to go, taking them by their arms" (Hos 11:3). "How shall I give thee up Ephraim? . . . mine heart is turned within me" (Hos 11:8).

Can there be a still deeper sense in this one word father? We are still more moved and astonished when we, thirdly, turn to the Gospels. There is something quite new, absolutely new – the word *abba*. With the help of my assistants I have examined the whole later Jewish literature of prayer, and the result was that in no place in this immense literature is this invocation of God to be found. How came this about? The Church Fathers Chrysostom, Theodore, and Theodoret, who originated from Antioch and had Aramaic-speaking nurses, tell us that *abba* was the address of the small child to his father. And the Talmud confirms it, when it says: The first words for a child when it leans to eat wheat (i.e. when it is weaned) are: *abba, imma*, dear father, dear mother.[5] *Abba* was a homely family word, the tender address of the babe to its father; O dear father – a secular word. No Jew would have dared to address God in this manner. Late Judaism never addressed God as *abba* – Jesus did it always, in all His prayers – with one single exception, the cry from the Cross: "My God, my God, why hast thou forsaken me?"

The invocation of God as *abba* is not to be understood merely psychologically as a step towards a deeper cognition of God – rather we learn from Mt 11:27 that it is the expression of Jesus' Messianic authority. He alone, the only begotten Son, had the Messianic privilege of this invocation of the heavenly father: *Abba*.

And this is the fourth and the last and most astonishing fact: In the Lord's Prayer Jesus gives His disciples a share in this privilege to address God as *abba*, a share in His position as the only begotten. He empowers them to speak to their Heavenly Father literally as the small child speaks to his father, in the same confident and childlike manner. This one word *abba*, if it is understood in its full sense, comprehends the whole message of the gospel. This St. Paul has understood, when he says twice: There is no surer sign or guarantee of the possession of the Holy Spirit and the sonship than this: that a man "makes bold" to repeat this one word *Abba*.

2. *The Two Thou-Petitions*. The first words which the child shall say to his heavenly father are: "Hallowed be thy name, Thy kingdom come."

This is a parallelism, both petitions having the same content. These two petitions recall the Qaddish, the sanctification, an Aramaic prayer which formed the conclusion of every service in the synagogue. It runs in its probably oldest form: "Hallowed be His great name in the world which He created according to His will. May His kingdom be established in your lifetime, speedily, soon, so say: Amen."

We see that the two Thou-petitions are eschatological. They implore God to reveal His final glory, they ask for the coming of the hour in which God's profaned and misused name shall be hallowed for ever, and in which the triumphant call sounds: "The kingdoms of this world are become the kingdoms of our Lord, and of his Christ; and he shall reign for ever and ever" (Rev 11:15). Their contents are identical with the prayer of the first community *Maran-atha* (1 Co 16:22), "Come, Lord Jesus" (Rev 22:20).

But the two Thou-petitions are not the same as the Qaddish, in spite of the similar wording. There is a great difference. For those who pray in these words as disciples of Jesus ask for the coming of the consummation as people who know that the great turning-point of the ages has already taken place. God has already begun His saving work. It is only the full accomplishment which is lacking.

These petitions are an expression of an absolute confidence. The disciples of Jesus, standing in the struggle between Christ and Antichrist, seemingly a prey of evil and death and Satan, lift their eyes to their Father. In spite of all the demonic powers they take God's power seriously, they throw themselves upon His promise and His infinite mercy and give themselves completely into God's hands in unshakeable confidence. *Abba*, father, Thou wilt perform Thy wonderful work.

3. *The Two We-Petitions*. The two We-petitions lead us one step further along the same road. They hang together as closely as the two Thou-petitions, they also form a pair of parallelisms. Here, it is important to remind ourselves that the two first petitions recall the Qaddish – for we must conclude, that the accent of the whole prayer lies on that part which is new, that is, on these two We-petitions. They are the real heart of the prayer, the two Thou-petitions forming the introduction.

(*a*) The first of the We-petitions asks for the ἄρτος ἐπιούσιος. There has been a long discussion about the meaning of the word ἐπιούσιος, and it is not yet finally settled. In my opinion, it is decisive that Jerome tells us that in the lost Aramaic gospel of the Nazarenes the translation *mahar* appears "for tomorrow". It is true, this gospel of the Nazarenes is not older than the Gospel of St. Matthew, but it was a translation of the First Gospel into the Aramaic. In spite of this, the translation *mahar* – "bread for tomorrow" – must be older than the gospel of the Nazarenes, even than the Gospel of St. Matthew. For the translator, when coming to the Lord's Prayer, of course stopped translating – he simply gave the holy words in the wording which he prayed day-by-day. In other words, the Aramaic speaking Jewish-Christians among whom the Lord's Prayer lived on in its original language in unbroken usage since the days of our Lord prayed: "Our bread for tomorrow give us today". Jerome tells us even more. He adds a remark telling us how the word "bread for tomorrow" was understood: *mahar quod dicitur crastinum id est futurum*, "*mahar* is: for tomorrow and that means future". As a matter of fact, in later Judaism *mahar* meant not only the next day, but also the future, the final consummation. Accordingly, says Jerome, the bread for tomorrow was not meant as earthly bread but as the bread of life. This eschatological understanding was indeed, as we know from the old translations, the dominating sense given to the word in the first centuries in the whole Church, the Eastern as well as the Western Church. They all understood the bread for tomorrow as the bread of life, the bread of the salvation time, the heavenly Manna. The bread of life and the water of life have been since ancient times symbols of paradise, an epitome of the abundance of all the corporal and spiritual gifts of God. It is this bread which our Lord meant when He said: "Man shall not live by bread alone, but by every word that proceedeth out of the mouth of God" (Mt 4:4), and again "if any man eat of this bread, he shall live for ever" (Jn 6:51). This bread of life, symbol, image, and fulfilment of the salvation time, this bread will He give to His own in the consummation (Lk 22:30) when He, the Master of the house, will minister to them (12:37) and give them the broken bread and the cup of blessing (always He the giving one and His own the recipients).

This may be a surprise, or even a disappointment for us. I have often heard the remark: There was one request in the Lord's Prayer leading into the plain work-day, the petition for daily bread. Don't we become poorer, if it is taken metaphorically? No, it is, in reality, an enrichment. Earthly bread and heavenly bread are no contrasts for our Lord. In the realm of faith all earthly things are hallowed. The bread which Jesus broke when He sat at table with the publicans and sinners, as well as the bread which He gave His disciples at the Last Supper, was earthly bread and yet it was more; it was bread of life. The bread of life embraces all we need for body and soul. It includes the daily bread. For Jesus' disciples every earthly meal was a Messianic meal, symbol and anticipation of the heavenly feast. In the same way, for all His followers, every meal is a meal in His presence. He is the host who fills the hungry and thirsty with the fulness of His blessings. Only if we realize all this do we understand the incredible boldness of the petition "Give us *this* day our bread for the morrow".

This is an antithesis: tomorrow/today, the whole accent lying on the words "this day". In a world of slavery under Satan, in a world where God is remote, in a world of hunger and thirst, the disciples of Jesus dare to say, this day give us the bread of life, now already, here already, this day already. Jesus gives to the children of God the privilege of stretching out their hands, to grasp the glory of the consummation, to fetch it down, to believe it down, to pray it down – right into their poor life: now already, here already, this day already.

(*b*) Now already – this is also the meaning of the petition for forgiveness. This request looks upon the great reckoning which the world must expect, the disclosure of God's majesty in the final judgment. Jesus' disciples know how they are involved in guilt and sin; they know that only God's forgiveness can save them from the wrath. But they ask not only for mercy in the hour of the last judgment – rather they ask: forgive us our debts – now already, here already, this day already. Through Jesus their Lord they belong to the salvation time. Forgiveness is the one great gift of salvation time. The Messianic time is the time of forgiveness. Grant us, O Father, this one great gift of the Messiah time – this day already, here already.

This petition, too, has two parts which form an antithesis (Thou-we): forgive us our debts as we forgive our debtors. This is not a comparison, how should Jesus' disciples compare their poor forgiving with God's mercy? What, then, is the meaning of this sentence "as we forgive our debtors"? A grammatical observation may give the answer. As we have seen, Matthew has here a past tense ($\dot{\alpha}\phi\acute{\eta}\kappa\alpha\mu\epsilon\nu$); in Aramaic the perfect is often a so-called *perfectum praesens*, indicating an action which takes place here and now. Thus, the correct translation would be "as we herewith forgive our debtors". This is a reminder for him who asks for God's forgiveness that he must himself be ready to forgive. God can forgive only if we are ready to forgive. "And when ye stand praying, forgive, if ye have ought against any: that your Father also which is in heaven may forgive you your trespasses" (Mk 11:25). This willingness to forgive is the outstretched hand, by which we grasp God's forgiveness. Jesus' disciples say: "O Lord, we belong to the Saviour, to the Messiah, to the Redeemer. We are ready to return the mercy we get to our fellow-brethren. Give us the gift of salvation time, Thy forgiveness. We stretch out our hands, forgive us our debts – now already, here already."

4. *The Conclusion*. Up to this point, the petitions have been in parallelism, the two Thou-petitions as well as the two We-petitions, but this last petition is only one single line: "And lead us not into temptation." This sounds abrupt, and that is intentional. But why?

Let us first briefly consider the wording and make two remarks. Firstly, "Lead us not" does not mean that God Himself tempts us. Rightly St. James rejects such a misunderstanding; he probably has this petition in mind when he says: "God cannot be tempted with evil, neither tempteth he any man" (Ja 1:13). The meaning is rather: "Do not permit that we be overcome by the temptation." This is to be seen from an old Jewish evening prayer which Jesus may have known and which says: "Do not lead me into the power of a sin, a temptation, a shame," where the request is clearly that

God might not permit that he who prays may be overwhelmed by sin or temptation or a shameful thing. Secondly, the word temptation ($\pi\epsilon\iota\rho\alpha\sigma\mu\acute{o}s$) does not mean the small temptations or everyday life but the great last test, which stands before the door, the revelation of the secret of evil, the abomination of desolation, Satan sitting on God's throne, antichrist's power revealed – the last temptation of God's saints by pseudo-prophets and false saviours. Who can escape?

This last petition, then, means: "O Lord, preserve us from falling away!"

Now, perhaps, we understand the abruptness of this last petition. Jesus has led His disciples to ask for the fulfilment, when God's name is hallowed, His kingdom comes. More, He has encouraged them to bring the gifts of the salvation time down into their own poor lives – now already, here already. But with the soberness which is characteristic of all His words, with the absence of all false enthusiasm, Jesus takes them back into the reality of their lives, abruptly, and this abruptness lends redoubled force to His words.

This is a cry of distress, a resounding cry for help out of the depth.[6] We are so weak and the danger is tremendous: "O Father, this one request grant us: preserve us from falling away." It is not by chance that this last petition has no parallel, neither in the Old Testament nor in the prayers of the time of our Lord.

Clement of Alexandria has preserved a saying of Jesus, which is not written in the Gospels. It says: "Ask ye for the great things, so will God grant you the little things."[7] Ye are praying falsely, says the Lord. Always your prayers are moving in a circle around your own small I, your own needs and troubles and desires. Ask for the great things – for God's almighty glory and Kingdom, and that God's great gifts, the bread of life and the endless mercy of God may be granted to you – now already, here already, this day already. That does not mean that you may not bring your small personal needs before God, but they must not govern your prayer: for you are praying to your Father. He knows all. He knows what things His children have need of before they ask Him, and He adds them to His great gifts. Jesus says: Ask ye for the great things, so God will grant you the little things. The Lord's prayer teaches us how to ask for the great things.

NOTES

1. T. W. Manson, "The Lord's Prayer", in *Bulletin of the John Rylands Library*, Vol. XXXVIII (1955–1956), Pt. 1, pp. 99–113; Pt. 2, pp. 436–448.

2. Jean-Paul Audet, *La Didachè. Instructions des Apôtres* (Paris, 1958), p. 219.

3. *Loc. cit.*, pp. 101 f.

4. Cf. the retranslations of the Lord's Prayer in C. C. Torrey, *The Translations made from the Original Aramaic Gospels* (Studies in the History of Religions Presented to Crawford Howell Toy by Pupils, Colleagues, and Friends) (New York, 1912), pp. 309 ff.; *The Four Gospels* (New York and London, 1933), p. 292; E. Littmann, "Torrey's Buch über die vier Evangelien", in *ZNW*, Vol. xxxiv (1935), pp. 20–34, especially pp. 29 f.; C. F. Burney, *The Poetry of Our Lord* (Oxford, 1925), pp. 112 f.; G. Dalman, *Die Worte Jesu*, Vol. i (Leipzig, 1930), pp. 283–365; K. G. Kuhn, "Achtzehngebet und Vaterunser und der Reim", in *Wissenschaftliche Untersuchungen zum Neuen Testament*, Vol. i (Tübingen, 1950), pp. 32 f.

5. *b Ber.* 40a, *b Sanh.* 70b.

6. H. Schürmann, *Das Gebet des Herrn* (Leipzig, 1957), p. 90.

7. J. Jeremias, *Unknown Sayings of Jesus* (London, 1957), pp. 87 ff.

7

DID JESUS REALLY RISE
FROM THE DEAD?

Wolfhart Pannenberg

Wolfhart Pannenberg is Professor of Systematic Theology on the Protestant Theological Faculty at Munich University, Germany. The present provocative essay is reprinted from the Spring issue 1965 of Dialog *by permission. The subject is worked out in greater detail in Pannenberg's book* Jesus – God and Man *(German 1964, English 1968). The position taken in the book is less conservative than this essay has led some to believe. Also in English are* Revelation as History *(1968),* Theology and the Kingdom of God *(1969).*

THE ANSWER to this question is absolutely decisive for any Christian proclamation and for the Christian faith itself. This was the case from the very beginning of Christianity. And it cannot be expressed more distinctly than it was by Paul in I Corinthians 15:14: "If Christ has not been raised, then our preaching is in vain and your faith is in vain." It could be shown in detail that the early Christian traditions, preserved in the New Testament writings, were formed from the experience of the risen Lord appealing to the apostles. Neither the message of Jesus' cross as a medium of salvation nor the Synoptics' witness of the pre-Easter activity of Jesus would have been developed without the Easter event, nor the early Christian conviction that Jesus is the One by whose appearance the expectation of God's Messiah and of the future Son of Man, who will come from Heaven to judge the living and the dead, is fulfilled. Only because of the resurrection of Jesus were the Synoptics able to describe his earthly cause to be the cause of the Messiah or of the Son of Man.

Thus, the resurrection of Jesus is the decisive ground for the proclamation and for faith; however, it cannot be considered as a single event, for it has to be considered in connection with Jesus' whole course of life. It is only by this event that everything else in Jesus' appearing is illuminated. Every previous event would have been something else than it is now, but for Jesus' resurrection. The importance of the question of whether or not Jesus really rose from the dead should be clear enough. But how can it be answered? Could the answer be left to a mere decision of faith? This must be absolutely denied. Jesus' resurrection is the basis of faith, but this again cannot owe its certitude to a decision of faith, otherwise faith would find its basis in itself. Faith cannot exist by its own decision. It can only live out of a reality which provides the basis and reason for faith. This must be the presupposition for a decision of faith. If the certitude of faith would not have its roots in a certainty of its presuppositions, it could scarcely be distinguished from superstition.

Thus, Paul in his first letter to the Corinthians, chapter 15, did not think a mere demand for faith was enough, but he gave the list of the witnesses of the resurrection of Jesus. This is a proof as it was commonly used in legal proceedings. The Greek historians, for instance Herodotus, also gave their proofs in such a way. Historical evidence was obtained by an interrogation of the eyewitnesses. It is not without reason that Paul emphasized the point that most of the witnesses were still alive and could still be submitted to an interrogation (I Corinthians 15:6). The proof Paul gave was for his time a historical proof, a first-hand proof beyond doubt. However, today this argumentation is no longer satisfactory for us without further explanation. We cannot hear these eyewitnesses any more to make sure that they were not deluded. But by means of modern historical research, we are able to gain positive knowledge of these events in the past, for which we have no witnesses. We examine the literary and archaeological witnesses in the same way as Herodotus interrogated his contemporaries. By doing this the modern historian tries to find out the tendencies in his sources, and from this conclusions are drawn. The real fact, then, is gained by that description of the events which covers in the best possible way all available evidences.

The question is whether we can, with the methods and criteria applied everywhere else today, achieve what Paul achieved by his first-hand proof for his time: a proven knowledge of the resurrection of Jesus as an event that happened at a certain time, a knowledge which can be the basis of our faith, as it was the basis for Paul and his congregations?

I. The Meaning of Resurrection

Before we can answer these historical questions in detail, we have to decide about the precise meaning of the expression, "resurrection from the dead". Only if we have a precise notion of this, will we know whether this question has any importance.

First it has to be stated that the expression "resurrection from the dead" has a metaphorical character. This expression stands for something we can experience in our everyday life like a mountain or a tree, like waking or sleeping. It is rather a metaphor, a way of speaking in an image. Just as we arise from sleep in the morning, in a similar way those who are dead shall also rise. This is not a literal expression for a reality which can already be experienced, but something which normally cannot be experienced directly and, therefore, must be described by a metaphor, in analogy to our rising from sleep daily. This metaphorical sense of the expression could already be found when the notion of resurrection is first mentioned in the Old Testament (Isaiah 26:19). The terms "rise" and "awake" are used in parallel. The frequently used interpretation of death as sleep has similar implications. (Daniel 12:2; Paul; I Thessalonians 4: 13, 15; I Corinthians 11:36; 15:6, 20, 51.)

One could be tempted in following the analogy of sleep and rising to think that the resurrection of the dead is a simple revivification of the corpse, an arising and walking of those who formerly were dead. This certainly is not intended in the early Christian image of the resurrection of the dead; in any case, Paul does not follow this line. For him resurrection means the new life of a new body, not a return of life into the physical body that died but has not yet decayed. Paul explicitly discussed the question of the corporality of those who rose from death (I Corinthians 15:35–56). For him there is no doubt about the fact that the future body will be another body than our present body, not, as he says, a physical body but a spiritual body (I Corinthians 15:44). The relation between the imperishable spiritual body and the present perishable physical body is described by Paul as a radical transformation: "I tell you this, brethren: flesh and blood cannot inherit the kingdom of God, nor does the perishable inherit the imperishable" (v. 50). But on the other hand it is the present perishable body that will undergo this "transformation" according to Paul: "For this perishable nature must put on the imperishable, and this mortal nature put on immortality" (v. 53). On the one hand, the transformation of the perishable into a spiritual body will be so radical that nothing will be left unchanged. There is no substantial or structural continuity from the old to the new. But on the other hand, the physical body itself will undergo this transformation. Nothing else shall be produced in its place, but a historical continuity relates the old to the new.

Here Paul does not refer especially to Jesus' resurrection but to the resurrection for which all the Christians were waiting. But Paul must have had the same mental image of the resurrected Jesus, for he has described the resurrection of Jesus and that of the Christians to be completely parallel events in every item (e.g. Romans 6:8; 8:29; Philippians 3:21). Paul also understood the resurrection of Jesus to be a radical transformation, not a mere revivification of his corpse. This is especially important for the reason that Paul's report is the only one we have, written by a man who saw the resurrected Lord with his own eyes. The appearance of Christ which Paul experienced must have been of a kind that could not be mistaken for a revivified corpse, but could only be understood as a reality of a completely different kind.

From this we conclude that the resurrection of the dead in the Christian hope for the future and in the Easter faith has to be sharply distinguished from those resurrections from the dead which are reported elsewhere in ancient literature as miracles and also from those which Jesus himself accomplished according to the gospels, e.g. the raising of the widow's son (Luke 7:11–17; Matthew 8:5–13) and the raising of Lazarus (John 11:38–44). Quite apart from the question of the trustworthiness of these legendary reports – probably of a later period – there is no doubt that these reports were intended to describe events of quite another kind than that intended by the testimony about the resurrection of Jesus and by the early Christian eschatological hope. In the case of Lazarus and the widow's son, we have a transitory return to life of one already dead. There is not a moment's doubt for the narrator that these persons, who were raised in this way again to life, had to die again. In the resurrection of Jesus and in the Christian eschatological hope, life means quite another thing – an imperishable life not limited by any death, which must be in any case completely different from ordinary organic structures.

II. THE APOCALYPTIC EXPECTATIONS

If one puts the next question: How could Paul know what the life of the resurrection would be like, one cannot simply answer that he knew it because of the apparition he had of the resurrected Jesus. We have to realize that already before Paul there was a tradition in which the expectation of the resurrection of the dead (be it for all men or only for the righteous ones) was alive. This is the Jewish apocalypticism which gained more and more ground after the time of the Babylonian exile and had penetrated deeply into the thinking of the Jews, e.g. the Pharisees. The beginnings of this movement are found already in the Old Testament, in Isaiah 24–26, and in Daniel. It can also be seen in other books which are hardly less important but do not belong to the Old Testament Canon, e.g. the book of Enoch, a collection of different apocalyptic writings. The apocalyptic expectations of a future resurrection of the dead, in association with the last judgment, is perhaps influenced by Persian ideas. Palestine had been under Persian rule after the breakdown of Babylon and the return of the exiled Jews.

Evidently the apocalyptic expectation of the resurrection was connected already very early with the idea of a transformation, of the resurrected righteous ones like the angels in heaven or like the stars. More precise reflections on the process of transformation, however, as in I Corinthains 15, can be found only later in the apocalyptic literature of the first century A.D. Jesus himself also shared this idea of the transformation. In Mark 12:25, Jesus answers the question of the Sadducees who ask about the life of those who are resurrected: "For when they rise from the dead, they neither marry nor are given in marriage, but are like angels in heaven"; Luke 20:36 adds: "for they cannot die any more". In any case, the explanation "like angels in heaven" was intended to say that there is a completely different mode of existence, as Paul did when he spoke of a spiritual body. Both Jesus and Paul with their ideas of the life of resurrection thus stood in a specific tradition of the apocalyptic theology.

Only because of this expectation of Jewish apocalypticism, did Paul have the possibility of designating this special event that occurred to him and before him to other disciples of Jesus as an event in the mode of existence proper to the life of resurrection. Paul, therefore, made the expectation of the general resurrection of the dead the presupposition of the acknowledgment of Jesus' resurrection. "For if the dead are not raised, then Christ has not been raised" (I Corinthians 15:16). The early Christian missions, therefore, also have to explain to the Gentiles the apocalyptic expectation of a general resurrection of the dead with a final judgment; the mission, indeed, accomplished this task (I Thessalonians 1:10; Hebrews 6:1). The truth of the expectation of the general resurrection of the dead was, thus, already presupposed in order to understand the particular message of the resurrection of Jesus. This is also valid for our historical judgment.

If one assumes that the dead cannot rise, that any event of this type can never happen, the result will be such a strong prejudice against the truth of the early Christian message of Jesus' resurrection, that the more precise quality of the particular testimonies will not be taken into consideration in forming a general judgment. Only if the expectation of the future general resurrection of all men from death, whether for life or for judgment, makes sense in itself, only if it also expresses the truth for us, will it then be meaningful to put the question of Jesus' resurrection as a question of historical importance.

We can here only mention briefly that the idea of the resurrection of the dead in fact contains a philosophical and anthropological truth. It seems to me that men cannot understand themselves as men without the conception of a resurrection from the dead. That man has to seek for his final destination beyond death is based on the specifically human structure of existence, on the so-called openness to the world. Philosophy, too, has known about this from its beginnings when it has spoken of the immortality of the soul. However, we can no longer use this expression because it is not adequate to our knowledge about the inseparability of body and soul. If men must seek their final destination beyond death, then it must be in the unity of body and soul. But just this is the content of the hope for a resurrection of the dead. This expression is – as mentioned above – metaphorical. We do not know what is awaiting us beyond death in another dimension of reality. In spite of this, however, we have to form an idea of it in order to become aware of our destiny. We can only form such an idea of what is completely hidden from us by analogy with known factors, that is, in the image of arising from sleep. It is necessary for a clear self-understanding of our human existence to form such an idea. This connection is the proof for the truth of the expectation of the resurrection of the dead.

Only if one takes this general presupposition as a starting point is it at all significant to put the question of the resurrection of Jesus as a historical question. Then we must ask if it is not possible to explain in some other way for our historical understanding that which the disciples experienced at the time and expressed as a resurrection from the dead, i.e. by this metaphorical expression through which we think of the final destination of man.

III. The Easter Appearances

Now we come to an examination of early Christian Easter traditions. They form two different lines independent of each other; the traditions of the appearances of the resurrected Lord and the traditions of finding the empty tomb of Jesus. It is only in the latest reports in the Gospel of John that both groups have fused. The oldest texts report either appearances only (I Corinthians 15) or a narrative of the empty tomb (thus the original report of Mark, in 16:1–8; Mark 16:9–20 is later attached as an appendix with reports from the other Gospels).

Both traditions thus have to be examined separately and I begin with the *Easter appearances*.

This historical question is completely concentrated on the Pauline report I Corinthians 15:1–11. The appearances reported in the Gospels, which Paul does not mention, have in their whole literary form such a strongly legendary character that it is hardly possible to find any particular historical root in them. Those reports of the Gospels which correspond to something in Paul have also been shaped by strong legendary influences, mainly by a tendency to underline the *bodily* appearances of Jesus, a tendency becoming stronger in the later reports.

In examining the Pauline reference to the Easter witnesses in I Corinthians 15:1–11, an argument which has the explicit intention of giving a proof, as is especially true of v. 6, we must first emphasize the following fact: this text is very close to the events. We can tell this by who the author is as well as by the formulation itself. The first epistle to the Corinthians was written in the spring of 56 (or 57) A.D. at Ephesus. But Paul speaks out of his own experiences which are to be dated even before this time. According to Galatians 1:18, Paul had been in Jerusalem about three years after his conversion. There he saw at least Peter and James. If Paul's conversion is to be dated in the year 33 – according to Galatians 1 – and Jesus' death in the year 30, it is evident that Paul arrived in Jerusalem, at the latest, six years after the event which took place in Jerusalem, and he certainly spoke with the other witnesses of the resurrection of Jesus about the appearances to them in comparison with the one which had happened to him. Thus, Paul had a first-hand knowledge of the events which the reports in the Gospels did not have.

Furthermore, we have to notice that in I Corinthians 15 the center of the enumeration is constituted by several pre-Pauline formulations: ". . . (that) Christ died for our sins according to the scriptures; *And* that he was buried, *and* that he rose again the third day according to the Scriptures, *and* that he was seen of Cephas, then of the twelve" (15:3b–5). Paul put together these single pieces and completed them by the reports of the appearance in v. 6, perhaps according to the information he gathered in Jerusalem. From this it follows that the single pieces of the formulation must have been developed in the first years after Jesus' death, in any case before Paul's visit to Jerusalem, that is, during the first five years after Jesus' death. Thus, we have here quite a number of formulations that were given a fixed form and were verbally transmitted shortly after the events.

That the events reported by Paul really took place is doubted by hardly any of the present historians. Much more complicated, however, is the question of the real character of these events. First, we have to discuss the contents of the appearances; secondly, we have to ask about the character of the experiences corresponding to them.

For the contents we have to consult Paul again – the Gospels with their tendencies to understand the incorporality of Jesus' appearance do not offer reliable grounds for historical considerations, and, moreover, at this point they contradict Paul. Paul evidently presupposes in I Corinthians 15 that the appearances he had had were of the same character as the appearances the other Apostles had experienced. Paul himself gives us some indications of the appearance which occurred to him near Damascus (Galatians 1:12 and 16).

A more detailed report was not written until thirty to forty years later in the Acts of the Apostles, in three different versions (9:1–22; 22:3–21; 26:1–23), which do not coincide with each other at several particular points.

In spite of this, these reports are not without value from the historical point of view. Earlier traditions can be recognized in them, because they stand in tension with Luke's own understanding which he gives of the Easter events in his Gospel. But they have to be used with caution and only as far as they coincide with Paul's own statements. For in any case, these reports seem to be stylized in a way similar to apocalyptic visions (as, for instance, Daniel 10). However, we will consider five points as probably true.

1. For Paul, the relation of the appearance which he had to the man Jesus was evident. He says himself that he has seen the Lord Jesus Christ (I Corinthians 9:1), that God has revealed his Son to him (Galatians 1:16).

2. We have stated earlier that Paul must have seen a spiritual body, not a physical one, near Damascus.

3. Most probably this was not an encounter which took place on earth, but an appearance that came from heaven, from above. This point in the story of Damascus in Acts 9 corresponds to the observation that the earliest Christian testimonies did not distinguish between the resurrection and ascension (Philippians 2:9; Acts 2:36; 5:30 f.; Mark 14:62). The appearance of the resurrected Lord then could be understood only as an appearance from heaven. If one takes the last two points together, the glorified form and the appearance from above, the result is:

4. That the appearance near Damascus may well have been a phenomenon like a bright light, as Acts 9:13 f. reports. Perhaps Paul refers to this, when in II Corinthians 4:6, he speaks of the light of the glory of God in the face of Christ.

5. Certainly the appearance of Christ to Paul was connected with an audition, but it seems that, there as otherwise, the content of what was heard was identical with what the appearance itself meant to Paul in his particular situation. This is not less than the Pauline "gospel" of the freedom from the Law and of his mission to the Gentiles (Galatians 1:12).

These five points, perhaps with the exception of the first, hold also for the other appearances of the resurrected Lord. In every case, all the witnesses recognized Jesus of Nazareth in the appearances. That this strange reality, which occurred in these appearances, could be understood and proclaimed as an encounter with one resurrected from the dead can only be explained by the above-mentioned apocalyptic expectation of a general resurrection of the dead, and that in the near future.

IV. THE MODE OF APPEARANCE

I shall come now to the mode of the Easter appearances. Evidently they were not events which could be seen and understood by everybody, but they were exceptional visions. In any case, this must be said of the Damascus event if it is to be understood as it is reported in the Acts, that is, that those who were in Paul's company either only saw something and did not hear anything (22:9; 26:13 f.), or only heard something and did not see anything (9), but in any case without understanding the appearance. There are many reasons for holding that we have to understand what really happened in a similar way.

But then the question arises as to whether such an event should not be considered as a vision, if the appearance in question could not be seen in the same way by all who were present. Certainly we hear that Paul's companions noticed something that frightened them, but without understanding it. The notion of "vision", however, is not sufficiently clear. If it implied nothing but an extraordinary view, nothing could be said against its application here. But generally one understands by a vision a sort of illusion, an event rooted only subjectively in the visionary, and that does not correspond with reality. In this sense, and also in the psychiatrical sense, the notion of a vision cannot be used for the Easter appearances of the resurrected Lord.

Again and again persons have tried to explain these experiences of the appearance of the resurrected Lord which the disciples had by psychological and historical circumstances of those experiences, without accepting a specific reality of resurrection which here was experienced. Historical–critical thinking must certainly try this way again and again. But precisely the failure of all these subjective theories about visions secures the historical credibility of speaking about the 'resurrection of Jesus". It becomes evident that a presentation can do justice to those events, only if it takes the specific reality into account which is signified by the symbolical expression "resurrection of the dead".

I shall mention the two most important difficulties for all attempts which try to explain the Easter appearances by the psychic and historical situation of the disciples:

(a) That the appearances may have been caused by the enthusiastic imagination of the disciples is, in any case for the first and basic appearances of Jesus, not convincing. All constructions holding that the faith of the disciples of Jesus remained unshattered after Jesus' death are problematical even from a psychological point of view. This is also true if one considers the anticipation of an imminent end of the world, which Jesus must have had when he died and in which his disciples lived. That the death of Jesus exposed the faith of the disciples to an extreme stress cannot be doubted. In this situation one can hardly suppose that the disciples of Jesus produced these appearances through their enthusiastic imaginations.

(b) The second basic difficulty of the "subjective vision hypothesis" consists in the plurality of the appearances and in their being distributed over a long time. One would have to maintain that the disciples of Jesus were men with a special visionary gift and explain the plurality of appearances by a sort of psychic chain reaction arising out of the enthusiastic atmosphere after Peter's experience. But the image of a chain reaction is questionable here because "the single appearances did not succeed each other so quickly" (Grass). The enthusiastic experiences of the early Christians were – as far as we can see – only the effects of the appearance of the resurrected

Lord. That the appearances of the resurrected Lord were different in kind from those later enthusiastic and visionary experiences, common in early Christianity, is already expressed by Paul. According to I Corinthians 15:8, such an encounter with the resurrected One occurred only once to Paul, and this was at the same time the very last appearance. However, even later on Paul had "visions and revelations of the Lord" (II Corinthians 12:1).

V. THE EMPTY TOMB

Now we have to examine the traditions of the empty tomb of Jesus. Paul does not mention anywhere the empty tomb. This, however, does not necessarily mean that these reports which appear in their earliest form in Mark 16:1–8 are not at all reliable. For the empty tomb is not among those features of Jesus' destiny which Paul thought believers shared with Jesus, and yet it seems that Paul was only interested in just such parallel items. The empty tomb, *if* it is a historical fact, belongs only to the unique aspects of Jesus' destiny.

We can take it for granted that Paul counted on the emptiness of the tomb, whether he knew the Jerusalem tradition of the tomb or not. In the apocalyptic text of the resurrection, it is held throughout that the earth will return the dead. For the early community in Jerusalem, the situation was quite different in comparison to Paul's silence concerning the empty tomb. We have only to try to imagine how Jesus' disciples could proclaim his resurrection if they could constantly be refuted by the evidence of the tomb in which Jesus' corpse lay. Without having a reliable testimony for the emptiness of Jesus' tomb, the early Christian community could not have survived in Jerusalem proclaiming the resurrection of Christ (P. Althaus). Otherwise, the Easter message would have taken a thoroughly spiritualistic character, and it could not have been proclaimed precisely in Jerusalem. On the other hand, the Jewish anti-Christian polemics would have had a great interest in the preservation of the report of the tomb, which would have still contained Jesus' corpse. But nothing of this is to be found in the tradition. On the contrary, the Jews agreed with their adversaries that the tomb was empty.

Thus, out of general historical considerations regarding the resurrection-kerygma in Jerusalem, the supposition is inevitable that

Jesus' tomb was empty. In this case the mere analysis of the text of Mark 16 is not decisive. It is justified to lay stress on the fact that (because of several legendary motives) one cannot with certainty infer from this text the historical reality of the empty tomb. But even more decisive here is the consideration of the historical situation of the first community in Jerusalem, which cannot be understood without the tomb having been found empty. This general historical consideration, however, will be justified rather than called into question by the analysis of Mark 16.

There is a theory, however, that reconstructs the cause of the events in the following way. The disciples of Jesus had returned to Galilee after Jesus' arrest already before his death. Only several weeks after they had seen the resurrected Lord in Galilee did they return to Jerusalem to proclaim the Messiah. The lapse of several weeks meant, according to this hypothesis, that precise information about the place where Jesus' corpse could be found was no longer available, and no special efforts were made to find it, "because one was certain of the resurrected Lord through the appearances" (Grass, 184). But this recent hypothesis is extremely unlikely, as I have shown above. Moreover, no vain search for the tomb of Jesus is mentioned nor is there anything that could be understood as an indication in this direction, not even in the Jewish polemics, and this again is very important. The Jewish polemics had only the intention of proving that the disciples themselves had carried away the corpse, but they did not emphasize the fact that the tomb of Jesus was unknown. However, the hypothesis about stealing the corpse can only be judged as adventurous. The enthusiasm of an ultimate devotion in the face of all obstacles which leads to sacrificing one's own life could not arise out of deceit.

Of great importance for the historical judgment is the question of the connection between the finding of the empty tomb and the appearances of the resurrected Lord. Today it is widely accepted that the basic appearances took place in Galilee, while the empty tomb naturally was found in Jerusalem, Now we have to see how these two things are connected: whether the discovery of the empty tomb was the reason the disciples of Jesus went to Galilee in the hope of meeting the resurrected Lord there (thus Campenhausen) or whether the disciples returned to the Galilean home because their journey to Jerusalem had come to such a catastrophic end (perhaps already before the execution of Jesus?) so that they met the resurrected One in Galilee, while in the meantime women (as we find everywhere in the tradition) discovered that Jesus' tomb was empty. This latter version is very probable because of the original independence of each of the two traditions, the finding of the empty tomb, on the one hand, and of the appearances of the resurrected Lord, on the other hand. Furthermore, this is supported by the fact that, according to the earliest reports, the disciples were not present at the execution nor at the burial and that they were not interested at first in the empty tomb, according to Mark 16. It would be difficult to explain these facts if one maintains that the disciples were still in Jerusalem. On the other hand, one cannot see why they should have gone to Galilee after the discovery of the empty tomb, because Jesus evidently thought Jerusalem would be the place of God's final decision regarding the imminent end of the world. And just for this reason the disciples did come back to Jerusalem in order to form, precisely in this city, the first community. Therefore, it is very likely that the appearances and the discovery of Jesus' empty tomb happened independently of each other and became connected only in later stages of the tradition. The independence from each other of the two traditions forms a last and weighty reason for the fact that the Easter events were not only imaginations of disturbed men, but the starting point in a unique but real event which occurred prior to all human experience of it.

VI. THE HISTORICITY OF THE RESURRECTION

I now come to the conclusion. We saw that something happened in which the disciples in these appearances were confronted with a reality which also in our language cannot be expressed in any other way than by that symbolical and metaphorical expression of the hope beyond death, the resurrection from the dead. Please understand me correctly: Only the *name* we give to this event is symbolic, metaphorical, but not the reality of the event itself. The latter is so absolutely unique that we have no other name for this than the metaphorical expression of the apocalyptical expectation. In this sense, the resurrection of Jesus is an historical event, an event that really happened at that time.

Up to a very recent date it has repeatedly been said that this would violate the laws of nature. But contemporary physicists have become much more careful before making such statements, not because of special microphysical results, but because of more precise consciousness of the fact that general laws do not make possible an absolutely certain prediction about the possibility or impossibility of single events, except in the case where all possible conditions can be taken into account. This might be possible in an experiment, but not in the process of the world as a whole.

If resurrection would mean revivification of the corpse, then we must really say this would hardly be thinkable from the point of view of the natural sciences. The range of the possible conditions in this model could be surveyed, so that such an event, although not entirely impossible theoretically, must practically be excluded. The beginning and end of an event which is understood in this way lie in the realm of the world known to our experience. After life has ceased for several seconds, or in special cases, for several minutes, irreversible processes of dissolution have begun. The concept of transformation is different, however, since we only know the starting point, but not the final point of this process. We speak of this on the basis of the appearances and, indeed, only in a metaphorical language.

Now, someone may ask: Even if the resurrection of Jesus is certain as an event that really happened, what would that mean? Would it be possible to recognize by this that Jesus was the Son of God, that he was the One who died on the cross for the sins of all men? This is precisely the case. If the resurrection of the dead really happened with Jesus and if one understands the meaning of this event in connection with the pre-Easter activity and destiny of Jesus, then all the assertions of the early Christian message of Christ are only a development of the meaning included in this event – also expressed in a way relative to that time. That can be proved and shown step by step, if one follows the way in which the message of Christ developed out of the proclamation of the resurrection of Jesus, thus expressing the inner meaning of this event in its original context. That this event has such an absolute meaning consists in the fact that the resurrection of Jesus stands in a close connection with the final destiny of man. With the resurrection of Jesus, what for all other men is still to come has been realized. Therefore, now man's attitude toward Jesus as a man is decisive for his future destiny, this was the claim made by Jesus before the events in Jerusalem. Thus, man has a hope beyond death through community with Jesus. In his destiny the final destiny of all men became an event, and through this Jesus proclaimed that the destiny of all people will be decided by the attitude they have toward him.

Thus, Jesus is the final revelation of God and, therefore, he himself is God. This doctrine adds nothing essential to the events of the resurrection of Jesus; it only makes clear the inner meaning of that event.

8

DISSENSIONS WITHIN THE EARLY CHURCH

Oscar Cullmann

Oscar Cullmann is Professor of New Testament and Patristics at both the University of Basel and the Sorbonne, Paris. He is widely esteemed for his significant contributions to the field of New Testament theology. A few of his most important works are: Christ and Time (*2nd edn.*, *1952*), The State in the New Testament (*1956*), The Christology of the New Testament (*1959*), Salvation in History (*1967*), Vatican Council II: The New Direction (*1968*). *The present essay is reprinted with permission from* Union Seminary Quarterly Review (*January 1967*).

THE USUAL manner of presenting the history and the theology of early Christianity is much too simplistic. It is not a matter of Palestinian Jewish Christianity on the one hand and the Gentile Christianity of Paul on the other. Under the influence of Hegel's philosophy the Tübingen School of the nineteenth century subsumed all history under the scheme "thesis-antithesis-synthesis" and applied it to the history of Christian origins: Jewish-Christianity–Gentile-Christianity–and the reconciliation of the two trends in Catholicism. Although this conception has been abandoned in principle, it continues to color the accounts of the history of the early Church.

E

There was, in fact, a greater diversity of trends within the Palestinian community itself, and this diversity gave rise to conflicting tensions. The earliest and strongest currents, precisely those which represent and develop the viewpoint of Jesus himself with regard to the law and the temple, were gradually eliminated by the Jewish Christianity which was dominant during the early days of the Church. As it hardened itself more and more by the elimination of those trends which were the most vital to nascent Christianity, Jewish Christianity in fact became detached from the source which gave impulse to the propagation of the gospel. Thus Jewish Christianity, by becoming rigid, affirming its authority, and triumphing over all opposition to its own traditionalism, became in the end, paradoxically, a sect.

This process likewise proves that the early Church was not the ideal and perfectly united Church ("one heart and one soul" – Acts 4:32) which we usually picture. Actually, the "unity of the Church" did not exist at the beginning, and the three decisive stages attesting the Jewish-Christian intransigence, which we shall examine, show the absence of solidarity within the first community. This Jerusalem church, which, on the one hand, was the place of the first manifestations of that unifying power which is the Holy Spirit (Acts 2), was equally the place of tragic dispute. The earthly Church has never been a perfect Church.

The three stages which we distinguish are: the elimination of the "Hellenists" of Jerusalem (Acts 6–8); the elimination of James, the son of Zebedee, and of Peter (Acts 12); and, finally, the arrest of the apostle Paul in Jerusalem (Acts 21), which ended in his martyrdom (I Clement 5). In all three cases the Christians were persecuted by the Jews because of their opposition to the temple or to the law. In all three cases the Jewish-Christians not only were *not* persecuted, but seemed to dissociate themselves from their brothers. The Book of Acts, while minimizing this, in keeping with its tendency to reconcile opposing viewpoints, has retained traces of these sources which enable us to catch intimations of the depth of the differences.

This three-fold lack of solidarity has its origin partly in the narrow legalism of the Jewish-Christian group represented by James, the brother of Jesus; partly in the vigorous polemic by Stephen and the other Hellenists opposing worship in the temple and every prescription concerning the localization of the cult; partly in the universalism of Peter, undoubtedly shared by James, son of Zebedee (not to be confused with James, the brother of Jesus); and, finally, partly in the anti-legalism of Paul.

The diverse trends prevailing in the first Christian community derive from the diverse trends at the center of Palestinian Judaism during the same era and correspond to them exactly. Just as it is a mistake to consider Palestinian Judaism a unified structure alongside of the Judaism of the Diaspora, it is likewise a mistake to contrast the Jewish-Christianity of Palestine with the Hellenistic Christianity of the Dispersion. Actually, the Palestinian Judaism of Jesus' day includes not only the Pharisees and the Sadducees, as we too often have assumed, but also nonconformist groups, more or less esoteric, whose existence we suspected for a long time but whose importance appears much greater since the discovery of Qumran.[1] Similarly, in early Christianity the Jerusalem community from the beginning comprised diverse trends and even strongly differing groups.

The differences which we notice – for example, between the Synoptic embodiment and the Johannine formulation of Christianity – were until now too readily explained by the current oversimplified schema: Jewish Christianity/Hellenistic Christianity. I have reacted, in my critical work on the Johannine gospel, against this schematized approach in analysis; and I have insisted on the harmony between the theology of John and the theology of Stephen's Jerusalem group by indicating certain points which both hold in common with the thought of the Qumran sect. I have also linked the Epistle to the Hebrews to this type of Christianity.

The early community, however, not only embraced the differences between the twelve and Stephen's group; but even among the twelve themselves there must have been rather profound differences, as proved by what happened at the martyrdom of James, son of Zebedee, and at Peter's arrest.

I am not able, within the limits of this paper, to retrace in detail the historical circumstances in which first the Hellenists, then Peter, and finally Paul were more or less abandoned to their persecutors by the inflexible Jewish Christians. I hope to do this in a future book. Here I wish to emphasize the general direction which seems appropriate for presenting the history of Christian beginnings in the light of our new-found insights.

The Elimination of the Jerusalem "Hellenists"

Today the great majority of critics acknowledge that Stephen's group (the "Hellenists" of Palestine) was infinitely more important than the book of Acts leads one to believe when it reduces its role to "serving tables" (Acts 6:2).[2] In fact, in spite of their subordination, the seven appear as a group comparable to the twelve. At the moment of Stephen's arrest the twelve were not in fellowship with him and had, no doubt, even rejected his bold ideas about "true worship" and the temple of Jerusalem. Did not Stephen and his followers go so far as to equate the construction of the temple of Jerusalem by King Solomon with the casting of the golden calf (Acts 7:41–50)? Did they not condemn all localization of divine presence as idolatrous in the light of God's revelation throughout the history of salvation, in which the great events took place *outside* every "holy" place?[3] Stephen's address (Acts 7:2–53), even after it was modified by Luke's editing, still reveals quite clearly the boldness of that theology which was inspired in the last analysis by the attitude of Jesus himself with respect to the temple.

Above all, Luke has fortunately let stand the account of Acts 8:1 (a tradition which he probably received from a special source). This account teaches us that after the martyrdom of Stephen his followers had to leave Jerusalem, even though the twelve were able to stay there. This short account is very revealing. It proves that the twelve were not in full fellowship with the persecuted members of their community. The succeeding chapters in the book of Acts relate how the Hellenists then preached the gospel in Samaria. This half-Jewish, half-pagan country also rejected (although in another way, it is true) the worship of the temple at Jerusalem.[4] But again at this point disunity breaks out: The leaders of the Jerusalem church distrust the accomplishments of these valiant preachers of the gospel. They send two from their group into Samaria in order to investigate their work and (in a sense) to "legalize" the conversion of the Samaritans already won by the Hellenists' mission (Acts 8:14 ff.). In the same manner the apostles of Jewish Christianity afterward penetrated everywhere that the Hellenists had already worked. Thus Philip is the first to arrive in the coastal cities on his way to Caesarea (Acts 8:40); Peter then follows (Acts 9:32 ff.). Later, the Hellenists who are dispersed preach the gospel at Antioch (Acts 11:19); Barnabas, the emissary of the community of Jerusalem, follows him (Acts 11:22).

I have tried to show elsewhere that the injustice done by the Jewish-Christians to the Hellenists' group, whose credit for propagating the gospel cannot be exaggerated, was stressed specifically in the Johannine gospel (4:38) where Jesus says, "Others have labored, and you have entered into their labor." This is exactly what we hear in Acts 8:14; those who had labored (in Samaria) were those first missionaries. The twelve entered only afterward into their labor.[5] Further, the author of this gospel defends the same ideas as Stephen does concerning worship "in spirit and in truth" and concerning true worship, which is offered neither on Mount Gerizim nor in the temple at Jerusalem. The fourth evangelist must have been close to this group.

The Elimination of James and Peter

When Stephen was martyred and during the events which followed, Peter was still present in the community at Jerusalem, which he had led in the earliest period. But James, Jesus' brother, adhering to the strictest legalism, already seems to have shared the chief role with Peter. His authority – due partly to his family relationship with Jesus and partly to his conversion, which followed a resurrection appearance (I Cor. 15:7) – is an incontestable fact. We do not know exactly how he achieved this authority, however, since before the arrest of Peter his authority was first imposed beside Peter's and later, probably, against it. In any case, we know that Peter's viewpoint was very close to Paul's. Like Paul, he held to the universality of the gospel, and theologically he seems to have attributed the same role to the death of Christ as did Paul. I believe I have demonstrated this in my book on Peter.[6]

For a long time the relation between Peter and Paul has been mistaken. They have been considered as two antagonists because of the incident at Antioch, where Paul blamed Peter publicly for his insincerity (Gal. 2:11 ff.). Actually, Paul in this situation explicitly attributes to Peter a theology of universal scope, which they share. When Paul rebukes Peter, it is for his inconsistency, his weakness, and the fear he has of the people who have come "representing James".

The persecution of Herod Agrippa (Acts 12:1 ff.), especially, eliminates any doubt about the divergence which separates, *not* Peter from Paul, but Peter from James, the brother of Jesus. There again, our history is too much under the influence of the scheme: Jewish-Christianity over against Hellenistic Christianity. In particular, the ulterior tendency of the Jewish-Christians to appropriate Peter as an exponent of their narrowness (see the Pseudo-Clementine writings) has obscured the real profile of his person and of his preaching.

James, son of Zebedee, within the group of the twelve, seems to have shared the ideas of Peter. It is striking that Luke, in Acts 12:2, is so cursory in the attention he gives the martyrdom of James. He gives it six words! It is, after all, a question of the very first martyr among the twelve apostles. Is not the explanation for such a truncated reference once again Luke's tendency to present the early Christians as perfectly united? Is not this brevity inspired by the desire to cloak in silence the difference existing between the attitude of James, son of Zebedee, and of Peter, on the one hand, and that of James, the brother of Jesus, and the other apostles, on the other hand? Indeed, James and Peter alone are persecuted. James is put to death, and Peter after his deliverance had to depart from Jerusalem and leave the supervision of the community to James, Jesus' brother, and the other apostles.

If the book of Acts leaves so many open questions at this point,[7] it is undoubtedly because the author did not wish to enter too much into the details of these events in which, once more, the Christians were not united in the presence of the persecutors.

The Arrest of Paul in Jerusalem

The conflict between Paul and the representatives of narrow Jewish Christianity is familiar. All the missionary activity of the apostle is filled with the battle he had to wage against sabotage by the emissaries of that party who followed him everywhere and did not refrain from employing any weapon, including even personal slander and the contention of his right to the apostolate. There, again, the book of Acts seeks to minimize the facts which would indicate that there was conflict. But in this case we may be more certain in our judgment, for we have at our disposal the epistles of Paul himself, and by comparing them with the book of Acts we may see at once the already mentioned tendency of Luke and the very serious nature of the conflict. This permits us to draw from the account of the arrest and trial of Paul (Acts 21 ff.) historical information which withstands critical examination. Thus, we see that for the third time one of the most important figures of the early Christian community suffered persecution while the Jewish-Christian leaders (who became more and more fixed in their narrowness) did not intervene on his behalf.

There is much discussion of Jesus' trial. Much less attention, however, is given to the circumstances of Paul's trial.[8] To understand what happened in Jerusalem at the time of the last stay of Paul in that city, we must take as our starting point what he himself says about the purpose of that visit. We know the importance for the apostle of the collection for the community at Jerusalem. The council called by the apostles had decided that the two missions, Jewish-Christian and Hellenistic-Christian, would each work in its own direction but that a collection to be organized by the Hellenistic churches for the benefit of the Jerusalem community would form the bond between them. This was not simply a charitable work but a *sign of unity*, corresponding to the institution of the tax which the Jews of the Diaspora had to pay each year for the temple at Jerusalem in order to affirm the unity of all Jews.

In Rom. 15:25 ff. Paul tells us that he is going to Jerusalem in order to bring what had been received for this collection to the church there. But we do not generally give enough attention to the *fear* which the apostle expresses in this passage, fear lest that collection be refused by the leaders of the church in Jerusalem. He even asks the Christians at Rome to pray that the Jerusalemites might accept the collection which he is about to offer them, and at the same time he exhorts them to pray for his deliverance from the Jewish persecutors who are in Jerusalem. This means that he reckons with the possibility that the collection might not be accepted. Given its character as a symbol of unity, that would signify the break of the church at Jerusalem with Paul and his missionary work.

Was the collection accepted by the church at Jerusalem? We do not know. Perhaps the apostle was arrested before the matter could be discussed. Be that as it may, the precautions which Paul and his companions took permits us to surmise how great the tension was. They went *first* to Caesarea and stayed with the "Hellenist" Philip, who had been a member of the early community (Acts 21:8); and *then* they went to Jerusalem, again staying with a Hellenist, Mnason of

Cyprus (Acts 21:16). The prophetic act performed at Caesarea by Agabus, binding his own hands and feet with Paul's belt in order to signify the arrest of the apostle at Jerusalem, likewise could be based on the fear that the apostle could not expect any help from the Jewish-Christians at Jerusalem. According to the book of Acts (21:18 ff.), it was James himself who made Paul aware of the extreme distrust, not to say open hostility, which had existed in the community in regard to his mission. (The text mentions "many thousands" of believing Jews, "all zealous for the law", who have been stirred up against Paul – 21:20 ff.) James advised Paul, in order to dispel that hostility, to make a Nazarite vow to prove his observance of the very law which the Jewish-Christians accused him of wishing to abolish. The performance of this vow required that Paul present himself at the temple for purification and offerings. The Jews of Asia recognized him, and that was the signal for a general riot against the man who "is teaching men everywhere against the people and the law and this place [the temple]" (verse 28). The juridical grounds for the accusation were Paul's admission of an uncircumcised man into the temple. Here we do not need to examine the basis of the accusation which gave rise to the arrest of Paul. In any case, it launched all the action directed against him.

Some scholars have already offered the hypothesis that his Jewish-Christian adversaries had drawn Paul into an ambush by making him enter the temple. Regardless, it is certain that the Christians of Jerusalem once again made absolutely no attempt to come to the aid of their brother when he was arrested by the Jews, although this would have been possible for them because of their absolute fidelity with respect to the law and the temple.

The Martyrdom of Paul

Concerning the events which led directly to the martyrdom of Paul, we have only a single source, the first epistle of Clement, which is the same epistle that informs us of the death of Peter. I will not rehearse here the arguments that I have developed in my book on Peter.[9] I proved there that, according to this valuable and indisputable testimony, Paul and Peter were killed by the Romans following a *fraternal quarrel* which split the Christians at Rome – not jealousy between Peter and Paul, of course, but the jealousy of a Jewish-Christian group against them. This jealousy, which certainly was already at work when Peter was rejected in favor of James, the brother of Jesus, and when Paul was arrested at Jerusalem, had particularly grave consequences at Rome. Clement, writing his letter from Rome to the factious Christians at Corinth to exhort them to peace, reminds them that jealousy between brothers always entails the worst misfortunes and usually even death. First he cites them examples from the Old Testament, beginning with the jealousy of Cain against Abel, and then he alludes to what had happened in his own community about thirty years previous. Indeed, when he says that Peter had become the victim of an "unjust jealousy" and that Paul "in response to the jealousy demonstrated the price of patience" (suffering martydom), it is more than probable that this refers to the events which unfolded in Rome, for precisely in the epistle to the Philippians, which Paul wrote as a prisoner (at Rome, according to the most likely hypothesis), he says that certain men there "preach Christ from [a spirit of] envy and rivalry . . . thinking [thus] to make my captivity more painful" (Phil. 1 : 15–17). The discord among the Christians at Rome was conducive to the intervention of the Romans against the two great apostles. Therefore Clement, who recalls these tragic memories to the Corinthian Christians, divided by dissensions, says to them in chapter 47, "Your folly . . . drives you yourself into peril."

In the case of the martyrdom of Peter and Paul there seems to have been more than simply a lack of solidarity. Everything leads us to the belief that, in the presence of the danger of persecution, there was even denunciation of Christians by Christians, which opinion has been confirmed elsewhere by other texts.[10]

The previous events, which happened at Jerusalem itself, and which we have examined in this paper, surrounding the arrest of Peter (Acts 2) and that of Paul (Acts 21), throw a new light on the passage in I Clement 5. The jealousy of which Peter and Paul suffered the consequences, according to Clement (although he refers especially to that which split the Christians at Rome), seems also to refer to the community at Jerusalem, from which this jealousy came.

The Irony of the Jewish-Christian Victory

Thus the whole history of the Christian beginnings is dominated, on the one hand, by manifestations of the Holy Spirit, who inspired both the love of the first disciples and the astonishing spread of the gospel, and, on the other hand, by regrettable dissension which actually helped to prepare the persecutions of the Christians by the Jews and the Romans.

But the triumph of Jewish-Christianity over those who defended the gospel of Jesus – Stephen, Peter, Paul – was a pyrrhic victory. As so often happened in the history of Christianity, good emerged from evil. Each of the three stages, characterized by the persecution of one group of Christians by the Jews (or the Romans) and the lack of Christian solidarity that it reveals, marks at the same time great progress in the expansion of Christianity.

The persecution of Stephen is itself a seminal event in the Christian mission. The "Hellenists" expelled from Jerusalem became initiators of the entire Christian mission by going to Samaria (Acts 8:4 ff., John 4:31 ff.), the first country not part of the Jewish community to which the gospel was preached. The persecution which drove Peter from Jerusalem resulted in his activity at Antioch and elsewhere. Paul's arrest at Jerusalem coincides with the definitive displacement of the center of gravity of Christianity from Jerusalem to other areas.

Jewish-Christianity, by its apparent victory in eliminating one after another of the free tendencies of authentic Christianity, in reality eliminated itself. It placed itself far from the major currents of Christianity to which the future would belong – those currents going back to the persecuted groups of which we have spoken. By its very intrenchment and isolation, Jewish-Christianity in the second century was exposed to the infiltration of gnostic ideas such as we find in the Pseudo-Clementines. It was no longer protected by the resistance which authentic Christian faith offered to syncretism elsewhere.

NOTES

1. Oscar Cullmann, *Le problème littéraire et historique du roman pseudo-Clémentin: Etude sur le rapport entre le Gnosticisme et le Judé-Christianisme* (Paris, F. Alcan, 1930).

2. Marcel Simon, *St. Stephen and the Hellenists in the Primitive Church* (New York, Longmans, Green & Co., 1958).

3. Bo Ivar Reicke, *Glaube und Leben der Urgemeinde* (Zürich, Zwingli-Verlag, 1957), pp. 19 ff.

4. Oscar Cullmann, "La Samarie et les origines de la mission chrétienne, Qui sont les αλλοι de Jean 4, 38?" *Annuaire de l'Ecole pratique des Hautes-Etudes*, 1953.

5. *Ibid.*

6. *Peter: Disciple, Apostle, Martyr* (Philadelphia, Westminster Press, 1953), pp. 66 ff.; cf. *The Christology of the New Testament* (Philadelphia, Westminster Press, 1959), pp. 73 ff.

7. Cf. the famous verse 17: "Then he departed and went to another place."

8. Maurice Goguel, *The Birth of Christianity* (London, George Allen & Unwin, Ltd., 1953), pp. 489 ff.

9. Cullmann, *Peter*.

10. Tacitus, *Annals*, XV, 14; see also Matt. 24:10: "They will betray each other."

CURRENT PROBLEMS IN
PAULINE RESEARCH

Hans Conzelmann

Hans G. Conzelmann is Professor of New Testament at the University of Göttingen, Germany. His exegetical work is well known to those who read German; available in English are: The Theology of St. Luke *(German 1954, English 1964),* An Outline of the Theology of the New Testament *(German 1967, English 1969). "Current Problems in Pauline Research" first appeared in English in* Interpretation *(April 1968) and is reprinted by permission. The original German text was published in* Der Evangelische Erzieher, *Vol. XVIII (July 1966).*

I. Introduction

AT THE moment Pauline research is not particularly flourishing. Real interest in the central theologumena of Paul (justification by faith alone, gospel, and law) has been displaced by other themes (the historical Jesus, history, and salvation-history). The last theme dominates the discipline of Old Testament study rather broadly today and has also appeared rather strongly in the area of New Testament study, partly in the selection of Pauline texts, above all, naturally, Romans 9–11.[1] However, the newer theology of history[2] has not yet entered

in any significant way into discussion with the reformed interpretation of Paul, which in my opinion is one of the most urgent of current
tasks. The failure is connected apparently with the new virulence of
historicism, which represents a real step backward in intellectual
history. To name only one symptom of the regression – the liberal
method of comparing one religion with another has returned in spite
of dialectical theology and modern hermeneutics, and has made its
way even among the following of dialectical theology. I have in mind
the procedure of demonstrating that a biblical or "Christian" idea
is without parallel in the history of religions and thus new, underi-
vable. Such a demonstration may be accurate in some cases, but it
becomes questionable when it is advanced as an argument for the
truth of the revelational character of this idea, for instance, for the
validity of the biblical understanding of history. Just how deep this
kind of thinking lies was demonstrably apparent in the panic following
the discovery of the texts from the Dead Sea (Qumran), when the
claim was advanced that the leader of this sect (the "Teacher of
Righteousness") was an authentic prototype, indeed the direct model,
for Jesus: He was killed, raised, and expected to come again. This
claim is, with respect to the content of the texts, untenable; but
suppose that it were correct – why panic? As if historical originality
were a category of faith! As if Christians had not long since discovered
a Jewish prototype for the suffering Jesus, the "servant of Yahweh"
of Deutero-Isaiah. As though it were not long since known that the
conceptional content of New Testament eschatology (the concept of
the resurrection of the dead) derived ultimately from Persian religion
and was mediated to Christianity through Jewish apocalyptic; that
christological conceptions have been appropriated from Hellenism
and Gnosticism; that "Christianity" is, with respect to its conceptional material, a "syncretistic religion".

It is high time to return to theological categories, and that means
that we have every reason to intensify Pauline research; for the sake
of "domestic politics" the dominant points of departure for research
must be reassessed, and for the sake of "international politics" the
relation to the Catholic position must be clarified. Today Catholic
exegetes admit baldly that Luther's translation of Romans 3:28 by
"through faith alone" (!) is actually correct (although the word
"alone" is not found in the original text). We can no longer mark out
a distinctive position for ourselves by using the formula "alone . . ."

but must, rather, spell out specifically what consequences the formula involves, for example, that there can be no man standing between God and the believer holding the position of a mediator of salvation. Further, it cannot be overlooked that Paul, not Jesus, will define the conversation with Judaism. The teaching of Jesus can be adopted by Judaism. Whether that would be right is discovered only when the work of Jesus is interpreted in the light of the Pauline teaching about the law.

This sketch of the problems facing Pauline research indicates which areas will be passed over or, at most, only marginally mentioned in this report; they are those which do not involve the central theological themes. Excluded are the questions of biography; chronology (concerning which there is nothing essentially new to report in any case); and, further, the current lively revival of discussion about problems of "authenticity" and literary unity of the individual epistles.[3] However, the question about the background of Paul's thought in the history of religions must be included because the texts from Qumran have created here a new situation.

II. The Situation Leading up to the Background of the More Recent Research Literature

A. Schweitzer, *Paul and His Interpreters*, 1912.

R. Bultmann, *Theologische Rundschau*, Neue Folge 1, 1929, pp. 26 ff.; 6, 1934, pp. 229 ff.; 8, 1946, pp. 1 ff.

W. G. Kümmel, *Das Neue Testament. Geschichte der Erforschung seiner Probleme*, 1958.

B. Rigaux, *Paulus und seine Briefe*, 1964.

K. H. Rengstorf and U. Luck, *Das Paulusbild in der neueren deutschen Forschung*, 1964. (Kümmel includes excerpts from the sources, while Rengstorf and Luck print complete reproductions of classic contributions.)

H. J. Schoeps[4] summarizes the result of his survey in the following agressive fashion: "From Marcion to Karl Barth, from Augustine to Luther, Schweitzer or Bultmann, Paul has always either been misunderstood or only partially understood." That results from Paul's ambiguity; his "was a self-contradictory nature". Moreover, he suffered the misfortune of falling "into the hands of the professional theologians of all times" (p. 13). Of course Schoeps' own attempt to understand Paul in terms of life-history is an anachronism hermeneutically, but deserves notice because it fits into contemporary historicism and psychologism.

Let us begin by recalling what is well known;[5] since the Reformation, justification by faith alone has stood as the center not only of Paul's teaching but of the Scripture as a whole, as the *articulus stantis et cadentis ecclesiae*. In the nineteenth century this interpretation was radically opposed. F. C. Baur interpreted Paul in the categories of Hegel; the center is the spirit's coming to itself through the antithesis ("flesh"); this is the "reconciliation". After Baur and under his influence the two dimensions of Paul's thinking were discovered, that is, spirit/flesh on the one side, law/sin/righteousness on the other.[6] They were defined as juridical in some quarters, as ethical/ physical or ethical/mystical in others. The eschatology and demonology were also discovered; that is, the temporally conditioned character of his thinking was more sharply seen. These beginnings were gathered together and methodically developed in the "history of religion school" (about the turn of the century: Gunkel, Weinel, Bousset, Heitmüller, Reitzenstein).[7] Paul's twofold conceptionality was explained historically in terms of the two sides of his intellectual origin, Judaism and Hellenism. It was finally recognized in all sharpness that, for instance, the "Spirit" in the Pauline sense is a *supernatural* power which comes upon men in a naturalistic way and produces ecstasy – a meaning far distant from spirit in the understanding of idealism. Paul's temporally conditioned apocalyptic image of the world was also clarified.

The history-of-religions interpretation crystallized into two types: (*a*) the Hellenistic-Gnostic (Reitzenstein, Bousset), in which the focus is no longer on theology but on religiosity, pneumatism, the relation of mysticism and ethic; (*b*) the Jewish-apocalyptic (A. Schweitzer). Both interpretations are agreed in taking, not justification, but mysticism, the "being in Christ" as central, as the authentically Pauline.[8] In this way it was possible to explain why Paul ignored the history of Jesus – because he was oriented to the Gnostic, mythical redeemer or to the apocalyptic figure of the one who comes again.

The way for a change was opened up by two approximately contemporary movements, the "Luther renaissance" and "dialectical theology". At the same time A. Schlatter hewed out his own solitary path in unrelieved debate with Luther. K. Holl claimed once again that justification is the center of Pauline thought, and so related anew Luther's theology (primarily that of the young Luther as seen in the lectures on Romans) to Paul. Dialectical theology (K. Barth, R. Bultmann) took up once again *theology* as its thematic task (instead of religious experience); and Schlatter, by means of a constant critique of Luther, maintained that "the righteousness of God" constituted the meaning of Paul. In the process it was primarily Bultmann who did not surrender the insights of history-of-religions research. He sought to uncover the message which Paul articulated in his temporally conditioned forms of thinking.

Up to the present the investigation has been determined by the two monumental presentations of the subject by A. Schweitzer and R. Bultmann. Their formulation of the problem persists – mysticism or justification, being in Christ or faith/grace/righteousness of God. Each, following consistently his own point of departure, has a different focus; Schweitzer is concerned with the reconstruction of the historical form of Paul's thinking, Bultmann with *existential* interpretation through which he presents the theology of Paul as anthropology in order to do justice to its own intention.[9] Currently, Bultmann's pupils are raising a protest against this latter interpretation. The situation becomes all the more exciting as Luther's understanding of the "righteousness of God" is drawn back into the field in the process; Schlatter's critique has been taken up again, so that the lines of battle are formed with Luther/Bultmann against Schlatter and the pupils of Bultmann. What is at stake in the debate?

Our survey has identified as the two most important themes: (1) Mystic interpretation or theology of the "righteousness of God"? (2) The meaning of the "righteousness of God".

III. MYSTICISM OR THEOLOGY OF JUSTIFICATION?

We can begin with the book of Schoeps. On the whole his position is quite near to that of A. Schweitzer; he sees Paul as a man defined by Judaism, though he does not, like Schweitzer, rigidly contest every Hellenistic influence. Going beyond Schweitzer, he traces the presuppositions of Paul's thinking, not only in apocalyptic, but primarily in rabbinical, literature and emphasizes here the conditions of the doctrine of the law. It is this rather than mysticism with which Schoeps is concerned, for it is here that the decision falls concerning the relationship of Judaism to Christianity. Schoeps' thesis is that the whole presupposition of the Pauline polemic against the law is a misunderstanding. Paul comes out of Hellenistic (not the genuine rabbinical) Judaism. In Hellenistic Judaism the understanding of the law was depraved. The genuine Jewish understanding is defined by the priority of salvation, of covenant before the statute. The law is not primarily regulation, but instrument of the covenant. In Hellenistic Judaism a legalistic narrowing had prevailed. It was in this environment that Paul grew up, and from this point of view that he polemicizes against the law. Therefore his critique is off the target of authentic Judaism. But through the centuries his misunderstanding has falsified the relationship of Judaism and Christianity. According to Schoeps, Paul had not grasped the fact that the law serves the creation of the "fear of God". He had regarded it merely as a sum of statutes, had "played sin off against the law as a breach of regula- tions" (p. 188). His doctrine of justification is nothing more than "a partial aspect of the law unjustifiably lifted out of its broader saving context, when judged from the point of view of the rabbinical under- standing of the law" (p. 196). The alternative, "faith or works", is an untenable exaggeration of the issue (pp. 206 f.). The authentic word is "faith *and* works".[10]

That the texts are violated by this interpretation is apparent. Paul does not conceive the law in a casuistic, rabbinical fashion as a sum of regulations, but as a complex entity. That is apparent in the locu- tion "the law"; and sin is not the single transgression, but the power under which man has fallen through his sinning, that is, through the confusion of Creator and creation. Paul speaks of "sin" in the sin- gular.[11] When he does introduce a single commandment, then it stands representatively for the whole; compare Romans 7:7: "Ye shall not covet." Thus he polemicizes, not against individual com- mandments, but in opposition to the use of the law as a way to salvation. Thereby every possible Jewish understanding of the law is attacked.

However, the question is whether the doctrine of the end of the law – speaking positively, justification through faith *alone* – really stands in the center of the problem.

An answer is more likely when we inquire not only concerning *Jewish* presuppositions but also concerning Paul's relationship to the *Christian* forms of doctrine which were already available to him. These are to be found where he cites and expounds stereotyped doctrinal formulae. There are philological criteria for distinguishing such traditional material.

Sometimes Paul says expressly that he quotes: I Corinthians 11: 23, 15:3. Sentences can be distinguished from their context by style and content, and identified by un-Pauline concepts and ideas: Romans 1:3 f., 3:25 f., 4:25. Moreover, they may coincide with the sentences of other authors: Romans 10:9.

Romans 10:9 may serve as example and paradigm. Here Paul combines two basic forms of the primitive Christian confession. Using the terms of the text itself, the two may be distinguished as the "homology" (or "confession" in the more technical form-critical sense, or "acclamation"): "Jesus is Lord" and the "credo": "God has raised Jesus from the dead." Paul does not content himself with citing such formulas; he expounds them and thereby affords us a chance to look into his workshop and to form an opinion concerning the direction of his thinking and of his theological judgment.

Examples

Romans 3:24–26. This text is the *locus classicus* of the Reformed doctrine of justification, but a precise analysis[12] shows that the material contains two strata. Paul reaches back to a formula which deals with the "demonstration" of God's righteousness, namely, through the institution of Christ as the means of atonement. The effect is the forgiveness of the "former" sins, those that had occurred up to the atoning act of Christ's death.[13] It is clear that this is an undeveloped preform of Paul's thinking; the formula says nothing about the sins of the time after the atoning sacrifice. Naturally it cannot be said that the believer thereby learns nothing about his current status; the formula clarifies his situation in that it identifies him as a member of the new covenant community founded through the death of Jesus. But in the long run this latent indication will have to be formulated more clearly, and it is that which Paul does by adding his own exposition: (*a*) He introduces the quote by verse 24: We receive righteousness without earning it, from grace alone. (*b*) He inserts in verse 25 the indication that righteousness is received through faith. (*c*) He explains that God's righteousness happens today. How? That is answered precisely by the concept of faith. (*d*) Finally, he expounds *how* God is righteous: in that he declares a man just = makes a man just. The Pauline agenda appears thus in these points: grace, faith, contemporizing, definition of God's righteousness as the act of declaring just – today for faith.

Romans 4:25. Paul attaches the comprehensive analysis of existence in Romans 5–8 to a formula of congregational tradition, 4:25. The style is that of the *parallelismus membrorum*. The idea manifests a pre-Pauline stage: The negative side of the work of salvation, the elimination of sins, is connected with the death of Christ; the positive side, the conveyance of righteousness, with the Resurrection.

Paul's intention appears in his comment in Romans 5:1 ff. Immediately he points again to faith and the contemporary result of salvation: "Thus being made righteous by faith we have peace with God."[14] Then follows the exposition of this peace, first of all as an exposition of the triad faith–hope–love.

The congregational credo shines through the interpretation of baptism in Romans 6. The credo runs: Christ has died and is risen. Paul expounds in this fashion: we have (in the baptism) died "with him"; then he continues contrary to the *ductus* of the formula: we shall (!) rise "with him". Here appears a new specifically Pauline motif, the "eschatological reservation": the resurrection will occur in the future. The meaning for existence is that the new life does not become a *Habitus*. We do not possess it in the form of seeing, but of faith. The eschatological reservation is nothing less than another form of the concept of faith. In Romans 6 this is made clear by verse 8.

Romans 14:7–9 is nothing other than an actualization of the credo: "If we live, we live to the Lord. . . ." The eschatology is established by demonstrating that it is a consequence of the christological credo. In the two thematic statements in I Thessalonians 4:13 ff. and I Corinthians 15 Paul develops the same credo. Eschatology is constructed christologically, not developed from an apocalyptic world picture.

From these observations, which can be multiplied, the conclusion may be drawn that where Paul expounds the tradition of the church it is his consistent intention to work out the significance of "faith" in its connection with justification and not in relationship to mysticism.

The old controversy can be decided by a methodological analysis of the text; Paul is to be interpreted along the lines of the Reformation. He is no mystic.

But what does the "righteousness of God" mean?

IV. The Righteousness of God

Bultmann[15] interprets the genitive in the expression "the righteousness of God" as a *genitivus auctoris*, that is, the righteousness bestowed by God. That corresponds essentially to the Reformed understanding and is supported by Philippians 3:9 which Luther rightly translated "die Gerechtigkeit, die aus Gott kommt". This interpretation is now, following Schlatter, again contested.[16] Bultmann underscores the kerygmatic meaning of the concept, pointing out that righteousness is a gift which is conveyed in the Word. For Käsemann that does not suffice. The point of departure for thinking about the problem should not be the communication of righteousness (thus the "making righteous"), but God's being righteous. Orientation ought to be worked out "first in terms of God's saving action which manifests itself in the gift without exhausting itself completely" (p. 185). I admit that I can appreciate the tendency of this last statement, but can find in it no clear meaning. Further, for Käsemann the gift has "the character of power"; righteousness appears as personified power, and he refers here to Romans 1:17, 10:6 ff. Paul does in fact speak in these texts in poetic, personifying style; but there can be no talk of the personification or hypostasis of righteousness. The assertion that the righteousness can be identified with Christ (I Cor. 1:30) is also not to the point. On the contrary, Paul says that *Christ* "is" God's righteousness, that is, he interprets Christ as the gift of salvation and presupposes the gift-character of righteousness. To say the least, it is dangerous and misleading to declare that the "connection between power and gift" is the basic characteristic of Pauline theology. "When God intervenes we ourselves [sic!] experience in his gifts his dominion" (p. 186). Perhaps I do not understand aright this enigmatic interpretation of the nature of God (as *potentia absoluta*?). But is not here once again a metaphysical background postulated, not in the sense of Luther's *Deus absconditus* from which we are driven to the *Deus revelatus*, but precisely in the reverse direction of thought so that we must conceive of the metaphysical "nature" behind the word as we think of the word. The same line is followed when justification is interpreted as the imposition of the power "of Christ over our life". One may accept the formulation, but it is "correct" only when it is immediately explained what "power" is in terms of the meaning of the revelation – not power in itself, but power as defined by the Cross. But then one cannot assert that as a result of this imposition of power there exists "no longer any real tension between sacrament and ethics" (p. 188).

In my opinion this sentence discloses the consequences of this interpretation of Paul, which will play a considerable role in the discussion of the coming years. The directions of the impulses in this interpretation are clear. It opposes "anthropology" (what is meant is individualism). The righteousness of God is not related primarily to the individual, but to the world (p. 188). Pauline anthropology is not identical with his theology, but only with a part thereof (in opposition to R. Bultmann, F. Gogarten, H. Braun, and actually, finally, also against Luther). It also opposes "enthusiasm". Over against this is set "the unheard of radicalizing and universalizing of the *promissio* in the doctrine of the *justificatio impii*" (p. 190). Thereby, Käsemann believes that he validates the "by grace alone" radically.

We raise two questions: (1) Can this interpretation be maintained exegetically? (2) What is to be made of the systematic consequences?

What is missing in the whole presentation is the notion of faith. Apparently it is not required in order to define the nature of the "righteousness of God".[17] That the motif of power participates in Paul's concepts of revelation has been long recognized (spirit, grace, glory). But the question is what function it has and in which direction it is developed by Paul. When Paul appropriates a concept, he does not necessarily employ it in its conventional meaning. It is not the history of the concept which is decisive, but the context in which it is used.

An example is furnished by Käsemann's own illuminating analysis of Romans 3:24–26. He shows that here a pre-Pauline formula lies in the concept "God's righteousness" in which the genitive is subjective, that is, the righteousness belonging to God. But it is not a power aspect of God or of the revelation that is worked out, but the institution of atonement, the forgiveness of sins. This, instead of an idea of power belonging to apocalyptic style, is the presupposition of the Pauline construction of the concept. The same holds good for the other texts in which "subjective" meaning is reflected, that is, where Paul asks whether God is "unjust" (Rom. 3:5, 9:14). He does not raise the question in order to give a definition of the "nature" of God, but, rather, in order to reject the question as inappropriate – there is no definition of the nature of God outside of the interpretation of his saving act "in Christ".

The chapter on the "reckoning" of righteousness, Romans 4, forms the connection between the thesis in Romans 3:21 ff. and the exposition of existing in the world which follows therefrom, and which does not begin with a formal statement concerning God's being righteousness, but with the anthropological assertion that we are pronounced righteous. That corresponds to Paul's method of interpretation in Romans 3:24, 26 (see above). When Paul interprets here God's righteousness as his pronouncing someone righteous today, that means in fact a specific "individualism"; this communication can at first only concern the individual. Paul detaches the individual from its former corporate existence in Judaism and paganism. It constitutes the presupposition for salvation's being universal, as Paul shows in Romans 3:27 ff. The message is aimed at the individual in order to lead him into the new community, the church.

If one defines the "world" instead of the individual as the partner of God's declaration, then a subtle remnant of free will is introduced into the saving event between God and me; for a moment the individual is isolated from God and world in the choice of whether or not to accept God's declaration. For this declaration concerns (in Käsemann's understanding who here takes up Schlatter), not primarily the man who is addressed, but God in his being in himself. In the meaning of the Pauline theology of the word however (and Luther has understood that), the word informs me that God was already with me before my "decision". Thereby, faith consists exclusively in the hearing of this communication. The psychological components of faith have become theologically unimportant. Instead of pursuing that problem, one has now to work out the relation of gift and demand (ethic). When the end of the tension between these two is proclaimed, I can understand that only as enthusiasm. With Paul, the "imperative" of God's demand is never absorbed by the "indicative" of the communication of salvation. Otherwise, the "indicative" would itself become law. The gospel would become a formalized proclamation of supernatural power; and faith, a formal subjection to a "claim". Paul avoids this formalization since faith exists only as a hearing of the salvation and thus is accompanied *a priori* by understanding as self-understanding in salvation. One can say that "by grace alone" becomes "saving" only when it is concretized by "by faith alone". This can be clarified by a look at the thinking of the Qumran sect.[18] Contacts in terminology are so close that a *sola gratia* at Qumran has been referred to:[19] ". . . And without thee nothing occurs; and without thy will nothing is recognized" (Psalm Book, Col. X, line 9). "For my justification lies with God, and in his hand is my perfect behavior with my integrity of heart. And by his righteousness (!) my sin is blotted out . . . yet I belong to wicked humanity and to the multitude of sinful flesh. . . . And if I stumble because of the sin of the flesh, yet my justification by God's righteousness abides forever" (Manual of Disc., Col. XI, lines 2 ff.).

Here the pious admits his sinfulness in radical fashion and knows himself to be fully dependent on God's "righteousness". But Qumran knows no "from faith alone"; here justification means radical submission to the law and not liberation from it. Paul not only can assert the freedom from the law, but because for him the understanding of God's righteousness coincides with Christology, he can declare that God's righteousness is – Christ.[20]

V. "In Christ" – "In the Lord"

In spite of all the contradictions in its interpretation, broad agreement prevails today that the conceptual cluster turning around "righteousness" is the center of Paul's theology. What about the probe in the other direction, the investigation of the "mystical" way of speaking of "being in Christ"? Recently interest has turned once again more strongly to this problem. "In Christ" stood for a long time as *the* formula of Pauline mysticism (Deissmann, A. Schweitzer). The proof for its mystical meaning appeared to be obvious. It lies in the inversion "Christ in us" (Gal. 2:20). Moreover, there is the alternative expression "in the Spirit", and here also a reciprocal turn of phrase, "the spirit in us" (Rom. 8:2–11). The mystical sense appears further to be confirmed by the sacramental formula "with Christ"; we have died with Christ and are therefore now "in him" (Rom. 6). In view of this material, how does Bultmann substantiate his assertion that "the *in Christo* (in Christ), far from being a formula for mystical union, is primarily an *ecclesiological* formula and designates the incorporation in the *soma Christou* (the body of Christ) by baptism" (*op. cit.*, p. 311)? According to Bultmann, the formula expresses the definition of the individual life of the believer "who lives not out of himself but out of the divine saving act" (p. 328).

Several new works concern themselves with this formula.[21] They have made progress with the problem by investigating the connection of the preposition "in" with the use of christological titles (Christ, Son of God, Lord). Kramer works out the various aspects of the saving event which are expressed in them (though, of course, one may not schematize; no strict separation between the titles prevails, nor do the aspects stand alongside each other in isolation). "Christ" indicates the completed work of salvation; "Christ (subject) has died and is risen", for which a paradigm would be the use of language in I Corinthians 15 in connection with the formula in 15:3 ff. "Lord" points to the present position of the Exalted One, is the title of acclamation (I Cor. 12:3; Phil. 2:6 ff.). "Son of God" contains the idea of pre-existence and "sending" (Rom. 8:3). Kramer tests this interpretation by checking the prepositions "in" and "with" when they are connected with "Christ" and "the Lord". This is also the theme of Neugebauer, who limits himself to the preposition "in". They conclude that in these phrases no mystic meaning is expressed. "Christ" and "the Lord" designate the *Christus extra nos* ("besides us", the one "in whom" God objectively inaugurates salvation). When Paul says that we possess our righteousness "in Christ" that means that we have it as "alien" righteousness. The new life which is given to us we cannot see in ourselves. We can believe in it, that is, learn of it through the alien word. We can grasp its nature in the crucified Christ.

Nor does the "with" formula, which may well be too sharply distinguished from the "in" formula, have any mystical meaning. That is the common result of investigations of Paul's understanding of baptism in Romans 6. Two types of interpretation stand opposed to each other, but both "unmystic". E. Fuchs (*Die Freiheit des Glaubens*, 1949) explains the thought of Paul thus. It is not that the death of Christ is conveyed to me in the baptism, but that my death is anticipated in the death of Christ. The movement is not that of bringing over the past work of salvation into the present, but rather runs in the other direction, of anticipation.[22] G. Delling (*Die Zueignung des Heils in der Taufe*, 1961) on the other hand prefers to maintain that baptism is the appropriation of the crucifixion event for the baptized. In this case the truth appears to me for once to lie between the two positions. As concerns Romans 6, Fuchs and Bornkamm may well be right. But in other texts the other idea of the conveyance of salvation (I Cor. 6:11) also appears, and what is Pauline may be found precisely in the interplay of both ideas. Thereby, Paul escapes both the mystic understanding of the sacrament as well as the one connected with the mysteries.[23]

As proof for the mystical interpretation there remains its *locus classicus* II Corinthians 3:17: "The Lord is the spirit", as well as the interchangeability of "Lord" and "spirit" in the "in" formulae.[24]

The following observations speak against the mystical identification of "Lord" and "spirit". The notion is not the same everywhere. For Paul the spirit is not a person and until the Parousia the Lord has his place in heaven. The spirit represents him in the world. It is the way the Exalted One works in the church, but in such a manner that the *extra nos* remains protected. For that reason one should not speak of identity because "Lord" is not a definition of being, but the title of status. This title is bestowed on Jesus for a definite period, for the time from the Resurrection (which for Paul is identical with the exaltation), until the completion of the work of salvation, that is, the submission of all powers. It is for just this time that the Spirit is given to the church as "earnest" of the future.[25]

VI. THEOLOGY OF THE CROSS

In the two letters to the Corinthians[26] Paul develops his theology less by use of the terminology of law and justification (although it emerges here and there) than by the terminology of the Cross, a dialectical definition of "wisdom" and "foolishness" as a dialectical interpretation of existing in the world. The model is the existence of the Apostle, but the analysis applies to believers in general. This shift of language is naturally connected with the actual controversy in which Paul is involved; in the documents of "justification"-terminology Paul is involved in discussion with Jews and Judaism; in the Corinthian correspondence, with a Christian religiosity of Hellenistic type. In Corinth there proliferated an enthusiasm which based itself on ecstatic experiences and grew out of the "knowledge" of its freedom mottoes: " We have the knowledge" (I Cor. 8:1); "all things are allowed" (I Cor. 6:12, 10:23).[27] Schmithals has shown that the problem is not that of the propagation of a general amoralism; this freedom had its own spheres of application which were fixed by the world view lying behind it, conduct in relationship to the heathen gods and sexuality. One can manifest disdain of the gods by participating in their cults without any reverence for them in doing so; sexual freedom is a way to demonstrate that one has already soared above and beyond world and flesh.

Our concern is not so much with the reconstruction of the Corinthian position, but rather with the question about Paul's response. In the formal sense his answer was the exposition of tradition already formulated in the church. In I Corinthians 11 he expounds the traditional formula of the Lord's Supper in terms of the idea of the church: The church is the body of Christ. That means a crisis for fanatical individualism and the possibility of a historical common life for the believers. In I Corinthians 12:1-3 he introduces the confession "Jesus is Lord" as the criterion of ecstatic spirituality and shows in I Corinthians 15 that the credo is the key to the foundation of hope. But already at the beginning of First Corinthians Paul takes his point of departure from christological tradition in his critique of Greek "wisdom" and of the analogous Jewish demand for miraculous proof. This tradition ("Christ has died and is risen") is interpreted by the Corinthians in a direction that leads to the exaltation; through the exaltation, the death of Jesus is quasi annulled. Faith is participation in the Exalted One, in his glory. He manifests himself in the appearances of the Spirit, in the demonstration of freedom against gods and "flesh", in spiritual soaring above the world (I Cor. 4:8).

In response Paul reverses the direction in which the credo is to be evaluated; the Exalted One we see now as the Crucified One. Preaching is "the word of the cross" – and nothing else (I Cor. 1:18 ff., 2:1 ff.).[28] Faith is not a religious soaring away from life, and the believer is no religious superman. Faith is exclusively related to the Cross. The believer has his superiority over the world in the paradoxical fashion of "having as though one did not have" (I Cor. 7). God's power appears in the form of weakness (I Cor. 4:9 ff.; II Cor. 4; 11 f.).[29]

VII. CONCLUSION

This survey had to be limited to the question concerning the center from which systematic constructions emerge. The lines of thought which radiate from this center and the way in which they are actualized cannot be pursued here. These areas can only be listed: for instance, the actualization of the understanding of the world and the paraenesis, the understanding of church and office, anthropology, eschatology. All these themes are held together and normalized by the one central theme of justification. In it the criteria for current tendencies in theology will have to be sought: the increasingly renewed undertaking to form a synthesis of faith and world view, of a theology of history and of personality. When viewed from the perspective of Paul, they show themselves to be questionable from the ground up.

NOTES

1. J. Munck, *Paulus und Israel*, 1956; O. Cullmann, *Salvation in History*, 1967 (the German form of the title, *Heil als Geschichte*, is characteristic); W. G. Kümmel's essays were published under the title *Heilsgeschehen und Geschichte*, 1965.

2. This expression should be understood only as a neutral abbreviation. The distinctions between different sketches of an understanding of history are not to be overlooked. At stake here is only the matter of the confrontation pointed to the article.

3. Examples are furnished by the debate over II Cor. and Phil. Extensive information is offered by W. G. Kümmel, *Introduction to the New Testament*, 1966, and more briefly by W. Marxsen, *Introduction to the New Testament*, 1968.

4. H. J. Schoeps, *Paul*, 1961.

5. Cf. the presentation in R. Bultmann, *Theologie des neuen Testaments*, 5th edn. (1965), pp. 589 ff.

6. A. Schweitzer, pp. 22 ff.

7. A broad critical presentation in C. Colpe, *Die religionsgeschichtliche Schule*, Vol. I (1961).

8. A. Schweitzer terms the doctrine of justification a "secondary-crater". In opposition, W. Wrede declares in his brilliant study "Paulus" which appeared in the collection *Religionsgeschichtliche Volksbücher*, 1904, and was reprinted by Rengstorf-Luck, pp. 1 ff.: "The religion of the Apostle itself is theological throughout; his theology is his religion" (the new edn., p. 42). A liberal must regret this situation, but the dialectical interpretation of Paul could relate itself to such insights.

9. The arrangement of his presentation of Paul is instructive: "Man prior to the relevation of *pistis* (of faith)" – "Man under *pistis*."

10. One thinks here of the eternal Catholic argument against Luther which contrasts the richness of the synthesis with the one-sidedness of the "alone". These voices find an eager ear in current pietism, as well as in the "una-sancta" camp.

11. The plural only where he depends on tradition.

12. E. Käsemann, "Zum Verständnis von Röm. 2, 24–26", *Exegetische Versuche und Besinnungen*, Vol. I (1960), pp. 96 ff.

13. I differ from the analysis of Käsemann in taking v. 24 for a Pauline transition while Käsemann attributes the basic material of the verse to tradition and reckons to Paul only the expression "by his grace as a gift". Actually, this difference in philological judgment is immaterial. The pre-Pauline material can be distinguished as follows, putting the additions of Paul in parenthesis: (". . . since all have sinned and fall short of the glory of God, they are justified by his grace as a gift through the redemption which is in Christ Jesus), whom God put forward as an expiation by his blood (to be received by faith). This was to show God's righteousness, because in his divine forbearance he had passed over former sins (and it was to prove at the present time that he himself is righteous and that he justifies him who has faith in Jesus").

14. The MSS. predominantly read the subjunctive: ". . . let us have peace with God"; the indicative is to be preferred for objective reasons.

15. *Theology of the New Testament*, Vol. I, p. 285.

16. A. Schlatter, *Gottes Gerechtigkeit*, 3rd edn. (1959); E. Käsemann, "Gottesgerechtigkeit bei Paulus", *Exegetische Versuche und Besinnungen*, Vol. II (1964), pp. 181 ff.; Chr. Müller, *Gottes Gerechtigkeit und Gottes Volk* (1964); P. Stuhlmacher, *Gerechtigkeit Gottes bei Paulus* (1965). Against Käsemann, see R. Bultmann, *DIKAIOSUNÉ THEOU*, *Journal of Biblical Literature*, Vol. LXXXIII (1964), pp. 12 ff.

17. The thematic word "faith" scarcely appears in Käsemann's essay, and in connection with the concept "righteousness" not at all.

18. H. Braun, "Röm. 7, 7–25 und das Selbstverständnis les Qumran-Frommen", *Gesammelte Studien zum Neuen Testament und seiner Umwelt* (1962), pp. 100 ff.

19. Paul is not directly dependent on the sect, but he manifests a common Jewish background. On *sola gratia*, see S. Schulz, "Zur Rechtfertigung aus Gnaden in Qumran und bei Paulus", *Zeitschrift für Theologie und Kirche*, Vol. LVI (1959), pp. 155 ff.

20. Concerning the connection of justification and law, see E. Jüngel, *Paulus und Jesus* (1962).

21. F. Neugebauer, *In Christus* (1961); W. Kramer, *Christos, Kyrios, Gottessohn* (1963); M. Bouttier, *En Christ* (1962).

22. Similarly, G. Bornkamm, "Baptism and New Life in Paul" (Romans 6), in *Early Christian Experience* (1969), pp. 71 ff.

23. The comparative material from the mysteries of antiquity is presented by G. Wagner, *Das religionsgeschichtliche Problem von Röm. 6, 1–11* (1962).

24. Some exegetes take the sentence for a harmless exegetical comment on the preceding sentence. There Paul cites Exod. 34:34: "Whenever Moses went in

before the Lord to speak with him he took the veil off." Verse 17 would then merely remark that the word "Lord" in the cited text means the spirit. But if the sentence is to be understood in this way, the question arises how Paul came upon this exegesis at all. According to the context it is more likely that Paul here interprets the nature of the spirit as the spirit of freedom, so that the meaning can be put in this fashion: The Lord "is", i.e. means freedom. A further modification is presented by I. Hermann, *Kyrios und Pneuma* (1961).

25. The existence of the spirit does not mean that according to the opinion of Paul the "new aeon" had already broken in. Quite apart from the fact that the expression "new aeon" is not found in Paul, the spirit is a signal of the character of the present as interim time, the time of faith and hope, not of seeing.

26. In reality, the two present letters may contain other authentic writings of Paul to Corinth; cf. the discussion in the Introductions of Kümmel and Marxsen.

27. W. Schmithals, *Die Gnosis in Korinth*, 2nd edn. (1965), goes a step further; he finds in Corinth a developed scheme of Gnostic mythology and Christology. This assumption is contradicted by the fact that the formal Christology of Paul and of the Corinthians is the same. That is presupposed by Paul in I Cor. 15:1–3.

28. U. Wilckens, *Weisheit und Torheit* (1959).

29. Here we can only point to the instructive discussion by Wilckens of H. Schlier's Catholic-ontological understanding of Paul.

IO

ST. PAUL AND THE LAW

C. E. B. Cranfield

C. E. B. Cranfield is Reader in Theology at the University of Durham, England, and received his M.A. degree from the University of Cambridge. He is the author of The Gospel According to St. Mark *(3rd impression, 1966) in the "Cambridge Greek Testament Commentaries" and contributed the volume* I and II Peter and Jude *(1960) for the "Torch Bible Commentaries". The essay reprinted here by permission was originally published in* Scottish Journal of Theology *(March 1964).*

THE PURPOSE of this article is to offer a few notes and observations on one part of this subject only, namely, on the attitude of St. Paul to the law, which H. J. Schoeps has called "the most intricate docrinal issue in his theology",[1] in the hope of clarifying some of the issues and perhaps stimulating others to join in the work of a full and thorough re-examination of the whole subject of the New Testament understanding of law and of the law's place in the Christian life.[2]

The reader should bear in mind throughout the following pages that Paul, as has quite often been pointed out,[3] nearly always uses the word "law" ($\nu\acute{o}\mu o\varsigma$) either (i) of the Old Testament Law (without distinguishing between the legal parts and the rest of the Pentateuch) or (ii) of the Old Testament as a whole viewed as law (as clearly in Rom. 3.19, the quotations in the preceding verses being from the

Psalms and from Isaiah), but in a few places uses it (iii) with the general sense of "norm" or "principle" (e.g. Rom. 3.27) or (iv) in the sense of "compulsion", "constraint", "necessity" (Rom. 7.21, 23, 25, and 8.2), while in Gal. 6.2 he uses it (v) in the phrase, "the law of Christ"; and that in a few verses he substitutes for "law" the word "commandment" (ἐντολή), which properly denotes one of the particular commandments contained in the law.

1. The first point to be noted is that for Paul *the law*[4] *is God's law*. In Rom. 7.22, 25, 8.7 it is explicitly called "the law of God" (cf. 1 Cor. 7.19 – "the commandments of God"). Being God's law, it is "spiritual" (Rom. 7.14), "holy", "righteous", and "good" (Rom. 7.12 – "the law is holy, and the commandment holy, righteous, and good"). In the RV the adjective "good" is again used of the law in Rom. 7.16; but in the Greek a different word is used from that represented by "good" in verse 12 (in 7.12 ἀγαθός is used, in 7.16 καλός). All this the law not only is originally but also continues to be, even when it is being misused and dishonoured by men (as is implied by the context of the statements in Rom. 7.12 and 14). It is God's word – the phrase "the oracles of God" in Rom. 3.2 certainly includes the law. As the revelation of God's will, the law has for its true and proper purpose "life" for men (Rom. 7.10), whatever other results it may have when it is met by human sin. So "the giving of the law" is reckoned by Paul among the great and glorious privileges of Israel (Rom. 9.4). Though C. H. Dodd writes on Rom. 3.2: "The logical answer on the basis of Paul's argument is, 'None whatever!',"[5] Paul is true to his own understanding of the law when to the question, "What advantage then hath the Jew? or what is the profit of circumcision?" he gives the answer, "Much every way." In his view, to have been entrusted with the law of God is an altogether real, and in no way illusory, though it is a dangerous, privilege. And it is consonant with his conviction that the law is God's, that throughout his epistles he treats the Old Testament as a whole with the greatest respect as having divine authority.[6]

2. As the revelation of God's will for men, *the law makes sin manifest as sin, as disobedience to God*. According to Rom. 5.13 f, sin was already in the world and men were already sinners before the law was given. Their thoughts, words, and deeds were contrary to the will of God, objectively disobedient, and as a result of their sin they died. But they did not disobey a known commandment in the way that

Adam did (Gen. 2.17) and Israel after the law had been received. In the absence of the law sin, though real, is not clearly visible; it is not registered.[7] But, when the law is given, sin becomes plainly and unmistakably visible, manifest, registered. The point which this paragraph is making is concisely summed up in Rom. 3.20: "through the law cometh the knowledge of sin". The law makes men recognize sin as sin, and themselves as sinners.[8]

3. But this means that *the law actually enhances sin*; for, by showing men that what they are doing is contrary to God's will, it gives to their continuing to do such things the character of conscious and wilful disobedience, thereby increasing their sin in the sense that it makes it more sinful. And that it should have this effect was part of the divine intention in giving the law (cf. Rom. 5.20*a* – "the law came in beside, that (ἵνα) the trespass might abound" – and the statement in Gal. 3.19 that the law "was added because of transgressions" (τῶν παραβάσεων χάριν), that is, in order that there might be transgressions, the conscious disobeying of definite commandments (cf. Rom. 4.15*b*)).

4. But *the law* not only increases sin in the sense that it makes it more sinful, it also *increases sin in the sense that it makes men sin more*. In Rom. 7.11 Paul no doubt has Gen. 3 in mind (his "deceived" is reminiscent of Gen. 3.13). In the Genesis story the serpent found in God's explicit prohibition (Gen. 2.17) the very opportunity he wanted and was able to use the commandment as a means of deceiving and ruining Adam. Thus the law provides sin with an "occasion" or, better, a foothold, a base of operations (the word ἀφορμή, which Paul uses, is a military term); for its presence makes it possible to inveigle men into deliberate disobedience, into deliberate rebellion against God. (Compare 1 Cor. 15.56*b* – "and the power of sin is the law".) In the absence of law sin is in a sense "dead" (Rom. 7.8), that is, relatively impotent; but when the law comes, then sin springs into activity (Rom. 7.9 – "sin revived"). And the opposition which the law offers to men's sinful desires has the effect of stirring them up to greater fury. So Paul speaks of "the sinful passions, which were through the law" (τὰ παθήματα τῶν ἁμαρτιῶν τὰ διὰ τοῦ νόμου) in Rom. 7.5, on which Calvin comments: "The work of the law, in the absence of the Spirit, . . . is to inflame our hearts still more, so that they burst forth into such lustful desires," and adds that the "perversity and lust" of man's corrupt nature "break forth with greater fury, the more

they are held back by the restraints of righteousness".[9] Man's self-centredness, aware that it is being attacked and called in question by God's claim to man's allegiance, seeks feverishly to defend itself and to assert its inviolability.

5. *In particular, the law makes men sin more, in that it establishes the possibility of legalism.* The very existence of the law is necessarily for sinful man a temptation to try to use it as a means to the establishment of a claim upon God, and so to the defence of his self-centredness and the assertion of a measure of independence over against God, He imagines that he can put God under an obligation to himself, that he will be able so adequately to fulfil the law's demands that he will earn for himself a righteous status before God. But the legalist's confidence of being "justified by the works of the law", "justified by works", "justified by the law" – Paul's terminology varies – is altogether vain; for "by the works of the law shall no flesh be justified in his sight" (Rom. 3.20), since fallen man can never adequately obey the law of God. When Paul says of himself in Phil. 3.6, "as touching the righteousness which is in the law, found blameless", he is indicating, not how he sees himself now that he is a Christian, but how he seemed to himself and to his fellows before his conversion. That "righteousness of mine own, even that which is of the law", to which he refers in verse 9, is an illusion of the Pharisee's heart (cf. the rich young ruler's reply to Jesus: "Master, all these things have I observed from my youth" in Mark 10.20) – an illusion supported by a constant tampering with the law. Such a tampering with the law the Jewish oral law largely was – Jesus bluntly called it "the traditions of men" (Mark 7.8); for, instead of recognizing in the demands of the law the absolute demand of God, by which He claims us wholly for Himself and for our neighbour, and with which men cannot live on terms of merit but only on terms of the divine forgiveness, it sought to turn them into something manageable and achievable.[10]

6. *The law pronounces God's condemnation and curse.* So in 2 Cor. 3.9 the giving of the law is referred to as "the ministration of condemnation". The condemnation from which, according to Rom. 8.1, Christ has freed us, is the condemnation pronounced by the law. In Gal. 3.10 Paul writes: "For as many as are of the works of the law (i.e. as many as refuse to accept the righteousness God has made available in Christ and insist on trying to earn their own righteousness by their fulfilment of the law's demands) are under a curse: for it is

F

written, Cursed is every one which continueth not in all things that
are written in the law, to do them"; and in Gal. 3.13: "Christ redeemed us from the curse of the law, having become a curse for us:
for it is written, Cursed is every one that hangeth on a tree." And the
condemnation and curse of the law involve death. So on 2 Cor. 3.7
the giving of the law is called "the ministration of death". It is not
that the law is injurious to us in its own nature, but, as Calvin says,
"because our corruption provokes and draws upon us its curse".[11]
It is because it encounters our sin that the law, which was intended
"unto life", actually results in "death" (Rom. 7.10).

7. But *the ultimate goal and the innermost meaning of the law are* not
the condemnation of sinners, but *Jesus Christ*. We begin here with
Rom. 10.4 ("For Christ is the end of the law unto righteousness to
every one that believeth"), which is a key verse for the understanding
of Paul's attitude to the law. Unfortunately the word τέλος, which can
have an unusually wide variety of meanings – consummation, fulfilment, supreme power, efficacy, completion, cessation, achievement,
goal, purpose, tax or due, to mention only some of the meanings
listed by Liddell and Scott [12] (though not all of these are to be found in
the New Testament), is ambiguous here. The AV and RV translation,
"end", reproduces something of this ambiguity; for "end" can be
used in the sense of termination or in the sense of goal, purpose.
Those who think that Paul's attitude to the law was predominantly
negative are naturally inclined to choose the meaning, "termination",
as does the N.E.B., which translates: "For Christ ends the law . . .",
thus getting rid of the ambiguity of the AV and RV. This interpretation has many supporters; but, in view of such passages as Rom.
7.12, 14*a*, 8.4, 13.8–10, and of the categorical statement in Rom. 3.31,
and also of the fact that Paul again and again appeals to the Pentateuch in support of his arguments (specially suggestive perhaps is the
fact that he does so in Rom. 10.6–8), it seems extremely probable
that it should be rejected, and the translation "goal" preferred.[13] We
may render the verse: "For Christ is the goal of the law, so that
righteousness is available to every one that believeth" or "For Christ
is the goal of the law, and this means that righteousness is available
to every one that believeth". This makes excellent sense in the context. Verse 4 explains verse 3 – hence the "For" with which it begins.
The Jews in their legalistic quest after a righteous status of their own
earning have failed to recognize and accept the righteous status which

God has sought to give them; for Christ, whom they have rejected, is the goal towards which all along the law was directed, and this means that in Him a righteous status before God is available to every one who will accept it by faith. Verse 5 may then be interpreted as explaining (again "For") how Christ is the goal of the law. In accordance with Lev. 18.5, He has fulfilled it by doing perfectly that which it required and has thereby earned eternal life not just for Himself but also for all those who will believe in Him. (This is at any rate one way in which He is the goal of the law.) Verses 6–10 will then be contrasting the righteous status which men have through faith in Christ with the righteous status which Christ Himself has by His obedience.[14]

At this point, therefore, we accept provisionally the translation "goal" for $\tau \acute{\epsilon} \lambda o s$ in Rom. 10.4, and go on to inquire whether there is support for it elsewhere in Paul's epistles: if there is, and if in the rest of our survey we do not find any clear evidence that he believed that Christ had put an end to the law, we may regard our provisional interpretation of Rom. 10.4 as confirmed.

What content, then, can we give, on the basis of Paul's epistles, to the statement that Christ is the goal of the law?

(i) The law has Christ for its goal, is aimed at, directed towards, Him, bears witness to Him (cf. Rom. 3.21),[15] by virtue of the promises which it contains. In Gal. 3.8 Paul writes: "And the scripture, foreseeing that God would justify the Gentiles by faith, preached the gospel beforehand ($\pi \rho o \epsilon v \eta \gamma \gamma \epsilon \lambda \acute{\iota} \sigma a \tau o$) unto Abraham, saying, In thee shall all the nations be blessed," the quotation being from the Pentateuch – from Gen. 12.3. (In view of this passage and of the fact that Moses was regarded as a prophet (cf. Deut. 18.15), we should probably not exclude a reference to the law in Rom. 1.2: ". . . the gospel of God, which he [i.e. God] promised afore ($\pi \rho o \epsilon \pi \eta \gamma \gamma \epsilon \acute{\iota} \lambda a \tau o$) by his prophets in the holy scriptures, concerning his Son . . .".) Highly significant is Rom. 10.6–10 in this connection; for there Paul discerns the voice of "the righteousness which is of faith" speaking in Deuteronomy, and refers what is spoken to Christ. For St. Paul, the law with its promises points forward to Christ, and Christ is the goal of the law, in that in His person and work He is the fulfilment of its promises – "For how many soever be the promises of God, in him is the yea" (2 Cor. 1.20).

(ii) The law has Christ for its goal, bears witness to Him, by virtue of its revelation of God's will for man, of God's absolute claim to man's life, man's allegiance, man's obedience. It points to one who will truly do the righteousness which is of the law (cf. Rom. 10.5), it draws the outline of a perfect obedience; and Jesus Christ is the goal, the meaning and substance, of the law, by virtue of the fact that He is the one and only Man, who has truly and fully loved God with all His heart, and with all His soul, and with all His might (Deut. 6.5) and His neighbour as Himself (Lev. 19.18), the one and only Man, who was completely and utterly "obedient" (cf. Phil. 2.8,[16] Rom. 5.19).

(iii) The law has Christ for its goal, bears witness to Him, by virtue of its ceremonies, and Christ is the goal of the law, in that He is the fulfilment, the meaning, the substance, of them. So Paul sees the work of Christ in the light of the sacrifices ordained by the law. In 1 Cor. 5.7 f. ("Purge out the old leaven, that ye may be a new lump, even as ye are unleavened. For our Passover also hath been sacrificed, even Christ: wherefore let us keep the feast, not with old leaven . . .") Christ is represented as the Church's Passover lamb: the implication is that He is the true and final Paschal Lamb, to whom all the Paschal lambs sacrificed according to the law were pointing forward. In Rom. 3.25 (". . . Christ Jesus, whom God set forth to be a propitiation, through faith, by his blood . . .") the death of Christ is again interpreted in terms of sacrifice, whatever be the exact significance of the word which the RV translates "propitiation". The ritual of the Day of Atonement (Lev. 16) is very probably in Paul's mind. Reference must also be made to 1 Cor. 11.25, in which Paul repeats the words ("This cup is the new covenant in my blood") by which Jesus had stamped a sacrificial significance on His approaching death. A number of other passages might be cited, but these will suffice.

(iv) The law has Christ for its goal, bears witness to Him, by virtue of its revelation of men's sinfulness and helplessness, and Christ is the goal of the law, in that He is the one and only remedy of men's desperate condition, which the law brings to light. By making objectively visible – though the legalists fail to see what is before their eyes – the impossibility of a righteousness earned by works, the law points to the righteousness of faith. So, for example, Paul writes to the Galatians (3.22): "Howbeit the scripture hath shut all things under sin, that the promise by faith in Jesus Christ might be given to them that believe." It is in this sense that "the law hath been our tutor to bring us unto Christ, that we might be justified by faith" (Gal. 3.24).

(v) Lastly, the law has Christ for its goal, bears witness to Him, by virtue of the fact that it sets the necessary forensic stage on which Christ's saving work is wrought, and Christ is the goal of the law, in that the justification which He achieves for us is not mere amnesty or indulgence, no caprice or sentimentality on the part of God, but acquittal "in God's severe and true judgment which searches the hearts and is no respecter of persons".[17] So far from it being true to claim, as G. W. H. Lampe does, that "St Paul realized the essential truth that the act of God in Christ had taken the whole question of man's relationship to God out of this area [i.e. of law]",[18] Paul underlines again and again by his language the legal framework of Christ's action. But, be it carefully noted, this legal framework is the framework, not of merely human law and, of course, not of legalism, but of God's law![19] Lampe regards it as disastrous that we should suppose "that God's action takes place within a framework of law";[20] but the fact that our justification is truly acquittal by the just Judge and not mere caprice is something that the Epistle to the Romans was designed to emphasize. And in this fact which Paul brings out so clearly is to be recognized God's respect for His creature man, His taking His creature seriously, His mercy which is truly mercy, His love which is truly love – and not sentimentality.[21]

8. The epistles reveal *Paul's radical rejection of legalism* (we have already seen in section 5 something of what legalism is) *and of* what is so inextricably bound up with legalism that we may treat the two things as one, *an understanding of the law which fails to recognise the fact, or the full implications of the fact, that Christ is its innermost meaning and goal.* Each of these two leads to the other: preoccupation with the quest for a righteousness of one's own by works of the law has the effect of blinding one to the righteousness which God has made available in Christ as a free gift (cf. Rom. 10.3), and failure to see that the substance of the law is Christ opens the way to the legalistic misunderstanding and perversion of the law.

For Paul the legalism which prevailed among the Jews of his day meant slavery. So in Gal. 4.25 he can say of "the Jerusalem that now is" that "she is in bondage with her children". The covenant "from mount Sinai", understood legalistically and without regard to Christ, bears "children unto bondage" (Gal. 4.24), and the Galatian Christians are warned against getting themselves "entangled again in a yoke of bondage" (Gal. 5.1*b*). It is a slavery from which Christ has freed us (Gal. 5.1*a*), and the men who are trying to make the Gentile Christians judaize are "false brethren . . . who came in privily to spy out our liberty which we have in Christ Jesus, that they might bring us into bondage" (Gal. 2.4).

To practise the observances of Judaism while rejecting Christ is to be left with the letter of the law only, without the Spirit (cf. Rom. 7.6, 2 Cor. 3.6); but the letter of the law in separation from the Spirit is the law – so to speak – denatured, for the law of God is by nature "spiritual" (Rom. 7.14). The literal observance of circumcision and other ceremonies of the law was valuable and significant as "a shadow of the things to come", a pointer forward to Christ; but to regard such things as having an independent value in themselves quite apart from Him is to be left with a mere empty "shadow" in isolation from "the body" which gives it meaning (cf. Col. 2.16 f.).[22]

While Paul seems to have made no objection to, indeed to have approved of (cf. 1 Cor. 9.20, Acts 16.3, 21.26), Jewish-Christians continuing to observe the ceremonies as a mark of their solidarity with their kinsmen according to the flesh, whose salvation he so earnestly desired, and may perhaps even have allowed the Gentile Titus to be circumcised (Gal. 2.3: Paul's Greek in this verse is far from clear) on the principle of "all things to all men, that I may by all means save some" (1 Cor. 9.22), he opposed the false teachers, who were troubling the Galatian churches, with uncompromising vehemence; for they were maintaining that circumcision was necessary to salvation, and thereby both propagating the legalistic notion that justification is by works – or at least partly by works – instead of by faith alone, and also calling in question the truth that Christ is the goal of the law (for to know that the goal of the law is Christ is to know that now that He, to whom the ceremonies pointed, has come, their literal observance cannot any longer be obligatory). So he writes about these false teachers, that their version of the gospel is a different gospel altogether, and in fact not a gospel at all (Gal. 1.6 f.), and, with them in mind, he warns the Galatian Christians: "Behold, I Paul say unto you, that, if ye receive circumcision, Christ will profit you nothing", and "Ye are severed from Christ, ye who would be justified by the law; ye are fallen away from grace" (Gal. 5.2 and 4).

With regard to the legalism of contemporary Judaism he seems even to go so far (however we understand the perplexing "rudiments of the world") as to put it on the same level as, or, at the least, to suggest that it has much in common with, paganism: this is the implication of Gal. 4.3 (cf. 4.9), for the first person plural links together under a common denominator the pasts of both Jewish and Gentile Christians. But this passage, together with a number of other passages which are relevant here, it will be more convenient to treat in the next section.

9. *For Paul, the law is not abolished by Christ.* This thesis is stated in full awareness of the widespread tendency today, observable not only in popular writing but also in serious works of scholarship, to regard it as an assured result that Paul believed that the law had been abolished by Christ. This "assured result", like so many others, needs to be re-examined.

There are, of course, a number of passages in the epistles which, at first sight, seem to provide support for the view we are opposing, and these we must now consider. In doing so, it will be well to bear in mind the fact (which, so far as I know, has not received attention) that the Greek language used by Paul had no word-group to denote "legalism", "legalist", and "legalistic". This means not just that he did not have a convenient terminology to express a key idea, but that he had no definite, ready-made concept of legalism with which to work in his own mind. And this means, surely, that he was at a very considerable disadvantage compared with the modern theologian, when he had to attempt to clarify the Christian position with regard to the law. In view of this, we should, I think, be ready to reckon with the possibility that sometimes, when he appears to be disparaging the law, what he really has in mind may be not the law itself but the misunderstanding and misuse of it for which *we* have a convenient term. It should also be borne in mind that in this very difficult terrain Paul was to a large extent pioneering. If we make due allowance for this fact, we shall not be so easily baffled or misled by a certain impreciseness of statement which we shall encounter.

The most obvious passage to refer to here is probably Rom. 10.4, which we have already considered (in section 7 above). The confirmation or otherwise of our provisional interpretation of that verse (we took "end" in the sense of goal, not termination) must to a large extent depend on whether we can give a satisfactory explanation of the other passages which have been held to justify the opposite view.

In Rom. 3.21 the phrase, "apart from the law", might at first sight suggest that Paul regarded the law as having been superseded, brushed aside, as it were, as something out of date by the manifestation of God's righteousness. But the words, "being witnessed by the law", in the same verse and the emphatic statement in verse 31 show the wrongness of such an inference. The simplest explanation of "apart from the law" is probably that it is shorthand for "apart from the works of the law" (cf. verse 28). The general meaning, at any rate, is that the righteous status which is God's gift has not to be earned by man's fulfilment of the law.

Rom. 6.14b ("for ye are not under law, but under grace") is often taken to imply that for Christians the law is altogether a thing of the past. But the contrast with "under grace" suggests rather, since "grace" means undeserved favour, that "under law" may include the two ideas of being under God's disfavour, under the condemnation of God pronounced by the law, and of labouring under the illusion that one has to earn a status of righteousness before God by one's works. We take Paul's meaning to be not that the law has no longer any authority at all over his readers, but that they have been freed from its condemnation and curse (cf. Rom. 8.1) and from the vain quest for righteousness by works of the law. And this interpretation, as well as giving a meaning consistent with Rom. 3.31, fits this context excellently; for to be reminded of this twofold freedom is indeed encouragement to seek after holiness of life with new strength and hope.

Rom. 7.4 and 6 are to be interpreted similarly. In "ye also were made dead ($\dot{\epsilon}\theta\alpha\nu\alpha\tau\acute{\omega}\theta\eta\tau\epsilon$) to the law through the body of Christ" and "But now we have been discharged ($\kappa\alpha\tau\eta\rho\gamma\acute{\eta}\theta\eta\mu\epsilon\nu$) from the law, having died to that wherein we were holden" "the law" is to be understood in a limited sense. The meaning is that Christians have through Christ's death died to, and been discharged from, the law's condemnation and also all legalistic misunderstanding and misuse of the law – or, to put it otherwise, they have died to, and been discharged from, the law in so far as it condemns them and the law in so far as, by men's perversion of it, it has become a bondage. That Paul does not mean here that the law is abolished for Christians is quite clear from verse 25b ("So then I myself with the mind serve the law of God . . ."). And verse 6b does not oppose the law itself to the Spirit; for only a few verses later (7.14) Paul says that the law is "spiritual".

The contrast is rather between the old way of the legalistic misunderstanding and misuse of the law, in which one was left with the letter bereft of the Spirit, and the new way of the right understanding and use of the law by the power of the Spirit.

Rom. 8.2 will be referred to in section 10. Suffice it here to say that by "the law of sin and of death", from which in Christ we have been made free, we understand not the law, but the inner necessity of our fallen nature (cf. Rom. 7.21, 23, 25 ("the law of sin"), in which "law" is used in the fourth sense listed at the beginning of this article).

We turn now to 2 Cor. 3. As this chapter contains a good deal that has often been taken to disparage the law and to imply that it is done away by Christ, we shall have to look at it in some detail. Verse 3 provides a transition from the subject of the letter of commendation to that of the ministry of the new covenant. The contrast between the old and the new covenants is already in Paul's mind when he speaks of "tables of stone" (cf. Exod. 24.12) and "tables that are hearts of flesh" (cf. Jer. 31.33, Ezek. 11.19 f., 36.26 f.). The reference to Jer. 31.31 ff. is picked up in verse 6: Paul is a minister of the "new covenant". There is no suggestion in Jer. 31.31 ff. of a new law to replace that given through Moses: the suggestion is rather that the same law of God – "my law" (Jer. 31.33) – will be given in a new way. What is looked forward to is not the abolition of the law, but its true and effective establishment. So far then there is nothing in what Paul has said in this chapter which need be taken as disparagement of the law. But what about verse 6*b*? The contrast here between "the letter" and "the spirit" (better "the Spirit") we take to be a contrast not between the Old Testament law which is written and a spiritual religion which knows no law, but between the legalistic relation of the Jews of Paul's time to God and to His law and the new relation to God and to His law established by the Holy Spirit and resulting from Christ's work. In the absence of the Spirit the law is misused and comes to be for those who misuse it simply "letter" (cf. what was said above on Rom. 7.6*b*), and this law without the Spirit "killeth" (verse 6*c*–cf. Rom. 7.10). Not until Christ's resurrection and the gift of the Spirit could the law come into its own as the law which is "unto life" (Rom. 7.10). So in verse 7 the ministry of service performed by Moses[23] at the giving of the law is referred to as "the ministration of death"; it was a service of death, in that the law, at the giving of which

Moses served, would indeed kill – though this is very far from being the whole of the story. Paul's point in verses 7–11 is that, since the service rendered by Moses at the giving of the law, which was actually going to effect "condemnation" (verse 9) and "death" (verse 7), was accompanied by glory (the glory on Moses' face – Exod. 34.29 ff.), the service of the Spirit rendered by himself (and other Christian preachers) in the preaching of the Gospel must much more be accompanied by glory. Verse 10 is difficult; but the general meaning would seem to be that the glory of the ministry of the Gospel is so surpassingly great that, in comparison with it, the glory which, according to Exodus, accompanied the ministry fulfilled by Moses can scarcely be called glory at all. In verse 11 the vital question is: To what does "that which passeth away" refer? In view of the use of "pass away" in verses 7 and 13, we might possibly be tempted to try to take it to refer to the glory on Moses' face; but the structure of verses 7–11 is clearly against this. It is best to take the reference to be, not to the law or "the whole religious system based on the law",[24] but to the ministry of Moses at the giving of the law; and we may translate with an imperfect as the RV does the same Greek in verse 13 – "that which was passing away". The service which Moses rendered was passing away, and yet it was accompanied by glory. How much more then must the service of the minister of the Gospel, a service "which remaineth", be clothed with glory! The key to the true understanding of this whole passage is to recognize that it is really the two ministries which are being contrasted rather than the two covenants themselves; when this is recognized the connection between verses 7–11 and verses 4–6 and 1–3 becomes clear. And the true explanation of the superiority of the glory of the Christian minister's ministry over that of Moses' ministry is not that the law which was given through Moses has been abolished, but that these two ministries are differently related to the ministry of Jesus Christ. Whereas Moses' ministry belongs wholly to the time of expectation, that of even the lowliest of Christian ministers belongs to the time of fulfilment, the time which is characterized by the fact that the work of Him who is the substance and the meaning of the law has been accomplished. What is said in Matt. 11.11b with regard to John the Baptist, who, though he lived to see Jesus, did not live to see the completion of His work, is even more clearly applicable to Moses, who had died many centuries before the Incarnation.

In verses 12 ff. Paul's thought is based on the detail of the veil which Moses wore (Exod. 34.33). Unlike Moses, the minister of the Gospel, since his ministry "remaineth" (verse 11) with its glory, does not need to veil his face. C. K. Barrett maintains that τὸ καταργούμενον ("that which was passing away") in verse 13 is "the whole religious system based on the law",[25] and appeals to Paul's use of the verb καταργεῖν in this verse and also in verse 11 (he explains τὸ καταργούμενον there in the same way) "in relation to the law" in support of his statement, "Paul knows that the law, and the covenant inaugurated on the basis of it, great as they are, are nevertheless in process of being done away."[26] But Barrett's interpretation here is surely impossible; for the contemporaries of Moses were in no danger of looking on the end of "the whole religious system based on the law".[27] What is meant must be the glory on Moses' face (cf. verse 7). In verses 14–16 another idea, suggested by the reference to Moses' veil, is brought out, namely, that up to the present time, when the law is read in the synagogue, a veil rests on the hearts of the Jews, so that they do not understand its true meaning; but, whenever "their heart" turns to Christ, the veil is taken away (in verse 16 Paul is echoing Exod. 34.34). There is here no suggestion that the law is done away, but rather that, when men turn to Christ, they are able to discern the true glory of the law. Calvin's comment is apt: "For the law is in itself bright, but it is only when Christ appears to us in it, that we enjoy its splendour."[28] (The N.E.B. translation of verse 14, ". . . because only in Christ is the old covenant abrogated", is perverse; for it is altogether more natural to take the subject (which is not expressed in the Greek) of καταργεῖται (RV: "is done away", N.E.B.: "is abrogated") to be the same thing as is described as μὴ ἀνακαλυπτόμενον (RV: "unlifted"; N.E.B.: "and it is never lifted"), i.e. the veil, than to supply "the old covenant" as the N.E.B. does. And the interpretation which is the natural way of taking the Greek in verse 14 is surely confirmed beyond all reasonable doubt by verse 16. The translation which the N.E.B. has given in verse 14 would scarcely occur to a translator who was free from preconceptions with regard to Paul's attitude to the law.)

Verse 17 is a notorious *crux interpretum*. It is, we believe, best interpreted thus: But the Lord (i.e. the risen and exalted Christ), of whom it may truly be said that, when Israel's heart turns to Him, the veil which prevents it understanding the law is taken away, is the

Spirit to whom reference has been made in verses 6 and 8, and where the Spirit of the Lord (i.e. of Christ) is present, there is liberty. The fact that the Lord and the Spirit, while they are identified in the first half of the verse, are distinguished in the second half, is an indication that we should not take "the Lord is the Spirit" to imply that, for Paul, the exalted Christ and the Holy Spirit are identical, but rather that to turn to Christ is to be introduced into the realm of the Spirit.[29] The point of verse 17*b* we take to be that the law, when it is understood in the light of Christ, when it is established in its true character by the Holy Spirit, so far from being the "bondage" into which legalism has perverted it, is true freedom (cf. Jas. 1.25 – "the perfect law, the law of liberty"). But with this verse, and with verse 18 which we need not discuss here, we have passed into the province of our next section.

We must turn now to Gal. 3.15–25, which – perhaps more than any other single passage – has encouraged readers of St. Paul to assume that he believed that the law is done away by Christ. We need not linger over verses 15–18, in which Paul argues that it is unthinkable that the law, which was only given four hundred and thirty years later, should disannul the promise made to Abraham, "a covenant confirmed beforehand by God". It is verses 19 and 20 which contain what G. S. Duncan has called Paul's "depreciatory account of the Law".[30] The details may be set out as follows:

(*a*) "was added". Duncan takes this to imply that the law " is a mere addition to the main stream of God's purpose".[31]

(*b*) "because of transgressions", i.e. to give to men's wrongdoing the character of conscious disobedience.

(*c*) "till the seed should come to whom the promise hath been made". On this Duncan writes: "its reign, so far from being eternal, is a strictly limited one, ceasing when in the promised 'Offspring', viz. Christ, the Promise began to receive its fulfilment", and "the reign of the Law is essentially temporary".[32] We may compare Gal. 3.25: "But now that faith is come, we are no longer under a tutor."

(*d*) "ordained through angels". We may quote Duncan again: "Paul's view is that they indicated that God was not present in person, and that a law which was merely transmitted by angels lacked the glory of the true life-giving Word. . . . Even those [angels] who were not essentially evil might, as on this occasion, exercise an evil influence by intervening between the worshipper and God, and by having their activities erroneously accepted as the activities of God Himself."[33]

(*e*) "by the hand of a mediator. Now a mediator is not a mediator of one; but God is one."

With regard to the details we have just listed the following points must be made:

(i) We must beware of the danger of exaggerating the depreciatory tendency of these verses. With regard to (*a*), Duncan reads more into "was added" than there is any firm warrant for doing: there is no need to see more in it than an indication that the law was, as a matter of fact, given after the promise (cf. verse 17). With regard to (*b*), Calvin's reminder is sufficient: "The law has manifold uses, but Paul [here] confines himself to that which bears on his present subject . . . The definition here given of the use of the law is not complete. . . ."[34] With regard to (*d*), it is not absolutely certain that Paul's mention of the angels has a depreciatory intention at all (in Acts 7.53 Stephen's reference to the angels' part in the giving of the law is meant to emphasize the majesty of the law). The tradition of the presence of the angels at the giving of the law goes back to the LXX version of Deut. 33.2. If, however, there is a depreciatory purpose here (and I am inclined to think that there is), it is probably simply to suggest a certain superiority of the promise, as given directly by God, over the law, as given by means of the angels. In detail (*e*) we probably should recognize a certain depreciatory flavour. The reference is of course to the part played by Moses. The point is probably the contrast with the promise given directly by God to Abraham.

(ii) In trying to evaluate the true significance of that element of depreciation which is present in these verses, it is of the first importance to bear in mind the polemical nature of Galatians. In this epistle Paul is seeking to undo the damage done by false teachers who have, in effect, exalted the law above the gospel. In arguing against their perverse, excessive exaltation of the law Paul naturally has to attempt to reduce the law's importance, in the eyes of those who have been led astray, to its true magnitude. It is not that Paul desires, absolutely, in any way to disparage the law, but that, in relation to this false exaltation of the law, he is forced in some measure to depreciate it. To fail to make full allowance for the special circumstances which called forth the letter would be to proceed in a quite uncritical and unscientific manner. In view of what has just been said, it should be clear that it would be extremely unwise to take what Paul says in Galatians as one's starting-point in trying to understand Paul's teaching on the law.

(iii) We should recognize a tendency in this passage to regard the law somewhat narrowly. Indications of this can be seen in the fact that Paul here distinguishes the promise from the law (verses 17 and 21), although the promise in question is contained in the Pentateuch, and in the concentration in verse 19 on just one purpose, "because of transgressions". In this connection it is worth quoting an interesting passage in Calvin's *Institutes*, in which, having just referred to Gal. 3.19, he goes on to say: Paul "was disputing with perverse teachers who pretended that we merit righteousness by the works of the law. Consequently, to refute their error he was sometimes compelled to take the bare law in a narrow sense, even though it was otherwise graced with the covenant of free adoption." [35] Perhaps we have here a clue to the right understanding of (c) above. This "bare law" (*nuda lex*) understood "in a narrow sense" (*praecise*) is not the law in the fullness and wholeness of its true character, but the law as seen apart from Christ. It is this law-apart-from-Christ, this law that is less than its true self, which is temporary. When once "the seed" has come, "to whom the promise hath been made", the One who is the goal, the meaning, the substance, of the law, it is no longer an open possibility for those who believe in Him to regard the law merely in this naked-ness (though even in this forbidding nakedness it had served as a tutor to bring men to Christ). Henceforth it is to be recognized in its true character "graced" or clothed "with the covenant of free adoption" (*gratuitae adoptionis foedere . . . vestita*).

It is sometimes argued, on the strength of the nowadays popular explanation of στοιχεῖα (translated "rudiments" in the RV) as denot-ing the spirits thought to rule the heavenly bodies, the "elemental spirits",[36] that the στοιχεῖα in Gal. 4.3 and 9 are to be identified with the angels referred to in Gal. 3.19. If this identification were accepted, the implication would be that the giving of the law was the work of elemental spirits which can be described as "of the world" (Gal. 4.3) and "weak and beggarly" (Gal. 4.9), and this would seem to carry with it a disparagement not merely of legalism but of the law itself, and also, in view of Col. 2.20, the implication that the law is done with as far as Christians are concerned. But it is to be noted that (i) this explanation of στοιχεῖα, though popular, is far from assured (it has recently been vigorously challenged by Gerhard Delling in the Kittel–Friedrich dictionary);[37] (ii) even if it is right, the identification of the angels of Gal. 3.19 with these "elemental spirits" is an unwarranted assumption; and (iii) if Paul really thought that the law had been given through the agency of "weak and beggarly" elemental spirits "of the world", it is strange that in Rom. 9.4 f. he sets "the giving of the law" (ἡ νομοθεσία) among the privileges of Israel in the company of the adoption, the glory, the covenants, the promises, and, finally, Christ Himself. We conclude that in Gal. 4.3 and 9 Paul is referring not to the law itself, but to the legalistic misunderstanding and misuse of it.

Col. 2.14 should perhaps be mentioned here, since it might possibly be thought that the law is meant by "the bond written in ordinances", and that Paul is saying that Christ has "blotted out" the law, and "taken it out of the way, nailing it to the cross". But this is not a likely interpretation. The word translated "bond" (χειρόγραφον) is the technical term for a signed "IOU", and the explanation given by C. F. D. Moule may be on the right lines: "The bond in question here is signed by men's consciences: for a Jew, it is his acceptance of the revealed Law of God as an obligation to abide by; for the Gentile, it is a corresponding recognition of obligation to what he knows of the will of God. In either case, it is an 'autographed' undertaking: 'I owe God obedience to his will. Signed, Mankind.' This χειρόγραφον is 'against us' because we have manifestly failed to discharge its obligations. . . ."[38] But, as χειρόγραφον can also be used in a general sense to denote a manuscript note or document, it is perhaps possible that the reference is to the law's condemnation of us: "that was against us, which was contrary to us" would fit this explanation equally well. Another explanation is that followed by C. Masson, which understands the reference to be to God's books in which men's deeds both good and bad were thought to be recorded (Masson explains the awkward "written in ordinances" as an addition to what Paul had written by the author of Ephesians, which, according to Masson, is non-Pauline).[39] In any case, it seems altogether unlikely that "the bond" is actually the law itself.

Eph. 2.15, containing as it does the very words, "having abolished . . . the law", looks at first sight like a clear statement that Christ has abolished the law. But, when one considers the way in which "the law" is qualified and the context of the verse, this interpretation looks much less convincing. The qualification, "of commandments contained in ordinances", is most probably to be explained as a rather clumsy way of limiting the meaning of "the law", of indicating that what is meant is not the law itself and as a whole; and the context suggests strongly that the meaning of verse 15a is simply that Christ has by His death abolished the ceremonial ordinances, in so far as they have the effect of maintaining the separation of, "the enmity" between, Jews and Gentiles, by doing away with the obligation to fulfil them literally. That the writer (whether Paul or another) did not mean to assert that Christ had abolished the law as such is clear enough from 6.2 f.

We have now completed our survey of passages which have been taken to support the view that, for Paul, the law is abolished by Christ. We submit that our exegesis of Rom. 10.4 has been confirmed, and that, when to our exegesis of these passages the clear positive evidence of such verses as Rom. 3.31,[40] 7.12, 14a, 8.4, 13.8–10, is added, a strong case has been made for our thesis that, for Paul, the law is not abolished by Christ.

10. *For Paul, the giving of the Spirit is the establishment of the law.* (One of the features which make Barth's shorter commentary on Romans[41] so outstandingly valuable – more valuable indeed as an exposition of Paul's epistle than his earlier and more famous commentary – is the clarity with which it shows this to be the meaning of Rom. 8.) The law, which God intended to be "unto life" (Rom. 7.10), which was essentially "spiritual" (Rom. 7.14), but which, encountering sin, pronounced God's condemnation and brought death, and, being misunderstood, misused and perverted by men, actually resulted in their sinning more and more, God has by the ministry of His Son and the gift of His Spirit re-established in its true character and proper office as "spiritual" and "unto life", as "the law of the Spirit of life" which sets us free from the tyranny of sin and death (Rom. 8.2). What the law, frustrated and abused by men's sin, could not accomplish, Christ has triumphantly accomplished in that He has dealt once and for all with our sin by taking upon Himself our condemnation (Rom. 8.3). But this He has done, not in order that the law might be done away, but "that the ordinance [i.e. the righteous requirement] of the law might be fulfilled in

us, who walk not after the flesh, but after the spirit [so RV wrongly: 'Spirit' is required]" (Rom. 8.4).

The gift of the Spirit is the establishment of the law, in that (i) the Spirit sets us free to give up tampering with God's commandments in the hope of making use of them for our own ends, to let go our "glorying' (Rom. 2.23, 3.27, 4.2) and our self-deceit, and humbly and frankly to allow the law to discover us to ourselves as the sinners that we are – a service we stand continually in need of so long as we are in this present life (as is recognized in the order of the administration of the Lord's Supper in the Book of Common Prayer).

The gift of the Spirit is the establishment of the law, in that (ii) the Spirit sets us free to allow the law to point us again and again to Christ its goal and to help to keep us in the way of faith in Him. This the law does no longer as a strict "tutor" (Gal. 3.25) giving commands which may seem harsh and arbitrary because their purpose is not understood; for now that Christ Himself has come the gracious purpose of the law is clearly seen.

The gift of the Spirit is the establishment of the law, in that (iii) the Spirit sets us free for obedience, enabling us to call God "Father" (Rom. 8.15) in sincerity – and therefore to desire wholeheartedly to be and think and speak and do what is well-pleasing to Him, what agrees with calling Him "Father", and to seek wholeheartedly to avoid all that displeases Him and is inconsistent with calling Him "Father". The Spirit enables us to recognize in God's law the gracious revelation of His fatherly will for His children, and therefore to accept it willingly and gladly as a guide to the expression of the gratitude we want to show Him – though this establishment of the law, be it noted, is as yet imperfect (for even those who have received the Spirit fall very far short of full obedience), and will not be perfected until the final coming of Jesus Christ, when that "revealing of the sons of God" at last takes place, for which "the earnest expectation of the creation waiteth" (Rom. 8.19).

Here it should be said that the slogan, "Not law but love", is hardly likely to increase the amount of true love in the world; for, while we most certainly need the general command to love (which the law itself provides in Deut. 6.5 and Lev. 19.18), to save us from understanding the particular commandments in a rigid, literalistic, and pedantic manner, we also need the particular commandments into which the law breaks down the general obligation of love, to save us from the sentimentality and self-deception to which we all are prone.

But it should, of course, be remembered that the Old Testament law is not one great uniform mass but is made up of diverse elements, and that the diverse elements are not all established in exactly the same way. We have already seen that, for Paul, the literal fulfilment of the ceremonial ordinances is no longer obligatory now that Christ has come and fulfilled His ministry. But the ritual regulations remain valid as witness to Christ, and they are established as we allow them to point us to Him and to help us to understand His work for us. And in the moral and civil spheres we must, of course, distinguish between those commandments which express God's absolute will and those which make provision for the limitation of the baleful effects of human sin in the actual conditions of a particular sinful society at a particular stage of development.[42] The latter are established and come into their own among us, not, for example, by our indulgence in an obscurantist defence of the retention of capital punishment on the grounds of Gen. 9.6, Exod. 21.12, 14, etc., but, when we seek resolutely to achieve their humane intentions in the changed conditions of the modern world and to build a society in which all those for whom Christ died and was raised from the dead are truly honoured. And those elements too, in which human weakness and limitation are most apparent, are in their own way established, in that they are recognized by us as a precious, abiding token of the gracious condescension of God, who has humbled Himself to speak to us in and through the broken and inadequate words of sinful men. This must also be said, that no part of the law is established in isolation, but each part only in relation to the whole and in relation to Jesus Christ, the goal of the law.

11. If the foregoing exposition of Paul's teaching on the law is substantially correct, it is clear that his authority cannot justly be claimed for that modern version of Marcionism which regards the law as a disastrous misconception on the part of religious men from which Jesus desired to set us free; nor for the view that the law was an unsuccessful first attempt on God's part at dealing with man's unhappy state, which had to be followed later by a second (more successful) attempt (a view which is theologically grotesque, for the God of the unsuccessful first attempt is hardly a God to be taken seriously); nor yet for the view (characteristic of Lutheranism) that in

law and gospel two "different modes of God's action are manifested",[43] the ultimate unity of which, while it may indeed be supposed to exist in God, has not yet been revealed to us men. On the contrary, it is clear that we are true to Paul's teaching, when we say that *God's word in Scripture is one*; that there is but one way of God with men, and that an altogether gracious way; that gospel and law are essentially one, and their unity, so far from being a mystery still hidden from us, has been once and for all revealed to us in that one gracious Word of God, whose name is Jesus Christ, in whom at the same time God gives Himself wholly to man, and claims man wholly for Himself.[44]

NOTES

1. *Paul: The Theology of the Apostle in the Light of Jewish Religious History* (London, 1961), p. 168.

2. Among the most recent publications on this subject the following should be mentioned: the paper, "Gospel and Law" in K. Barth, *God, Grace, and Gospel* (Edinburgh, 1959), pp. 3–27; W. D. Davies, "Law in the NT" in G. A. Buttrick (ed.), *The Interpreter's Dictionary of the Bible*, Vol. III (New York, 1962), pp. 95–102; and the valuable chapter, entitled "Gospel and Law" in W. Niesel, *Reformed Symbolics: A Comparison of Catholicism, Orthodoxy, and Protestantism* (Edinburgh, 1962), pp. 211–214.

3. E.g. R. Bultmann, *Theology of the New Testament*, Vol. I (London, 1952), pp. 259 f.

4. It may be assumed that "law" is used in this article in one of the senses (i) and (ii) listed above, unless the context indicates otherwise.

5. *The Epistle to the Romans* (London, 1932), p. 43.

6. When C. K. Barrett (*The Epistle to the Romans* (London, 1957), pp. 195 f.) in his translation of Rom. 10. 1 inserts the supplement, "Scripture or no scripture", as "an attempt to bring out the meaning of the particle ($\mu\acute{\epsilon}\nu$) which opens the paragraph", he is giving to Paul's sentence a nuance that is altogether foreign to it. This is certainly not Paul's attitude to Scripture, as a glance at chapters 9–11 of Romans in the British and Foreign Bible Society Greek text, in which the Old Testament quotations are printed in bold type, is in itself sufficient to prove. Paul is continually appealing to Scripture, and is certain that it supports his argument; and in 10. 21 he is going to quote a verse from Isa. 65 which strongly encourages the sentiment he is expressing at this point. The force of the Greek particle $\mu\acute{\epsilon}\nu$ in this sentence is adequately brought out by Blass–Debrunner (F. Blass and A. Debrunner, *A Greek Grammar of the New Testament and other Early Christian Literature*, translated and revised by R. W. Funk (Cambridge, 1961), § 447(4)): "so far as it depends on my desire".

7. In Rom. 5.13 "is not registered" (cf. K. Barth, *Christ and Adam: Man and Humanity in Romans*, Vol. 5 (Edinburgh, 1956), p. 26) is perhaps a rather more satisfactory translation of οὐκ ἐλλογεῖται than the RV "is not imputed", since the next verse makes it clear that Paul does not mean to deny that even in the absence of the law sin is punished.

8. That this (*pace* Bultmann, *op. cit.*, p. 264: "this sentence (coming after vv. 10–19) does not, of course, mean that *through the law* man is led to knowledge of what sin is, but does mean that by it he is *led into sinning*") is what Paul means in 3.20 is fairly certain; for there is, as far as I can see, no suggestion at all in this context of the thought of law as "occasion" (ἀφορμή) which is introduced by Paul in Rom. 7.5, 7–11. It is a mistake to read into "knowledge" (ἐπίγνωσις) in 3.20 a special meaning that perhaps adheres to the use of "know" (γινώσκειν and εἰδέναι) in 7.7.

9. J. Calvin, *The Epistles of Paul the Apostle to the Romans and to the Thessalonians*, translated by R. Mackenzie (Edinburgh, 1961), p. 141.

10. Cf. C. E. B. Cranfield, *The Gospel according to Saint Mark* (Cambridge, 2nd impression, 1963), pp. 243 f., 329.

11. *Op. cit.*, p. 145.

12. H. G. Liddell and R. Scott, *A Greek–English Lexicon* (revised and augmented by H. S. Jones and R. McKenzie, Oxford, 1940), pp. 1772–1774.

13. H. Lietzmann's comment on Rom. 13.8 ("That Paul here, as in 8.4, speaks without trace of embarrassment of 'fulfilment of the law' as something worth striving after and seems to have forgotten chapter 7 and 10.4, is characteristic of the unschematic nature of his discourse" – *An die Römer* (Tübingen, 4th edn., 1933), p. 113 (my translation)) surely indicates a certain deficiency of self-criticism.

14. An alternative interpretation takes v. 5 and vv. 6–10 to be setting forth the meaning of justification by works of the law and justification by faith, respectively. The strongly supported variant reading, which places ὅτι ("that") after νόμον ("law") instead of after γράφει ("writeth" – it could also mean "describeth") and so makes possible the AV translation ("For Moses describeth the righteousness which is of the law, That the man which doeth these things shall live by them"), perhaps reflects someone's desire for a smoother sense along the lines of this interpretation. The fact that a contrast between v. 5 and vv. 6–10 is clearly intended, together with an awareness of the way Paul uses the same OT quotation in Gal. 3.12, may well have misled readers of Romans at an early stage. The interpretation which we have adopted in the text gives a perhaps less obvious but a more closely knit sequence of thought. (Should the alternative interpretation be preferred, vv. 5–10 would then, as a whole, be an explanation of v. 4 thus: The fact that Christ is the goal of the law means that a righteous status is available for all who believe in Him; for, while justification by works is as Moses indicates (v. 5), justification by faith is in accordance with the passages quoted in vv. 6–8 and interpreted in vv. 9 f.)

15. Here Paul speaks of the righteousness of God as "being witnessed by the law and the prophets", but the righteousness of God, i.e. the righteous status which is God's gift, is, for Paul, so intimately bound up with the person and work of Christ (in 1 Cor. 1.30 he actually says that Christ "was made unto us . . .

righteousness" from God), that the implication is that Christ is borne witness to by the law and the prophets.

16. *Pace* F. W. Beare, *The Epistle to the Philippians* (London, 1959), p. 84, there is no justification in the context for taking the meaning to be that Christ was obedient to the "Elemental Spirits": the explanation that the meaning is "obedient to God" (e.g. J. B. Lightfoot, *Saint Paul's Epistle to the Philippians* (London, reprinted, 1908), p. 113) is surely to be preferred.

17. K. Barth, *A Shorter Commentary on Romans* (London, 1959), p. 43.

18. In *Soundings*, ed. by A. R. Vidler (Cambridge, 1963), p. 178.

19. It is not, of course, intended to suggest that there is no human element in the law. In the law, as in the rest of the Bible, God's word is given to us in human words – with all that that involves.

20. *Op. cit.*, p. 183.

21. The chapter entitled "The Gospel as the Divine Justification of those who believe" in Barth's *Shorter Commentary on Romans* should be read as a very necessary antidote to Lampe's essay in *Soundings*.

22. It should, however, be noted that in Colossians Paul seems to be dealing not with a simple judaizing but with some sort of amalgam of Christian, Jewish, and pagan elements.

23. The word which the RV renders in this chapter by "ministration" is διακονία, which means "service" or "ministry" (cf. 2 Cor. 4.1, and also, e.g. Rom. 11.13, 2 Cor. 5.18, Col. 4.17). In v. 7 Paul's language is elliptical: he does not mean that Moses' ministry was "written, and engraven on stones". We might supply something like "which was a ministry of that which was" before "written" in the RV translation, and substitute "was" for "came" (RV "came" renders ἐγενήθη).

24. C. K. Barrett, *From First Adam to Last: A Study in Pauline Theology* (London, 1962), p. 52, n. 1.

25. *Op. cit.*, p. 52, n. 1.

26. *Op. cit.*, p. 52.

27. This statement would be equally true, if we understood "end" in the sense of goal rather than termination; but to take τέλος here in the sense of goal is really not feasible.

28. *Commentary on the Epistles of Paul the Apostle to the Corinthians*, Vol. II (trans. by J. Pringle, reprinted Grand Rapids, 1948), p. 183.

29. Cf. E. Schweizer, in *Theologisches Wörterbuch zum Neuen Testament*, ed. by G. Kittel, continued by G. Friedrich, Vol. VI (Stuttgart, 1933–), p. 416.

30. *The Epistle of Paul to the Galatians* (London, 1934, and frequently reprinted), p. 115.

31. *Op. cit.*, p. 111.

32. *Op. cit.*, p. 112.

33. *Op. cit.*, pp. 114 f.

34. *Commentaries on the Epistles of Paul to the Galatians and Ephesians* (trans. by W. Pringle, reprinted Grand Rapids, 1955), pp. 99 f.

35. II. vii. 2 (quoted according to *Calvin: Institutes of the Christian Religion*, ed. by J. T. McNeill and trans. by F. L. Battles (London, 1961)). This passage is cited by W. Niesel, *op. cit.*, p. 218.

36. See, for example, Duncan, *op. cit.*, pp. 134–136; P. Bonnard, *L'Épître de Saint Paul aux Galates* (Neuchâtel, 1953), pp. 8 f.; and, for a different view, C. F. D. Moule, *The Epistles of Paul the Apostle to the Colossians and to Philemon* (Cambridge, 1957), pp. 90–92.

37. *Op cit.*, Vol. VII, pp. 670–687.

38. *Op. cit.*, p. 97.

39. *L'Épître de Saint Paul aux Colossiens* (Neuchâtel, 1950), pp. 127–129.

40. Rom. 3.31 would still be positive evidence in our favour, even if B. Gerhardsson's suggestion (*Memory and Manuscript: Oral Transmission in Rabbinic Judaism and Early Christianity* (Uppsala, 1961), p. 287), that "abolish" and "establish" are to be understood as Rabbinic technical terms, were accepted.

41. For details, see n. 17 above. Unfortunately the English translation sometimes misrepresents the original.

42. Cf. Cranfield, *op. cit.*, pp. 319 f.

43. Niesel, *op. cit.*, p. 212.

44. In this connection it is most instructive to note that all the initial statements of sections 2, 3, 4, and 6 with reference to the law can also be made with reference to the gospel. The gospel reveals sin – the Cross shows us our sin; the gospel enhances sin, giving to our continuing sin the character of wilful rejection of God's love; the gospel increases sin – for when God's claim on man is most clear and pressing, it enrages our sinfulness most, our self-centredness recognizing the seriousness with which it is threatened; the gospel declares God's condemnation – it is declared in the Cross even as it is being borne for us. (Incidentally, it would hardly be unfair to say that the arguments advanced by G. B. Caird (*Principalities and Powers: A Study in Pauline Theology* (Oxford, 1956), pp. 41–43) to prove that Paul regarded the law as a "demonic agency" could, for the most part at any rate, equally well be used to prove the demonic character of the gospel!)

II

DYING AND RISING WITH CHRIST

Eduard Schweizer

Eduard Schweizer is Professor of New Testament at the University of Zürich; he holds the Dr.Theol. degree from Basel University. Among his principal works available in English are: Lordship and Discipleship (*1960*), Church Order in the New Testament (*1961*), *and* The Church as the Body of Christ (*1964*). *This article originally appeared in* New Testament Studies (*October 1967*) *and is reprinted by permission of the Cambridge University Press.*

THE RELATION of the so-called "mystical" to the so-called "juridical" aspect of Paul's theology has been frequently discussed. While Albert Schweitzer thought that the doctrine of justification by faith was no more than a "side-crater" in the Pauline theology, Rudolf Bultmann considered the idea of a participation in the destiny of Christ a Gnostic influence not really fitting into the Pauline pattern of thought.[1] This disagreement is not of merely historical interest; behind it lies the central theological problem of the significance of Jesus' life, death, and resurrection for us today. Is this significance to be expressed in the categories of an example to be followed or a forerunner, who opens the way ahead for us, or are the categories of sacrificial or vicarious death more adequate? At first sight, the two patterns seem to contradict each other. According to the first, the believer dies with Christ; Christ's death becomes the believer's death; according to the second, Christ dies under the curse of divine judgment, lest the believer undergo this judgment. However, the first observation that we make in the Pauline texts is the coincidence of both lines in the same sentence: II Cor. v. 14: "One has died for all; therefore all have died"; I Thess. v. 10: "Christ died for us so that whether we wake or sleep we might live with him."[2]

We may add I Cor. vi. 11, where God's Spirit, effective in baptism, is connected with the concept of justification and forgiveness of sins: "You let yourselves be washed, you were sanctified, you were justified in the name of the Lord Jesus Christ and in the Spirit of our God." It might, therefore, be worth while trying anew to investigate Paul's conception of living "with Christ" and its connection with other parts of his theology. I shall suggest that, if we start from Paul's eschatology, that will elucidate the fundamental unity of both patterns.

I. THE ESCHATOLOGICAL BEING "WITH CHRIST"

A first group of sayings offers no great difficulties. Being "with Christ" describes the coming life after the parousia of Christ in I Thess. iv. 17 and II Cor. xiii. 4[3] (compare also Rom. vi. 8b; Col. iii. 4). Phil. i. 23 ("What I should like is to depart and be with Christ") is not really different.[4] Chapter iii, 20 f.,[5] in the same letter, proves that Paul is still expecting the parousia of Christ in the near future. Being imprisoned, he realistically considers the possibility of being executed, and he knows that the "being with Christ" which will characterize the final state of beatitude after the parousia will also determine any possible interval between death and resurrection. Paul probably never reflected on the question, whether this will be a time of unconsciousness which passes in the twinkling of an eye or a kind of peaceful sleep in the hands of Christ.[6]

I Thess. iv. 14, although different, does not pose great problems either. Paul expects that God will bring the deceased "with Christ" at his parousia, so that the believer will, even at the parousia itself, not only be with Christ, but share his destiny. This, however, corresponds with the Old Testament and Jewish passages to which, as Dupont showed, this group of eschatological sayings goes back. It is the Old Testament image of the Lord's epiphany with his saints, and more specifically its further developed form in post-biblical Judaism. So we read in I Enoch i. 9: "He (God) will come with myriads of his saints", and especially in lxii. 14: "And they shall eat, lie down and rise with that son of man." It is important to observe that Paul speaks of sharing "with Christ" only in the apocalyptic context of the parousia, whereas, in speaking of the death of the believer, he uses "through Christ": "God will bring with Jesus those who have fallen asleep through him." [7]

This shows that the formula "with Christ" describes, in the Pauline letters, the final being with him after his parousia, similarly to I Enoch lxii. 14, but also, parallel to I Enoch i. 9 and Old Testament phrases, the believer's participation in the event of the parousia, in which he shares the destiny of Christ.

That the eschatological meaning of the expression "with Christ" is the original one is also proved by II Cor. xiii. 4: "We are weak *in* Christ, but shall live *with* him." [8] This former phrase corresponds with the frequent formula "in Christ" that describes the earthly life of the member of the church, the latter is the eschatological formula. In a similar way, Paul declares that we are given over to death "because of Jesus", but shall be raised "with Christ" (II Cor. iv. 11, 14). This is buttressed by I Thess. v. 10, where Paul speaks of Christ's dying for us and our life with him. Unfortunately, the interpretation of this latter expression is debatable. If Paul means that, whether living or dead at the moment, we shall, after the parousia, live with Christ, it is just one more instance of an apocalyptic usage. However, after iv. 18 Paul is finished with the argument about the deceased sharing the parousia of Christ with the still living member of the church. From *v.* 1 on, he stresses the ethical point that expecting the near parousia leads to a new life in faith, love, and hope. Thus, verse 10 more probably means that, whether we are living or dead, we are "with Christ", because he has died for us. [9] If this be so, Paul, as early as I Thess, extended the meaning of the formula "to be with Christ" from describing the apocalyptic life after the parousia even further back than in iv. 14: namely to a description of the period between death and parousia and even to that of the earthly life of the Christian. The former is a perfect parallel to Phil. i. 23, the latter is closely paralleled by Rom. xiv. 8 f., where, however, in the Greek text "to be of the Lord" (namely: the property of the Lord) replaces "to be with Christ", because Paul stresses here the Lordship of

Christ and the obedience of the faithful. A similar passage is Rom.
viii. 32. That God "will grant us everything with Christ" relates,
probably, in the view of the context viii. 17–30 and of the reference to
the last judgment in *v.* 33, primarily to the still outstanding eschatological beatitude but may, in some vague way, also describe the
situation of the believer before the parousia.

II. BAPTISM AS ANTICIPATION OF ESCHATOLOGICAL
LIFE

Is it possible that the formulas which speak of the dying with
Christ as something which has already happened are to be explained
as a similar extension of the apocalyptic formula? The first fact which
should be noted is that the formula "with Christ" occurs only in
either apocalyptic or baptismal contexts. This is undoubtedly true
for the very formula "with Christ" which, apart from the apocalyptic
passages already discussed, is to be found exclusively where Paul
deals with baptism, namely Rom. vi. 8 and Col. ii. 13, 20 and iii. 3 f.
(whether written by himself or by one of his disciples); in all instances it is closely connected with apocalyptic statements. Even
when we turn to verbs composed with the preposition σύν ("with"),
the situation is not much different. Phil. iii. 21 stands in an apocalyptic context, Eph. ii. 5 f. definitely uses apocalyptic language, although
speaking of what has already happened to the Christian, probably
in baptism. Rom. vi. 4–8 and Col. ii. 12 f., iii. 1 clearly describe
baptism. For Gal. ii. 20 the same may be true, although Paul uses the
perfect tense in order to emphasize the continuing validity of what
happened once in baptism. "I have been crucified with Christ."[10]
The imagery of man becoming anew the image of God in Rom. viii.
29 f. shows also that Paul thinks probably of baptism.[11] Thus, only
Rom. viii. 17; Phil. iii. 10 and II Tim. ii. 11 f. are different. All three
passages declare that the apocalyptic glorification with Christ includes and presupposes a preceding suffering with Christ. All three
passages combine a reference to the baptismal experience of receiving
the spirit of sonship (Rom. viii. 15 f.) or dying with Christ (Phil. iii.
10, cf. 8 f. and II Tim. ii. 11) with the concept of daily suffering with
Christ.[12] This is also mentioned in II Cor. iv. 10 f., where, however,
the phrase "with Christ" is lacking, and, without any direct reference

to Christ, in Rom. vi. 36, I Cor. xvi. 30. Let us therefore turn to the understanding of baptism in the New Testament.

The baptism of John was undoubtedly shaped by a vivid expectation of the impending doomsday. It was probably more, even the anticipation of the imminent judgment by fire, saving the penitent, who underwent it voluntarily, from future damnation.[13]

Despite all differences Christian baptism stands historically and theologically in close relation to the rite of John.[14] This is especially true for the eschatological connotation. We start from the word of Jesus (Mark x. 15), which promises entry into the (coming?) kingdom of God to whosoever receives it like a child. Probably this saying had been related to baptism very early. Cullmann[15] has pointed to the formula "do not hinder them" in *v.* 14, which occurs also in early Christian baptismal liturgies from Acts viii. 36 on. Ferdinand Hahn[16] thinks that the position of this pericope in Mark x. may reflect an early catechism dealing with marriage, baptism, and Christian life. Be this as it may, John iii. 5 ("Unless one is born of water and spirit, he cannot enter the kingdom of God") shows at any rate a tradition which understood this saying in the light of Christian baptism. The formulation "to enter into the kingdom of God", totally foreign to John, who nowhere else speaks of the kingdom of God, proves that he quotes a traditional sentence. It is identical with the phrase used in Mark x. 15. This proves that the child-like receiving of the kingdom in the subordinate clause of Mark x. 15 has been interpreted by the early church in the light of its baptism as "being born from water and spirit".

Thus, in the interpretation of the pre-Johannine church, baptism, understood as a rebirth by water and spirit, guaranteed entry into the coming kingdom of God. John himself uses the same phrase in a different way. No longer does he expect a coming kingdom;[17] for him, it is, at least primarily, a present reality, which the believer is already able to see. Moreover, he accepts baptism as an ecclesiastical rite, but is not much interested in it and therefore drops all allusions to it in the remaining parts of the pericope iii. 1–21. Thus, his own reformulation is to be found in *v.* 3: "Unless one is born from above, he cannot see the kingdom of God." According to his understanding, birth from above, in the church connected with the rite of baptism, brings the kingdom of God. In it, what the apocalypticists expected from a future parousia, already happens. To say it in the terms of the

Pauline eschatology: baptism brings the eschatological being with Christ. As I Thess. iv. 14 stated that God will give the deceased their share in the parousia of Christ, John states that in baptism God lets the believer share in the destiny of Christ, that he will not only be "brought with Christ" in the parousia, but that he is already living with him.

Is John the first one with such an understanding? Certainly not. Even in the time of Paul, the Corinthians thought themselves to live in the new aeon, in the promised kingdom (I Cor. iv. 8), speaking in new tongues (xiii. 1 f., xiv. 27), irresistibly moved by God's spirit (xii. 2, xiv. 32), no longer expecting resurrection from the dead (xv. 12). It was not that they were denying the existence of a life after death, as Paul misunderstood them (I Cor. xv. 12, 32). If this were so, they would not have let themselves be baptized for the dead (xv. 29). Rather they thought, like Hymenaeus and Philetas in later times (II Tim. ii. 18), that the resurrection had already happened so that the life of the soul would go on eternally after the death of the body.[18] In Col. i. 13, the term "kingdom", which is very rare in the Pauline letters, turns up again. The close resemblance of verses 12–14 to Acts xxvi. 18 and to Qumran texts proves that we deal here with traditional liturgical phrases. The context is that of conversion, referring to the participation in the lot of the holy ones, in the light; to the salvation from the power of darkness; to the forgiveness of sins, and finally to the "son of his love", which reminds us of the baptism of Jesus (Mark i. 11).[19] Most interesting is the assertion that the baptized are saved from the power of darkness and already transferred into the kingdom of Christ. This kingdom is no longer a future reality to be hoped for; it is present, and the believers are now living in it. This means that Col. i. 13, like John iii. 5, expresses exactly the belief which we hypothetically presupposed for the history of the phrase "with Christ": baptism is the anticipation of the change of the aeons; by it the believer is transferred into the coming kingdom, into the eschatological life with Christ. The apocalyptic expectation of such a life with Christ may also explain why Col. i. 13 speaks of Christ's, not of God's, kingdom.

There is another, even more suggestive, text: Tit. iii. 5. Here baptism is called "the bath of rebirth". The term "rebirth", however, is not the usual one for "being reborn" known from popular Greek philosophers, occasionally also from mystery religions: it is the term

which occurs in the New Testament only once again, namely in Matt.
xix. 28: "In the rebirth (of the whole world) when the son of man
shall sit on his glorious throne, you . . . will also sit on twelve
thrones . . ."

This term, in Stoic usage, describes the rebirth of the whole cosmos
after the cosmic fire,[20] sometimes also the rebirth of man after the
cosmic cycle of 440 years.[21] Plutarch uses the word for the individual
rebirth in mystery religions[22] and occasionally the word occurs in a
figurative sense.[23] Judaism took it up in order to apply it to the
apocalyptic rebirth of the new earth under a new heaven.[24] Thus, in
this certainly traditional liturgical phrase we find again a probably
still apocalyptic terminology identifying baptism with the cosmic
rebirth of Stoic or Jewish apocalypticism.

In the same verse baptism is called the "renewal of the Holy
Spirit", which probably means the new, eschatological creation
effected by God's Spirit. This is an expression of the common
Christian belief that in the work of the Spirit given by baptism the
coming aeon has broken into this present one. This is what, for instance, Heb. vi. 4 f. clearly states: "It is impossible to restore again
to repentance those who have once been enlightened, who have
tasted the heavenly gift, and have become partakers of the Holy
Spirit, and have tasted . . . the powers of the age to come . . ."

III. THE PAULINE INTERPRETATION OF
DYING AND RISING WITH CHRIST

Let us turn to indisputably Pauline texts. The term "kingdom of
God", rare with Paul, as we said, is to be found in close connection
with baptism in I Cor. vi. 9–11.[25] According to this passage baptism
is carried out "in the name of the Lord Jesus Christ and in the Spirit
of our God", that is, in the realm or in the sphere which is dominated
by the exalted Christ and the living Spirit. The difficulty in which
Paul finds himself is obvious. On the one hand, he wants to emphasize,
contrary to the view of the Corinthians, that entry into the kingdom
of God is a future fact and will be barred to adulterers, idolaters,
etc. (*vv.* 9 f.). On the other hand, he cannot deny that baptism means
a real change. The old life in adultery, idolatry, etc., definitely came
to an end, and entry into the coming kingdom of God was definitely

given to them as a divine promise, when they were baptized. Hence, Paul solves the problem by asserting that dying to the old life of sin has already definitely happened in baptism, but rising to the final state of eternal life is still in the future. And yet, this is not all of the truth. In some way, this future life penetrates the still earthly existence of the baptized: the Spirit is present. II Cor. i. 21 f. tries to do justice to this. The baptized[26] have been transferred "into Christ", have been anointed and given the Spirit as a pledge, or according to Rom. viii. 23 as the first fruits of the coming eschatological gifts.[27] There are other Pauline texts showing a close connection between baptism and apocalyptic hope, which can only be mentioned: Rom. viii. 29 f.;[28] xiii. 11–14[29] and I Cor. xi. 1–11 with its concept of a second eschatological exodus.[30] It is clear: Paul fights against the Corinthian enthusiasm, an enthusiasm which leaves time and space behind it, by means of an understanding of baptism as the beginning of a way which leads to the final consummation; at the same time, he will not deny that in baptism the old aeon of sin has been ended definitely, and that in the Spirit the firstfruits of the coming life have been given to the church.

Let me summarize: Mark x. 15, John iii. 5, and I Cor. vi. 9–11 prove that baptism was understood in a broad area of the early church as giving admission to the kingdom of God. For Paul, and probably also for the tradition which was taken up by John, this was a future event promised and/or guaranteed by God to the baptized. For John, and even clearer for Col. i. 13, the seeing of God's kingdom, the transfer into Christ's kingdom has already been effected in baptism. Tit. iii. 5 shows even that this has probably been identified with the apocalyptic rebirth of the whole cosmos, which ends the old and initiates the new aeon, and the "new creation" in II Cor. v. 17 may well be a relic of such apocalyptic views. I Cor. v. 11 and Tit. iii. 5 prove that it was first of all the experience of the Spirit in and after baptism which led to such apocalyptic views. Heb. vi. 5 states explicitly that the baptized are already tasting the powers of the future aeon; and Paul's corrections of a more enthusiastic understanding show that ideas of this kind were widespread and that the Corinthians understood the presence of the Spirit, not as a mere pledge or firstfruits like Paul, but as the new, eschatological life itself, as the apocalyptic "living with Christ". It seems fair to me to draw the conclusion that "being with Christ" originally described the future life after the parousia of Christ. At the same time "being brought" or "coming with Christ" was what the baptized expected from that day on which he would share in Christ's triumph. Baptism was first conceived of as the divine promise or even God's guarantee for the participation in these coming events, for the entry into the kingdom of God. More and more it became the admission into the present kingdom of God or of Christ, and was understood as being raised with Christ to the life of the new aeon. The experience of the Spirit seemed to prove that the new aeon had in the church already broken into this world; resurrection was already an accomplished fact, since it had taken place in the rising with Christ in baptism. Against this enthusiasm, Paul emphasizes that the rising with Christ is still to be awaited. Asked whether, according to his preaching, nothing definite had happened in baptism, he would reply that indeed the dying to the old life of sin had definitely happened with Christ, into whose death they had been baptized. There was also a new life indeed, but in a paradoxical way. This life had to validate itself in the obedience of the believer. In the case of Paul himself, this led to imprisonment, scourging, defeat, death. And yet, even so, he knew himself to be going his way with Christ. It was "suffering with Christ" (Rom. viii. 17) and at the same time "walking in the newness of life" corresponding with Christ's resurrection (Rom. vi. 4). This new life, created in the midst of death, could already be seen in the revival of the congregations founded by Paul (II Cor. iv. 12) and would lead to the final glorification and the life "with Christ" (Rom. vi. 8, vii. 17).[31]

This scanty summary leads to the main question: how is the idea of this new life in obedience under the Lordship of Christ to be related to Paul's proclamation of justification by faith? If Christ died for us, why have we to die with him? Are we holy because of Christ's vicarious death or because of our new obedience, or is this a false alternative?

IV. The Theological Importance of Paul's View

We started from the observation of the fact that Paul combines very often in the same sentence both the statements just mentioned. According to I Cor. vi. 11, baptism is sanctification and justification at the same time; it is effected in the name of Jesus Christ and in the power of the Spirit. I Thess. v. 10 states that Christ died for us so that we might live with him. II Cor. v. 14 argues that just because he died for us, we all have died, and Rom. vi. 2 ff. runs very much the same way, when it takes for granted that we have definitely died to sin and are walking in a new life, because we are baptized into the vicarious death of Christ. Hence, is not the church's doctrine wrong when it places sanctification and obedience in a new life over against justification by mere faith? We shall therefore ask: (a) is not justification, with Paul, more than a mere act of divine jurisdiction? and (b) is not sanctification, with Paul, more than a mere performance of human good will?

(a) Undoubtedly, it is very important for Paul to emphasize that the foundation of all our living and dying is God's act, and God's act alone. Baptism is baptism into the death of Christ Jesus (Rom. vi. 3). In Rom. viii. 3 f. and Gal. iv. 4 f. Paul changes a pattern which originally described the incarnation of the pre-existent son, into a proclamation of his death on the cross.[32] There is indeed no other foundation than that which is laid, Jesus Christ, and him crucified (I Cor. iii. 11, ii. 2). And yet, it would be wrong to deduce from these passages a clear legal theory of substitution, of which man should only take cognizance in order to be saved. Even within the one letter to Romans, Paul uses five or six different images in order to express the importance of Jesus' death for us: that of expiation (iii. 24 f.)[33] or atonement (v. 10 f.), that of vicarious death (v. 6–11, xiv. 15, also in the passive voice iv. 25a), that of ransom (viii. 3 parallel to Gal. iv. 4 f.; probably also iii. 24, vii. 4), that of judgment over sin (viii. 3) and that of justification (iii. 24–26, etc.). But the death of Christ is also mentioned where Paul speaks of sharing Christ's destiny so that his death becomes our death (vi. 4–6, cf. v. 15–17; II Cor. v. 14) or where he considers Christ's example as effective in the life of the church (xv. 3–5). The abundance of these images shows that we should be wrong in selecting just one of them as *the* Pauline doctrine.

A further reflection may strengthen this point. As long as one deals with the canonical Old and New Testaments only, the idea of vicarious or expiatory death appears in the sacrificial rites of Israel, is taken up in an astonishingly new way in the figure of the servant of God in Isa. liii, and is fulfilled in a definite and comprehensive way in Jesus' death. However, since we have now a better understanding of the inter-testamental period, we have realized how common this idea was in many circles, although no Jew of this time would have thought of a vicarious death for the world, which would include the Gentiles. [34] Thus, when a Jewish-Christian preached Jesus dying for the sake of many, it meant nothing extraordinary. His hearers all believed that quite a number of innocent Jewish martyrs did the same. In order to proclaim the uniqueness of this death of Jesus, a preacher needed still other categories in addition to that of expiatory death. He had to say, at the same time, that this vicarious death of Jesus was unique, because it was the eschatological fulfilment of God's history with mankind. This, of course, is exactly what Paul did when he introduced the phrase "with Christ". If it is true that this formula goes back to the apocalyptic hope of an eschatological life with Christ, it guards us from dissolving Paul's statements into mere anthropological descriptions. For, more than anything else, the apocalyptic hope of the New Testament for the new creation of the whole world resists a mere existential interpretation. On the one hand, this shows, exactly in the same way as the doctrine of justification by faith does, that our hope lies outside of ourselves, of our experiences, of all the ups and downs of our faith, namely exclusively in God's deed, which will create a new world at the end of the times, and did so, in a proleptic way, in the death and the resurrection of Christ.[35] On the other hand, it shows that this creation of a new world on Good Friday and Easter was more than a divine decree merely giving a reprieve from all punishment for sins. It urges us to search for new theological categories in order to understand why Paul prefers the concept of living in a new world created by the death and the resurrection of Christ, or under a new lordship inaugurated by these events and anticipating the coming kingdom of God, to any merely anthropological statements.

(*b*) At the same time, the insight into the roots of the formula "with Christ" in apocalyptic expectancies warns us against misunderstanding the sanctification and the new life as a human effort. In Phil. iii. 3, Paul writes that we serve God by the Spirit, no longer trusting in the flesh. This means that the Spirit is the real power which is behind all our service to God, whereas the flesh gets its power only if we put our trust in it. Rom. viii. 13 f. contrasts those who live *according* to the flesh to those who *by* the Spirit kill the works of the body. Again, the Spirit is the actual power killing all that does not please God, whereas the flesh gets some power only if man chooses it

G

as his standard of life. According to Gal. iv. 23 f. one son of Abraham is begotten *according* to (the norms of) the flesh, the other *through* the promise of God. Again, the Spirit is the real begetting power, the flesh is the thing to which Abraham looked first, so that *he* let it dominate him. Never is it the reverse. This means that for Paul the power of the flesh and that of the Spirit are in no way to be seen on the same level. The flesh is a power by the grace of man; it is powerful only as long as man gives it its power, allows it to dominate him. Not so with the Spirit. It – or we should preferably say – *he* is the real power behind all work of the baptized, working in God's power, independently of man. This is, of course, the Old Testament influence, where the contrast to flesh is always God or God's word or God's Spirit. It is hence quite well possible, in the case of flesh, to reduce a mythological Pauline figure of speech to a mere anthropological attitude, since the work or thinking of the "flesh" is actually the work or thinking of man trusting in the "flesh", that is, in the created world instead of in the creator. But the same reduction is impossible in the case of Spirit. For the Spirit is, with Paul, always God's own activity, absolutely independent of man, breaking into human existence from outside, as a new power ruling over him not by man's grace, but by his own authority.[36]

Is this an additional event which follows that of justification? Should we distinguish the juridical and the mystical statement of Paul by distinguishing two subsequent stages of a Christian life? The three passages from which we started all describe, in the juridical language of atonement or justification, the inauguration of a new lordship. Living under justification by Christ, in the righteousness of God, means living under the lordship of Christ, in the life of the Spirit. Justification by the death of Christ, therefore, means, for Paul, always the conquest of man by the authority of the Spirit. With E. Käsemann,[37] I think indeed that the righteousness of God is interpreted correctly by the category of "power". It is the act which transfers man from the lordship of the Flesh, which is ultimately the lordship of his own will, to that of Christ, exercised by the Spirit.

V. The Unity of the "Juridical" and the "Mystical" Line in Paul's Theology

This, I suppose, explains our first observation, namely the fact that the idea of Christ dying for our sake and that of our living with him or our sharing his death with him, or our life in the realm of the Spirit, appear in the same sentence. Let me try to clarify my position by very shortly pointing to three outstanding pericopes at the beginning, at the end, and in the middle of the letter to the Romans, and by finally summarizing my view.

The first pericope is Rom. iii. 21–26. Paul certainly uses traditional vocabulary, whether or not he actually quotes a creed or liturgical formula, as Käsemann thinks. No less certain is the fact that Paul's own interpretation is to be found, first of all, in the emphasis which he puts on faith and the gratuitous gift of God's grace which does not demand the words of the law. Faith, however, is not simply the attitude of individual men; it came, according to Gal. iii. 23–25, into the world as a power superseding that of the Mosaic law. Without dealing with the numerous exegetical problems, we realize that the event of the righteousness of God inaugurates a new "time", a new aeon. The period of God's holding back his judgment[38] has definitely come to its end.

It is the law of faith which rules, and no longer the law of works, according to Paul's own exegesis in *v.* 27. As, after the victory of the allied forces in France, the law of the victors ruled over the country and no longer the law of the German occupation force, whether one realized it or not; so God's righteousness rules now over the world, whether one realizes it or not.

The second text is Rom. xv. 1–6. The introduction in *v.* 1, generalizing the concrete admonitions of Chapter 14, and the phrases "for the common good" and "for edification", both important for Paul and well known from I Cor. xii. 7, xiv. 3–5, show that this pericope is a kind of summary. The life of the church in mutual love is, according to *v.* 3, founded in the behaviour of Christ, who is described with a quotation from a psalm of the suffering righteous. This means that the passion of Christ, as the eschatological fulfilment of the Old Testament, is the foundation of the church's life, which, as verses 5 and 6 say, is now dominated by hope and praise of the Lord. Above all, it is a being "of one mind" or "thinking unanimously" of all "according to Christ Jesus". Paul does not write "as with Christ Jesus" or anything similar. He formulates "to think unanimously according to Christ Jesus", parallel to his phrase "to live according to the Spirit". This means that Christ is not simply an example to be followed. He is at least the standard according to which the church lives, but, as in the case of the other phrase "according to the Spirit", the meaning is rather comprehensive and includes the actual cause of such a life.[39]

Thus both texts, seemingly contradictory to each other, describe the change of the ruling power which transposes the church into the new righteousness of God and the new obedience of his people. Whereas, at the beginning of the letter, the stress is laid upon God's act not merited by any work of man, it is, at the end, laid upon the new situation of the church created by God's act.

This is buttressed by the third section, Rom. viii. 2–4. Here also, the change of the ruling power is central for Paul. In Christ Jesus, the law of the revivifying Spirit has superseded that of sin and death. It has done this because God has judged sin in the flesh of Christ, sacrificed on the cross.[40] And it has done this with the aim that the demands of the law should be fulfilled in those who, from now on, would live according to the spirit. Paul neither writes "for those" nor "by those" but "in those". Again, the "juridical" statement that God let Christ die for our sake is identified with the "mystical" statement that, by this, God has transplanted men into the realm of the Spirit, by whom the demands of the law are fulfilled in the believers. Again justification and sanctification cannot be separated; again the name of Jesus Christ, dying for the sake of the church, and the power of the Spirit, working in the church, cannot be separated.

Does this not mean that the contrast between imputed and effective justification or between a merely cognitive and a magically effective significance of baptism is somehow wrong? Should we not search for new theological categories? When God created the world, his word was identical with his deed. It is the same in the new creation. And yet, creating or new-creating is not identical with practising magic. It puts man under a new power, a new lordship, and it puts him by this into a new responsibility, where obedience is the only possible answer. When, to take up this example again, the allied forces took over control in France, it was a historical fact which could be dated exactly. Yet it was not an objective fact in the same sense as, for instance, the falling of a meteor in Siberia. This is true whether anyone realizes it or not and may, for centuries, not affect anybody. A lordship, however, is always lordship over men. They may know or not know about it, they may like or dislike or even hate it; it changes their lives from the very first moment. Whatever they do becomes, by the mere fact of the newly exercised authority of the ruling power, obedience or disobedience, co-operation or rebellion. There is, of course, no lordship without a people. Thus, the lordship of Christ is a fact since Easter and has changed the world, once for all. And yet it is, at the same time, still changing the world, since it creates obedience (or disobedience), new love (or hatred), devotion (or aggression) ever anew.[41] By taking up the traditional phrases for Christ's vicarious death, Paul keeps his readers from a mere existential understanding, in which the conversion of the believer, his engagement and his decision would become central. By taking up the traditional phrase of apocalyptic hope, Paul keeps his readers from a mere existential understanding, in which the new self-understanding of man, his attitude, his faith would become central. In "juridical" and "mystical" vocabulary Paul stresses *God's* act in Jesus and in the Spirit as the only foundation and the only reality of all new life.[42] And yet exactly this act claims and creates man's faith. Faith founds its certitude on God's deed, and just by doing so and by expecting everything from him becomes obedience. Such obedience gives way to the work of the Spirit and leaves him the space occupied hitherto by man's own works.

NOTES

1. A. Schweitzer, *Die Mystik des Apostel Paulus* (Tübingen, 1930), p. 220. Cf. R. Bultmann, *Theologie des N.T.* ch. 33, 3–5. The most recent and very helpful discussion of this problem is to be found in R. C. Tannehill, "Dying and Rising with Christ", Beiheft, *ZNW*, Vol. XXXII (1966). Cf. also W. Thüsing, "Per Christum in Deum", *Neutestamentliche Abhandlungen*, N.F. 1 (1965), and E. Güttgemanns, *Der leidende Apostel und sein Herr* (1966), also E. Schweizer, *Ev. Theol.* 26 (1966), pp. 239–257.

2. Cf. Tannehill (*op. cit.*, note 1), pp. 69, 133 f., who also refers to Phil. iii. 2–11 (p. 115).

3. Cf. note 8, below.

4. *Pace* J. Dupont, Σὺν Χριστῷ, *L'union avec le Christ suivant St. Paul*, Vol. I (1952), pp. 172–181.

5. Considered as a fragment of a pre-Pauline hymn by Güttgemanns (cf. note 1, above), pp. 240 f.

6. The same idea is probably expressed as early as I Thess. v. 10, cf. below.

7. Cf. Dupont (cf. note 1), p. 42; the New English Bible against RSV; and Thüsing (cf. note 1, above), p. 202.

8. Some manuscripts read "with Christ", some also "in him"; but the rendering given above represents probably the correct reading. Cf. Tannehill (cf. note 1, above), 99, n. 1.

9. To be sure, the verb is in the aorist (Tannehill (cf. note 1, above), pp. 133 f., who interprets therefore in the former sense); however, exactly the same is true for Rom. 6.4c.

10. R. Schnackenburg, *Das Heilsgeschehen bei der Taufe nach dem Apostel Paulus* (Münchener Theol. Studien, hist. Abt. 1 (1950)), pp. 57–60.

11. The idea of man becoming, through Christ, the image of God is for Thüsing (cf. note 1, above), pp. 122–124, etc., the key to understanding man's participation in the life of the Risen Lord. Cf. also note 37, below.

12. I agree with Tannehill (cf. note 1, above), pp. 7–14, 41–43, etc., that the baptismal context in Rom. vi belongs to a pre-Pauline tradition and that, on the whole, Paul himself does not emphasize baptism in most of the passages quoted above. Cf. note 1, above.

13. H. G. Marsh, *The Origin and Significance of New Testament Baptism* (1941), p. 28; C. H. Kraeling, *John the Baptist* (1951), pp. 117 f. Cf. also T. Gnilka, *Revue de Qumrân*, Vol. III (1961), pp. 204 f.

14. Kraeling, pp. 171–175.

15. O. Cullmann, *Vorträge und Aufsätze* (1966), pp. 529 f.

16. In a mimeographed paper: *Die Kindertaufe im ältesten Christentum* (1965), pp. 4 f.

17. I should not say that he expects nothing from the future, but certainly not the kingdom of God in the old sense which this connotation has in the Synoptists. I think that v. 28 f., vi. 51–58, xii. 48d are traditional sentences or phrases taken up by the evangelist, but cf., in his own language, xi. 25 f., xii. 25, xiv. 3, xvii. 24.

18. For a modern variant of this thesis, cf. Güttgemanns (cf. note 1, above), pp. 67–93; his presupposition that a fully developed myth of the Saviour's identity with the saved people was known in Corinth still seems to me a hypothesis without evidence.

19. It might be that this expression was borrowed from a first line of the hymn quoted in i. 15–20; for H. Wildberger has shown in *Theologische Zeitschrift*, Vol. XXI (1965), p. 500 that it occurs rather frequently in Egyptian texts (up to the time of the New Testament) together with the concept of the image of God (*v.* 15). For the meaning of baptism, cf. notes 30 and 41.

20. *V. Armin.*, II, 191; III, 265.

21. *M. Ant.*, II, 1; Terentius Varro (Augustinus, *Civ. Dei.*, 22, 28).

22. Kittel, *Theol. Wörterbuch*, Vol. I, p. 686, 8 ff. (F. Büchsel); *Corp. Herm.*, Vol. XIII, where it occurs ten times, is of a very late date.

23. Philo, *Post. Cain.*, 124; Cicero, *Att.*, 6; Josephus, *Ant.*, II, 66; cf. in the second century A.D., Lucianus, *Enc. Mus.*, 7 (the Platonic rebirth of the soul).

24. Cf. E. Sjöberg in *Studia Theol.*, Vol. IV (1951), pp. 60 ff., also G. Strecker, *Der Weg der Gerechtigkeit* (1962), p. 238, n. 3. For a Hebrew parallel, cf. 1QS 4, 25 (J. Dupont, *Biblica*, Vol. 45, p. 365).

25. The middle voice means "to let oneself be washed" (Schnackenburg (cf. note 10, above), pp. 1 f.; E. Lohse, *Taufe und Rechtfertigung bei Paulus, Keryma und Dogma*, Vol. XI (1965), p. 322).

26. Although "sealing" is not yet a technical term for baptism (Schnackenburg, pp. 81–83), the passage deals probably with it and not only with the apostolic vocation (against Schnackenburg, pp. 84 f.).

27. Cf. II Cor. v. 5; Eph. i. 13 f.

28. Cf. P. Stuhlmacher, *Gerechtigkeit Gottes bei Paulus* (1965), pp. 186 f.

29. Cf. the baptismal phrase "to put on the Lord" (Gal. iii. 27) in *v.* 14, and Lohse (cf. n. 25, above), p. 323.

30. Cf. the mention of baptism in *v.* 2 and J. Jeremias in Kittel, *Theol. Wörterbuch*, Vol. IV, p. 874. Again, the reference to baptism belongs, of course, to the tradition rather than to Paul himself (cf. note 12, above). For Paul, baptism marks mainly the beginning of the new way of faith.

31. Again, I agree with Tannehill's (cf. note 1, above) statement that the idea of dying with Christ is different from that of living with Christ in or after the parousia (p. 88, n. 14), and that the former is rooted in pre-Pauline tradition (cf. note 12, above). However, I am suggesting that the phrase "with Christ" (with which Tannehill is not dealing, p. 6) originates in an apocalyptic view of the future life and was, before and independently of Paul, transferred to the area of ideas about a new life gained by baptism. On the other hand, baptism was traditionally connected with the death of Jesus (Mark x. 38; Luke xii. 50), although not with the phrase "with Christ". Thus, it would be Paul, who in contrast to an understanding of baptism as a mere rising with Christ to a divine life, finally defined it as "dying with Christ".

32. That Gal. iv. 4 f. simply takes up the idea of iii. 13 is proved by the mention of the law and the term ἐξαγοράζειν, which, within Paul's undisputed letters, is restricted to these two passages. In Rom. viii. 3, the phrase περὶ ἁμαρτίας, going back to Lev. ix. 2 f., xii. 6, 8, xiv. 22, 31, xv. 15, 30, xvi. 3, 5, xxiii. 19; also v. 6, 11, vii. 37, is certainly not a later addition, but Paul's reinterpretation of the pattern in the light of Christ's sacrificial death. Cf. E. Schweizer, "Zum religionsgeschichtlichen Hintergrund der 'Sendungsformel', Gal. iv. 4 f., Röm. viii. 3 f., Joh. iii. 16 f., I Joh. iv. 9", *ZNW*, Vol. LXII (1966), pp. 199–210.

33. Cf., however, G. Fitzer, "Der Ort der Versöhnung nach Paulus", *Theologische Zeitschrift*, Vol. XXII (1966), pp. 161–183.

34. Cf. II Macc. vii. 38; IV Macc. i. 11, vi. 29, xvii. 21 f.

35. Cf. note 41, below.

36. Cf. E. Schweizer, in Kittel, *Theol. Wörterbuch*, Vol. VII, pp. 131, 20 ff.

37. "Gottesgerechtigkeit bei Paulus", in *Exegetische Versuche und Besinnungen*, Vol. II (1964), pp. 181–193. I should think that this category, used also extensively in Tannehill (cf. note 1, above), e.g. pp. 14–20, 123–129, is more adequate to Paul's thinking than either Thüsing's or Güttgemann's stimulating new formulations (cf. note 1, above). The former emphasizes the corporate body of the exalted Lord, to be conceived of in ontological terms, into which the believer is trans-

ferred in the sacrament (for Rom. vi., especially pp. 67–93, 134–143). However, his understanding of the life of the exalted Christ as directed towards God so that sharing it means sharing a life of obedience in which God becomes the only goal (262 f.), comes rather near to Käsemann's concept, and is a real progress in Pauline interpretation. The latter's emphasis on the Christological aspect of Paul's theology (203–206, for Rom. vi, cf. 212 f.) is certainly helpful. He also rightly opposes a merely mythological concept of the body of the risen Lord (e.g. 330–344). But I doubt whether his stress on the "eschatological" character of the time of Jesus' crucifixion and resurrection which bridges the gap between A.D. 30 and today, is sufficient for explaining Paul's view (cf. e.g. 118–121, 195–198, 222 f.). His strict denial of a concept of an individual body of the risen Lord (247–270) or of the apostle's membership in the body of Christ (323) does not seem to do justice to the texts.

38. I understand ἀνοχή as it is understood in ii. 4, and interpret πάρεσις as a provisional allowing to pass, not identical with ἄφεσις. Hence the formerly committed sins are those which had been committed before Christ's death.

39. Cor. xii. 8 f. διὰ τοῦ πνεύματος is totally synonymous with κατὰ τὸ πνεῦμα. Very similar is it in Rom. viii. 4–9 (cf. 13 f.), and in Rom. i. 4 κατὰ τὸ πνεῦμα designates the sphere which determines the new, heavenly existence of Christ. Cf. also Thüsing (cf. note 1, above), pp. 39–45.

40. Cf. note 33, above.

41. We cannot deal here with the difficult problem of the relation of the "once for all" of Christ's crucifixion and resurrection to the "once for him" of the individual baptism. For Paul, the establishment of the Lordship of Christ clearly took place around the year A.D. 30 in Palestine, although it becomes valid for us in our baptism as the beginning of our faith.

42. A last image may illustrate Paul's emphasis. If I want to know about a performance of Shakespeare's *Macbeth*, I must ask somebody who was present. A totally "objective" observer might tell me that 250 electric bulbs were burning, etc. Thus, I must ask somebody who really got engaged. If, however, this one told me merely about his subjective experiences ("I tell you, I had tears in my eyes during the second act, and my heart was beating wildly during the third . . .") he would not help me at all, since I want to know what happened on the stage and not in the hearts of the audience. Therefore, the witnesses of the New Testament, just because they are totally engaged, do not tell us about their own engagement, but about God's deeds.

12

THE DESTINATION AND PURPOSE
OF ST. JOHN'S GOSPEL

J. A. T. Robinson

*John A. T. Robinson is Dean of Trinity College Cambridge and holds
the D.D. degree from Cambridge University. His best known publica-
tions are* The Body *(1952),* Jesus and His Coming *(1958),* Honest to
God *(1963), and* Exploration into God *(1967). "The Destination and
Purpose of St. John's Gospel" is reprinted from* New Testament
Studies *(January 1960) by permission of Cambridge University Press.*

FOR WHOM and for what, to what audience and to what purpose,
were the four Gospels written? This is one of the most elementary
questions of New Testament study, and one might think that by
now the answers could be given with some degree of certainty and
consent. And of the first three Gospels I think this is broadly true.
Naturally there will always be room for fresh lines of development
and approach, but they are unlikely to modify very radically the
conclusions which can be found set out in any textbook. If one had to
reduce these conclusions to their barest summary, one could say,
without immediate fear of contradiction, that St. Matthew's Gospel
was evidently written for a Jewish-Christian community, and that its
overall purpose was broadly speaking *catechetical*; that St. Mark's

Gospel was composed for a predominantly Gentile community and that its primary purpose was *kerygmatic*, setting out, for the use of the Church, a summary of its proclamation; and that St. Luke's Gospel, as he himself indicates, was again addressed, though more generally, to the Graeco-Roman world, and that its purpose was *instructional*, with the defence and confirmation of the Gospel as a dominant motif.[1]

But when we come to the Gospel according to St. John there is no such broad agreement. On almost every question connected with this Gospel it is still possible for the most divergent views to command serious and scholarly assent. And after all this time the question of the destination and purpose of the Gospel is as wide open as it ever was. Was it addressed to a Jewish or a Gentile audience, or indeed to the inquiring individual whatever his background?[2] Again, was it intended primarily for a Christian or for a non-Christian public? Was its motive in the first instance to win the faithless, to establish the faithful, or to counter the gainsayers? And if John's primary purpose was to *defend* the Gospel, was the opposition Jewish, or Gnostic, or Baptist, or even Christian? All these opinions have been canvassed and seriously sustained, before one even reaches the questions that have most divided scholars, and which I must here leave on one side, questions namely about the cultural and intellectual *milieu* to which the author and his readers belonged, whether they were Jew, Gentile, or Christian.

The mere fact that none of these views has succeeded in establishing itself over the others shows that the evidence does not point decisively in any one direction. Nevertheless, I am persuaded that there is one solution that can be stated a good deal more compellingly than it has been and merits the most serious consideration. What I shall advocate is, of course, no new position – it would almost certainly be wrong if it were – and indeed it is substantially that to which Professor W. C. van Unnik of Utrecht gave the not inconsiderable weight of his support at the Oxford conference on the Four Gospels in 1957.[3]

Let us start from the statement which is constantly made, that St. John's Gospel is the most anti-Jewish of the four. In a very real sense this is true: the Jews' responsibility for the rejection and death of Christ is in this of all the Gospels the most solid and unrelieved: "He who delivered me to you," says Jesus to Pilate, "has the greater sin" (xix. 11). But there is no need to underline this. The term "the Jews" is found overwhelmingly in polemical contexts: they are the representatives of darkness and opposition throughout the Gospel.

But it is easy to assume without further discussion that because it is anti-Jewish it is therefore pro-Gentile. We jump to the conclusion that the logic underlying its appeal is that of St. Paul's speech to the Jews in Pisidian Antioch: "It was necessary that the word of God should be spoken first to you. Since you thrust it from you, and judge yourselves unworthy of eternal life, behold, we turn to the Gentiles." "And," we read, "as many as were ordained to eternal life believed" (Acts xiii. 46, 48). "These things are written that you may believe that Jesus is the Christ, the Son of God, and that believing you may have life in his name" (John xx. 31). The purpose of the two seems to be the same.

But this is going altogether too fast for the evidence. For nowhere in St. John is there any trace of this transition: the Jews have rejected, therefore we turn to the Gentiles. The remarkable fact is that there is not a single reference to "the Gentiles" in the entire book. The fourth Gospel, with the Johannine Epistles, is the only major work in the New Testament in which the term $\tau\grave{\alpha}$ $\check{\epsilon}\theta\nu\eta$ never occurs.[4] Moreover, so far from being anti-Semitic, that is, racially anti-Jewish,[5] it is, I believe, in the words of J. B. Lightfoot's magisterial but far too little known lectures on St. John, "the most Hebraic book in the New Testament, except perhaps the Apocalypse".[6] If Judaism is condemned, it is always from within and not from without. Such phrases as "your law" (viii. 17; (x. 34)) and "their law" (xv. 25) cannot be interpreted, as they often are, to imply that John wishes to dissociate Jesus from Judaism. For it is fundamental to the Gospel that Jesus himself is "a Jew" (iv. 9), that he should distinguish Jews from Samaritans as "we" (iv. 22). Indeed the heart of the whole tragic drama is that it is "his own" to whom he comes (i. 11) and "his own nation" by whom he is delivered up (xviii. 35, $\tau\grave{o}$ $\check{\epsilon}\theta\nu os$ $\tau\grave{o}$ $\sigma\acute{o}\nu$ – $\check{\epsilon}\theta\nu os$ in John being reserved always for the Jewish nation, not for the Gentiles).

And not only is Jesus very much a Jew, but the world of the Gospel narrative is wholly a Jewish world. While "the Jews" occurs nearly seventy times in John (compared with five times in Matthew, six in Mark, and five in Luke), the Gentiles as a group receive, as we have seen, no mention. Moreover, from the beginning to the end of the story there is only one individual Gentile – and he is Pilate, hardly the figure by whom to commend the Gospel to the Gentiles. Pilate with his soldiers is necessary because otherwise Jesus could not be sentenced to death (xviii. 31) or "lifted up from the earth" by the Roman penalty of crucifixion (xii. 32 f.; cf. xviii. 32). But Pilate makes it clear that he is a complete outsider to the world within which the drama moves: "Am I a Jew?" (xviii. 35).

The extent indeed to which the drama revolves exclusively round the crisis of Judaism is remarkable – and it stands in noticeable contrast with the Synoptists. In the Synoptic Gospels the centre of the stage is also occupied by the Jews. But we are conscious always of the Gentiles pressing in on the wings. At the very beginning of the Gospel of Matthew, the most Jewish of the Synoptists, come the Magi from the east, to make it clear that Jesus is not the king of the Jews alone (Matt. ii. 1 ff.). In Luke too he is hailed from the start not only as "the glory of God's people Israel" but as "a light for revelation to the Gentiles" (Luke ii. 32). Then, within the Ministry, there is the centurion whose faith is held up as an example and reproof to Israel (Matt. viii. 10 = Luke vii. 9). There is the Syro-Phoenician woman whose claim is allowed to eat of the crumbs that fall from the children's table (Mark vii. 28). There is the other centurion's testimony at the Cross, standing as the climax to the Marcan narrative (Mark xv. 39). There are the excursions of Jesus to non-Jewish territory, to the region of Tyre and Sidon (Mark vii. 24), to Caesarea Philippi (viii. 27). There is the damming comparison of the Jewish towns with these cities of Tyre and Sidon and "the land of Sodom and Gomorrah" (Matt. x. 15; xi. 20–24). There is the example of God's preference in the past for the widow of Zarephath in Sidon and for Naaman the Syrian (Luke iv. 25–27). There is the warning that foreigners like the Ninevites and the Queen of the South, a Negress, will stand up in the judgment with this generation and condemn it (Matt. xii. 41 f. = Luke xi. 31 f.). Many, again, are to come from the east and the west and sit down with Abraham, Isaac, and Jacob in the kingdom of heaven, while the sons of the kingdom will be thrown out (Matt. viii. 11 f.; Luke xiii. 29 f.). There is the recurrent threat which echoes through the later teaching of Jesus that the vineyard will be taken away and given to others (Mark xii. 9 and pars.). The Temple is cleared so as to perform its true function as "a house of prayer for all nations" (Mark xi. 17). Above all there is always the sense that, while the immediate ministry of Jesus and his disciples may of necessity be confined to "the lost sheep of the house of Israel" (Matt. x. 6; xv. 24), yet ultimately the Gospel must be proclaimed in the whole world (Mark xiv. 9). Released by the Resurrection, the apostles are to go to the ends of the earth (Acts i. 8), making disciples of all nations (Matt. xxviii. 19; Luke xxiv. 47). They will also have to make their defence before Gentiles (Matt. x. 18) – but this too can be turned into an opportunity for witness to them (Luke xxi. 12 f.). For ultimately the End cannot come till the gospel has been preached to the entire Gentile world (Mark xiii. 10; Matt. xxiv. 14).

But in John there is none of this. Jesus is not presented as a revelation to the Gentiles. The purpose of the Baptist's mission is simply that "he might be revealed to Israel" (i. 31). Instead of the Syro-Phoenician woman we have the Samaritan woman, who, though the Jews may refuse dealings with her (iv. 9), can still speak of "our father Jacob" (iv. 12), just as later the Jews speak of "our father Abraham" (viii. 53). In the story corresponding to that of the centurion's servant, the healing of the court official's son (iv. 46–54), there is no commendation of his faith as a Gentile, nor indeed any suggestion that he was a Gentile. (As a βασιλικός he was in all likelihood a Herodian.) Again, for all the piling up of witnesses, there is no Gentile witness to Jesus in the entire Gospel – not even the final testimony of the centurion to him as the Son of God, the very title round which the Gospel is written and which many have supposed to be chosen because it could come so easily to Gentile lips. Nowhere are Gentiles held up for favourable comparison with the Jews; nor is there any reference to them in the cleansing of the Temple, which is inspired solely by zeal for true Judaism (ii. 17). The Romans will indeed come and destroy the Jewish nation and its holy place (xi. 48), but there is no suggestion of the heritage of Israel being given to the Gentiles. There is nothing about the disciples' having to appear before Gentiles – only of their being expelled from the synagogues of Judaism (xvi. 2). Again, Jesus never leaves Jewish soil; there is no reference to a Gentile mission, nor anything about their coming in, even after his glorification. The "Greeks" do indeed ask to see Jesus – and this, as we shall see, is a point of decisive significance for the Evangelist. But it is important to insist that these Greeks are *not* Gentiles. They are Greek-speaking Jews, of whom it is specifically stated that they had 'come up to worship at the feast' (xii. 20) – and there is no suggestion that they are merely God-fearers or even that they had once been Gentiles. All that we can deduce with certainty is that they spoke Greek rather than Aramaic (and hence presumably the approach through Philip, with his Hellenistic name and place of origin (xii. 21)), and that they were in Jerusalem for a specifically Jewish reason. In fact, the Evangelist has already at an earlier point (vii. 35) equated the term "the Greeks" with "the Dispersion among the Greeks", that is, Greek-speaking Diaspora Judaism.[7]

Now to stress this unremitting concentration on Judaism is far from saying that John is narrowly nationalistic or religiously exclusivist. On the contrary, there is a cosmic perspective to the Gospel, which is introduced from the very first verse. Jesus is "the . . . light that enlightens every man" (i. 9), "the Lamb of God who takes away the sin of the *world*" (i. 29); and the purpose of his being sent is that "the world might be saved through him" (iii. 17). There are no more universalistic sayings in the New Testament than in the fourth Gospel: "I, when I am lifted up from the earth, will draw all men to myself" (xii. 32). Yet for all this there is no mention of, nor appeal to, the Gentiles as such. When Jesus is pressed to "show himself to the world" (vii. 4), it is not an urge to missionary expansion but to public demonstration – and that to "the Jews". The κόσμος is not the world outside Judaism, but the world which God loves and the world which fails to respond, be it Jew or Gentile. If as a whole the Jews are hopelessly blind and walk on in darkness, those who come to the light and hear Jesus' voice are still Jews, not Gentiles – both in general (there are repeated references to the Jews who believe in him: ii. 33; vii. 31; viii. 31; x. 42; xi. 45; xii. 11) and as represented by particular individuals: Nathanael, the ideal Israelite (i. 47), Nicodemus, "the ruler of the Jews" and "teacher of Israel" (ii. 1, 10), Joseph of Arimathea (xix. 38) and the man born blind (ix. 1–39), representing respectively the governing class and the common people.

The contrast for John is always between light and darkness, not between Jew and Gentile. There is no agony, as there is for Paul, about the relation between these latter as groups (as in Rom. ix–xi), no middle-wall of partition to be broken down between them (as in Eph. ii). For John the question is not how Jews and Gentiles can become one, nor even how the Gentiles *as such* can come in. In this respect, it is instructive to compare their use of the figures of the vine (John xv) and the olive (Rom. xi), recognized Old Testament symbols for Israel. For both branches must be cut off (John xv. 2; Rom. xi. 17) – but for John there is no grafting in of alien branches. For him the simple question is the relation of *Judaism* to the true Israel, the true vine – and that means, for him, to Jesus as the Christ. For to John the only true Judaism is one that acknowledges Jesus as its Messiah. Becoming a true Jew and becoming a Christian are one and the same thing.

But John is clear that this does not mean what the Judaizers meant, with whom Paul had to fight. It does not mean retaining the whole empirical system of Judaism and fitting Jesus into it. For Judaism to accept Jesus as its truth is no mere reformation, but a complete rebirth (iii. 3). In him its entire existing structure is challenged and transcended – its *torah* (i. 17), its ritual (ii. 6), its temple (ii. 19), its localized worship (iv. 20 f.), its sabbath regulations (v. 9–18). And yet John is insisting throughout that there is nothing in Jesus alien to Judaism truly understood. He is the true *shekinah* (i. 14), the true temple (ii. 21). Though Jerusalem is to be transcended as the place God chooses for his "name" to dwell (Deut. xii. 11) – for that place is occupied by Jesus (John xvii. 11 f.) – yet still "salvation is from the Jews" (iv. 20–22). And that is why the Old Testament plays such a vital part in the Gospel. The truth about Jesus is already present in the witness of Moses (i. 45; v. 39–47; vii. 19–24), Abraham (viii. 39, 56) and Isaiah (xii. 41), who condemn their own children because they do not listen to him of whom their scriptures speak. For he is the crown of everything in Judaism. It is as "the king of the Jews" that Jesus goes to his death (esp. xix. 19–22), and from the beginning he is hailed as "the king of Israel" (i. 49; cf. xii. 13), "the holy one of God" (vi. 69), "the prophet who should come into the world", that is, as the context implies,[8] the prophet like Moses (vi. 14; vii. 40; cf. Deut. xviii. 15).

But above all he is "the Messiah", "the Christ".[9] And this for John is not just a proper name, as it has become for Paul in his Gentile environment. Except in two instances, in the combination "Jesus Christ" (i. 17; xvii. 3), it is always a title, ὁ χριστός, retaining its full etymological force, as John insists by being the only New Testament writer to preserve it in its Aramaic form, ὁ Μεσσίας (i. 41; iv. 25 f.). We all recognize that Matthew is above all concerned to present Jesus as the Christ of Judaism. But it comes as a surprise to most to be told that John uses the title more frequently than Matthew (twenty-one times to seventeen), and more often than Mark (seven) and Luke (thirteen) put together. This, rather than "the Logos", is the category which controls his Christology in the body of the Gospel. This is obvious from a concordance. But the way of thinking reflected, for instance, in E. F. Scott's dictum that "in the Fourth Gospel the Messianic idea is replaced by that of the Logos" [10] has exercised a mesmeric effect.

Moreover, the understanding of St. John's other main category, "the Son of God", must start from the fact that it stands as epexegetic of "the Christ", especially in the crucial passage that explains the purpose of his writing (xx. 31). Indeed, I believe there is no other New Testament document more important for studying the Jewish sources of the term "Son of God" than the fourth Gospel. Nor should if be forgotten that John sides decisively with the Synoptic Gospels in retaining on Jesus' lips the title "Son of man", which evidently served no purpose in the Gentile mission of the Pauline churches.

Furthermore, the distinctive images which Jesus is made to use of himself in this Gospel – the Manna (vi. 32–35), the Light (viii. 1), the Shepherd (x. 11–16), the Vine (xv. 1–6) – all by their associations in the Old Testament and later Judaism represent him in his person as *the true Israel of God*. And the primary contrast implied in the epithet $\dot{a}\lambda\eta\theta\iota\nu\acute{o}s$ is with "Israel according to the flesh". The true Jew, whose "praise is not from men but from God", to use a Pauline distinction also made by John (Rom. ii. 29; cf. John v. 44), is the one who recognizes in Jesus the true Light (i. 9), abides in him as the true Vine (xv. 1), and follows him as the true Shepherd of God's flock (x. 27). The others may say that they are Jews, but are not: they are children not of Abraham but of the devil (viii. 30–47; cf. Rev. ii. 9; iii. 9).

But for the Jew who would remain loyal to his traditional faith, "How can this be?" (iii. 9). That is the question put by Nicodemus, the ruler of the Jews and the teacher of Israel. And Nicodemus, the person he is and the question he poses, represents the problem to which the fourth Gospel is addressed. Or, in the terms of the man born blind, how can a man say to Jesus, "Lord, I believe", without ceasing to be a Jew, even though he may be thrown out of the Synagogue (ix. 35–38)?

That is the problem which John sets himself to answer. There is not even a side-glance at the problem of the man who is not a Jew but wants to become a Christian, let alone at the problem of the Gentile who wants to become a Christian *without having* to become a Jew. John is not saying, and would not say, that such a man must first become a Jew – that was the answer of the Judaizers. His problem is not even considered. John is not a Judaizer; nor, like Paul, is he an anti-Judaizer: that whole issue never comes within his purview.

But again, how can this be? It is possible only if John is not involved, like Paul, in the Gentile problem as such. All the controversies in the fourth Gospel take place within the body of Judaism. The issues raised by the Judaizers are essentially *frontier* problems – of whether, in a frontier situation like that of Antioch, one lived as a Jew or as a Gentile (Gal. ii. 14). But John is not faced with this problem.[11] Consequently circumcision and law have a different significance for him and for Paul. For Paul they represent the fence between Judaism and the Gentile world, barriers of exclusivism to be broken down. For John they are what must be transcended by Judaism within its own life, because they belong to the level of flesh and not spirit, *whether a single Gentile wanted to enter the Church or not.*

This fits with the many other indications that the *Heimat* of the Johannine tradition, and the *milieu* in which it took shape, was the heart of southern Palestinian Judaism. There is nothing, as far as I can see, to suggest that the great controversies of Chapters 5–12, which comprise the hard core of the Evangelist's tradition, were not the product of discussion and debate with Jewish opposition in a purely Palestinian situation. The Gentile world, except as represented by the Romans, is miles away – as it is, incidentally, in the Qumran literature, where the sons of darkness and deceit are in the first instance not Gentiles (who are the Kittim) but faithless Israel. In this lack of contact with the Gentiles John differs from the Hellenists and the group round Stephen. John's is essentially an Aramaic-speaking background.

And yet quite patently his Gospel is in Greek and for a Greek-speaking public. Who are these Greeks? Precisely, I believe, the Greeks who appear in the Gospel. Again, it is necessary to emphasize who these are. For Paul, as for Luke, the distinction between Jew and Greek is the distinction between Jew and Gentile, the Circumcision and the Uncircumcision (cf. e.g. Rom ii. 9–14; iii. 9, 29). But for John, the distinction is between the Jews of Palestine (and more particularly of Judea) and the Jews of the Greek (as opposed, e.g., to the Babylonian) Diaspora.[12] The Ἕλληνες are for him the Greek-speaking Jews living outside Palestine – in distinction again from the Ἑλληνισταί of Acts vi. 1 and ix. 29, who are Greek-speaking Jews resident in Palestine (cf. Acts vi. 9). Naturally the word Ἕλληνες itself draws attention to them as non-Palestinians rather than as Jews, and indeed it is only from a Palestinian point of view that Jews could conceivably be described as Greeks – but then it is from that point of view that I believe the story of St. John's Gospel is written. The Hellenistic viewpoint which we have accepted as normative, as indeed it is in the rest of the New Testament, is clearly represented in Acts xxi. 27 f., where "the Jews from Asia" stirred up the Jerusalem crowd against Paul on the charge that he brought "Greeks" into the temple. In Johannine terms this would read "*The Greeks* stirred up *the Jews* against Paul because he had introduced *Gentiles*".

Now this division within Israel between Jews and Greeks, thus defined, is of the greatest importance to John and contains, I believe, the clue to his purpose in writing the Gospel. If the tension between Jew and Gentile is never felt (except in the purely external antagonism of the Jews' refusal to enter the Praetorium (xviii. 28)), the tensions within Judaism are never far from the surface. Nothing could be more false than to suppose, as has often been suggested, that "the Jews" is a blanket-term covering John's ignorance of or indifference to the divisions of Judaism. Indeed, it looks as though a deliberate part of his purpose was to show Judaism, faced with the claims of Jesus, as hopelessly divided against itself.

There is, first, the constant tension between the common people and the Jerusalem authorities (e.g. vii. 13, 25–32, 48 f.; ix. 22; xii. 19), who are themselves sometimes designated "the Jews" even against their own people (v. 10–15; vii. 13; ix. 18, 22).[13] And there is the more subtle division within these authorities between members of the Sanhedrin (the ἄρχοντες) and the Pharisees (xii. 42; cf. vii. 45–52; xix. 38 f.). Moreover, the various groupings – the Pharisees (ix. 16), the common people (vii. 12, 43), the Jews who believed on him (vi. 66), and the Jews who did not (vi. 52; x. 19–21) – are split among themselves.

Then there are the geographical divisions. Apart from the standing feud between the Jews and the Samaritans (iv. 9), there is a recurrent and bitter altercation between Judea and Galilee (i. 46; iv. 44 f.; vii.

41, 52). "The Jews" for this Gospel are not merely the Jews of Palestine, but, with two exceptions only (vi. 41 and 52), the Jews of Judea. Indeed, Ἰουδαῖος often appears to keep its strict meaning of Judean (as in the adjective, τὴν Ἰουδαίαν γῆν, in iii. 22). Thus, in vii. 1 we read, "After this Jesus went about in Galilee; he would not go about in Judea because the Jews sought to kill him," where the R.S.V. margin reads "the Judeans" (cf. also xi. 7, 54). And there is a sense, important for the Evangelist, in which Jesus himself is "a Jew" in the narrower sense. According to this Gospel, it is not Galilee but Judea which is Jesus' πατρίς (contrast John iv. 44 f. with Mark vi. 1–6 and pars.). Though he may come from Nazareth, it is to Judea that he really belongs, and vii. 42 probably presupposes that John knows the tradition of his birth at Bethlehem. In the strictest sense he comes to "his own", even though his own may not receive him (i. 11), but disown him as a Galilean (i. 46; vii. 41) and even as a Samaritan (viii. 48).

But behind these tensions within Palestine lies the still more far-reaching division between metropolitan Judaism and the Diaspora. We can hear the disgust and contempt behind the words of vii. 35: "The Jews said to one another, 'Where does this man intend to go that we shall not find him? Does he intend to go to the Dispersion among the Greeks and teach the Greeks?'"

But as well as disdain there is also here surely strong irony. For this is precisely where Jesus' teaching is now going through the words of the Gospel. The Gospel has a strong and reiterated evangelistic motive: it is written "that you may *believe*"[14] (xx. 31), and almost every incident ends on that note. But as we have seen, there is no indication that it is to Gentiles that John is primarily addressing his message. On the contrary, everything points to his appeal being to Diaspora Judaism,[15] that *it* may come to accept Jesus as its true Messiah, even though, to quote Paul's speech at Antioch, "those who live in Jerusalem and their rulers . . . did not recognize him" (Acts xiii. 27). This speech is in fact addressed to precisely such an audience as that for which I am arguing John is writing: "Men of Israel and you that fear God" (Acts xiii. 16), that is to say, Greek-speaking Judaism with its God-fearing adherents. In other words, the real situation is the exact opposite of that which was suggested at the beginning. John is writing for the Jews who thrust aside Paul's appeal, not for the Gentiles to whom he subsequently turns.

That John's primary concern is with the Jews is perhaps confirmed by Paul himself in a striking way. In the course of what is unquestionably our best piece of first-hand evidence about the history of the early Church, Paul speaks in Gal. ii. 9 of the division of apostolic labour between Barnabas, Titus, and himself, on the one hand, and James, Cephas, and John, on the other. It was agreed, he says, "that we should go to the Gentiles and they to the circumcised". Attention has been so concentrated on the division between Paul and Peter, which is the occasion of the whole narration, that the significance of John's name appears to have been overlooked. James is associated in any case with the Circumcision; but the passage tells us, on the highest authority, two things that we should not otherwise know about John: first, that he was alive and in Jerusalem at least fourteen, and more probably seventeen, years after Paul's conversion, which is surely the most decisive disproof, though it is seldom adduced,[16] of the tradition that he was executed with his brother James before the death of Herod in 44; and, secondly, that at that time at any rate he was committed to evangelism among the Jews. This fits exactly with what I believe to have been the *milieu* of the Johannine tradition *during this period*, namely, the Christian mission among the Jews of Judea. This of course will not impress anyone who does not think that John son of Zebedee was in some way connected with the tradition of the fourth Gospel, nor does it prove anything for a later period. But it does not seem to me entirely coincidental that the only three occurrences of the term διασπορά in the New Testament should be in the writings associated with the three persons specifically mentioned by Paul as concentrating on the Jewish mission, namely the Gospel of John (vii. 35), the first Epistle of Peter (i. 1), and the Epistle of James (i. 1). Even if traditional ascriptions of these writings cannot be sustained (and in no case do I regard this as proved), it is surely significant that this was the field of evangelism with which these particular figures were associated in the mind of the Church.

But the case for St. John's Gospel being addressed to Diaspora Judaism stands on its own merits. And once we are prepared to take this hypothesis seriously, it is surprising what light it throws upon many passages in the Gospel.

The Evangelist's peculiar understanding of the work of Christ at once becomes perspicuous. The purpose of this is carefully defined (again in context of heavy irony) in xi. 51 f. In an editorial comment on Caiaphas' words John writes: "He did not say this of his own accord, but being high priest that year he prophesied that Jesus should die for the nation, and not for the nation only, but to gather into one the children of God who are scattered abroad." "The nation" is, as we have seen, for this writer metropolitan Judaism. Who are "the children of God who are scattered abroad"? As in the case of "the Greeks", the reference is almost universally taken to be to the Gentiles.[17] But this is quite arbitrary. There is nothing in the Gospel to suggest it, and every reason, from the wealth of Old Testament parallels, to identify them with those of God's people, the Jews, at present in dispersion.[18] In the prophetic words of her own high priest, the purpose of Jesus' death, as Israel's Messiah, is to bring about the final ingathering of which her prophets so constantly spoke. And it is when Diaspora Judaism, in the persons of the Greeks at Passover, comes seeking him, that Jesus knows "the hour has come for the Son of man to be glorified" (xii. 23). Hitherto he has been confined to "his own" to whom he came; but once the seed falls into the ground and dies it will bear much fruit (xii. 24).

The supreme purpose of the laying down of Jesus' life is that all Israel should be one flock under its one shepherd (x. 15 f.). And once more this pastoral imagery in Chapter 10 is clearly modelled upon passages in Ezekiel (especially xxxiv and xxxvii. 21–28) and Jeremiah (xxiii. 1–8; xxxi. 1–10) whose whole theme is the ingathering of the scattered people of Israel. The "other sheep, that are not of this fold", whom also Jesus must bring in (x. 16) are not the Gentiles – again there is nothing to suggest this – but the Jews of the Dispersion. And the purpose, that "there shall be one flock, one shepherd", is reflected again in the repeated prayer of Chapter 17 "that they all may be one", the chapter above all which interprets the purpose of Jesus' going to the Father. Here once more we have the same distinction as that between "this fold" and the "other sheep", the "nation" and "the children of God who are scattered abroad". The prayer is not "for these only", that is for those already faithful to Jesus in Palestine, but "for those also who shall believe in me through their word", that is (in terms of the same distinction again from Chapter 20), for those who believe without having seen (xx. 29), for whom clearly the Gospel is being written. The prayer "that they may all be one" is, on Jesus' lips, not a prayer for broken Christendom but for scattered and disrupted Judaism, viewed as the true Israel of God.

"Brethren, my heart's desire and prayer to God for them is that they may be saved" (Rom. x. 1). That could be John speaking. His consuming concern is for the whole Jewish people, that they should find the life which is their birthright. Throughout the Gospel we can trace the anxiety of the pastoral evangelist that none of those should be lost for whom this life is intended (vi. 39; x. 28 f.; xvii. 12; xviii. 9). This theme is first introduced in vi. 12 f., where great importance is attached to the care with which the fragments must be gathered up after the feeding – "that nothing may be lost". Filling as they do twelve baskets, they symbolize the fullness of Israel still to be gathered in after "the Jews" have eaten their fill.

Again we must insist that John, with Paul, is the least exclusivist or nationalistic writer in the New Testament. The right to become the "children of God" is given to all who believe, exactly as in the Epistle to the Romans (John i. 12; cf. Rom. iii. 22). John is certainly not suggesting that Christianity is for the Jews only: it is for the whole world. Indeed, it is explicitly stated in xvii. 21 that the bringing in of "those who shall believe in me through their word" (those for whom the Gospel is written) is itself in order "that *the world* may believe". Nevertheless, he is directing his appeal in the first instance to a specific audience, and like a good evangelist is defining salvation in the terms of their own heritage. In the same way Paul, when he wants to, can so identify Christianity with the true Judaism as to say of the Church, "*We* are the circumcision" (Phil. iii. 3), and equate being "outside Christ" with being "alienated from the commonwealth of Israel" (Eph. ii. 12).

But, unlike Paul, John is not fighting on two fronts. He is not all things to all men, but limits himself voluntarily as an apostle to the Circumcision. Always he speaks as a Jew, and indeed, like Jesus, as a Jew of Palestine. In the course of his work he writes damningly of "the Jews" – yet never perhaps with quite the animosity that shows through Paul's words in I Thess. ii. 14–16. This passage indeed provides an instructive comparison with John.[19] It is constantly said that John's use of the term "the Jews" could come only from a man who stands outside Judaism and from a date when the break between the Church and the Synagogue was bitter and complete. Yet here in Thessalonians, in the early fifties, we see Paul, a Hebrew of the Hebrews, writing in exactly the same vein (though with a personal animus that John does not show) and actually differentiating "the

Jews" from Christians in Judea exactly as John does. "For you, brethren," he says to the Thessalonians, "became imitators of the churches of God which are in Judea; for you suffered the same things from your own countrymen as they did from *the Jews*, who killed both the Lord Jesus and the prophets, and drove us out, and displease God and oppose all men . . . so as always to fill up the measure of their sins. But God's wrath has come upon them finally and for ever (εἰς τέλος)." If John also speaks thus of "the Jews", it is always with the chastisement that comes from within, drawn out of him by the tragedy of his own people.

Sometimes too he speaks of them with a terrible objectivity, explaining their customs as though he did not belong to them, and indeed as though he were not writing to fellow-Jews at all. But should this seem a decisive objection to our thesis, we should remember two things.

(*a*) In the majority of such passages John is interpreting *Aramaic-speaking* Judaism to those who know nothing of its language and ethos. And by the very regularity with which he renders into Greek the most obvious words, like Μεσσίας (i. 41; iv. 25), or 'Ραββεί (i. 39) and 'Ραββουνεί (xx. 16), which Mark never even bothers to translate for his Gentile public (Mark ix. 5; x. 51, etc.), we know that he is not a man who fears being redundant. Indeed, his whole style bears this out: he would rather give superfluous explanations than fail to make his meaning clear.

(*b*) His explanations are frequently not as redundant as they sound. The fact, for instance, that he regularly designates the feasts as feasts "of the Jews" (as if anyone did not know it, let alone a Jewish audience) becomes intelligible when we observe that, in every case but one (vi. 4), this is put in in order to explain why it is that Jesus must go up to Judea (ii. 13; v. 1; vii. 1–3; xi. 55). It is precisely because they are feasts of "the Jews" that Jesus, a Galilean, must travel into the country of the Jews, and this is of great significance for the unfolding of the drama (cf., especially, vii. 1–9; xi. 7–16). Again, John's explanation of the customs of purification (ii. 6) and burial (xix. 40), on the face of it so unnecessary for an audience of fellow-Jews, is not given simply for its own sake – because otherwise they might not know (though doubtless the water-pots were distinctively Palestinian) – but because every detail is seen by him as supremely significant for the sign and its interpretation. He is concerned that nothing shall be missed which reveals Jesus as the true fulfilment of Judaism.

To say that the Gospel belongs to the world of Hellenistic Judaism is still, of course, to leave undefined what sort of level of Hellenistic Judaism. That must be settled by examination of its literary and cultural background, into which it has not been my purpose to go. But since the term "Hellenistic Judaism" immediately connotes for most Johannine commentators the world of thought most signally represented by Philo of Alexandria, I should like to dissociate my own conclusion from that inference. Mr. W. D. Stacey, in his admirable book *The Pauline View of Man*, uses these words: "Philo found in the Pentateuch . . . the wisdom after which Greek thinkers had been striving, and he tried to present the Pentateuch in such a way that Greeks would see in it their journey's end."[20] It is a widely held view that we should need only to alter that very little to have a perfect description of the fourth Gospel: "John found in Jesus as the Logos the wisdom after which Greek thinkers had been striving, and he tried to present Jesus as the Logos in such a way that Greeks would see in him their journey's end." I am convinced that this is in fact a serious misrepresentation of his purpose. Philo was commending Judaism to Greek-speaking paganism: John was commending Christianity to Greek-speaking Judaism. And between those two aims there is a world of difference.

Nor am I convinced (though this again rests on detailed considerations of language for which this is not the occasion) that the world he addressed was the world of speculative philosophy in which Philo was at home. He stood, I believe, much more in what has aptly been called the "pre-gnostic"[21] stream of Jewish wisdom-mysticism, new light on which is constantly coming before us. I confess, moreover, to seeing less and less evidence of a polemical motive in the Gospel, whether against Baptist, Jewish, or Gnostic groups. There is undoubtedly such a motive in the Johannine Epistles. But these were written specifically for the stablishing of those who had already accepted the faith (I John ii. 21), to the converts of his Gospel message, which is constantly presupposed in what they are stated to have "heard from the beginning" (I John ii. 24). The difference of aim between the Gospel and the Epistles is in fact summarized in the clearly connected statements which set out their respective purposes. Of the Gospel it is said: "These [things] are written that

you may believe that Jesus is the Christ the Son of God, and that
believing *you may have life* in his name" (xx. 31); while of the first
Epistle the author says: "I write this to you *who believe* in the name
of the Son of God, that *you may know that you have* eternal life"
(v. 13). Professor E. C. Colwell's title *John Defends the Gospel* would
be appropriate enough for the Epistles; but the Gospel itself has an
evangelistic purpose. It is composed, I have no doubt, of material
which took shape as teaching *within* a Christian community *in Judea*
and under the pressure of controversy with "the Jews" of that area.
But in its present form it is, I am persuaded, an appeal to those
outside the Church, to win to the faith that Greek-speaking *Diaspora
Judaism* to which the author now finds himself belonging as a result
(we may surmise) of the greatest dispersion of all, which has swept
from Judea Church and Synagogue alike. His overmastering concern
is that "the great refusal" made by his countrymen at home should
not be repeated by those other sheep of God's flock among whom he
has now found refuge.

NOTES

1. Cf., more fully, C. F. D. Moule, "The Intention of the Evangelists", *New
Testament Essays*, ed. by A. J. B. Higgins (Manchester, 1959), pp. 165–179.

2. It has even been doubted recently whether it was consciously addressed to
any audience. Cf. C. K. Barrett, *The Gospel According to St. John* (London, 1955),
p. 115: "It is easy, when we read the Gospel, to believe that John, though doubtless aware of the necessity of strengthening Christians and converting the heathen,
wrote primarily to satisfy himself. His gospel must be written: it was no concern
of his whether it was also read."

3. *Studia Evangelica*, ed. by K. Aland, etc. (Berlin, 1959), pp. 382–411.

4. Οἱ ἐθνικοί occurs once in III John 7, but in its regular Jewish sense of "the
heathen". In this passage, indeed, as in Matt. xviii. 17, the ἐθνικοί are specifically
contrasted with the ἐκκλησία: they are not contemplated as part of the Church.

5. So J. Knox, *Criticism and Faith* (New York, 1952), pp. 75–77.

6. *Biblical Essays* (London, 1893), p. 135.

7. The words μὴ εἰς τὴν Διασπορὰν τῶν Ἑλλήνων μέλλει πορεύεσθαι καὶ
διδάσκειν τοὺς Ἕλληνας; are unfortunately ambiguous. "The Diaspora of the
Greeks" could mean "the Greek-speaking Diaspora" (i.e. Jews) and "the Greeks"
be an abbreviated way of referring to the same group. Or it could mean "the
Diaspora resident among the Greeks", in which case "the Greeks" would be
Gentiles. H. Windisch comes down in favour of the latter in Kittel, *T.W.N.T.*
(art Ἕλλην), Vol. II, p. 506. But K. L. Schmidt, *ibid.* (art. διασπορά), Vol. II, p.

102, insists on leaving both possibilities open (cf. H. J. Cadbury in *The Beginnings of Christianity*, Vol. V, pp. 72 f.). The decision between them can in fact only be made in the light of the Johannine context as a whole. As there is no other reference in the Gospel or the Epistles to a Gentile mission, the probability would seem to be heavily in favour of the first interpretation.

8. For he too provides manna from heaven and water from the rock.

9. For a fuller discussion of this neglected Johannine category, see van Unnik, *op. cit.* pp. 389–405.

10. *The Fourth Gospel, its Purpose and Theology* (Edinburgh, 1920), p. 6.

11. In saying this I must dissent from the very interesting suggestions made by C. H. Dodd in his article "A l'arrière-plan d'un dialogue Johannique", *Revue d'Histoire et de Philosophie Religieuses*, Vol. I (1957), pp. 5–17. Dodd would see the background of John viii. 35–58 in the Jewish-Christian controversy of the early Church, and he points out a number of parallels with the Epistle to the Galatians. But in the Judaizing controversy the crucial question was "Who is the true Christian?" (Need he observe the whole law to qualify?) In the Johannine controversy the question is rather "Who is the true Jew?" (Is sonship of Abraham automatic by race?) This latter is the question posed also by John the Baptist (Matt. iii. 7–10; Luk. iii. 7–9) in a purely Jewish context; and the Pauline parallels to John would appear rather to be Rom. ii. 17–29 ("Who is the true Jew?") and iv. 9–22 ("Who is the true son of Abraham?"), where the Apostle is addressing himself to the Jews rather than to Judaizers. For the Judaizer the underlying question is "What does it involve for the Gentile to become a Christian?" For John it is always: "What does it involve for the Jew?" And his answer is: "Birth, not from Abraham (nor anything 'of the earth'), but from above." There is a close parallel between Chapters viii and iii. Both recount the approach of Jews who believed in some way that Jesus came from God and that God was with him (cf. viii. 29 f. with iii. 2); and viii. 23 shows the issue to be the same as in that of the conversation with Nicodemus. Neither dialogue has any apparent connection with the Gentile controversy.

12. Cf. the letter of R. Gamaliel I (*Jer. Sanh.* 18d) "to our brethren, the sons of the diaspora of Babylon, the sons of the diaspora of Media, the sons of the diaspora of the Greeks, and all the rest of the dispersed of Israel" (quoted A. Schlatter, *Der Evangelist Johannes*, p. 198). It is to be observed that the phrase "the diaspora of the Greeks" (where the parallels would lead us to expect "the diaspora of Greece") is exactly that which John also uses in vii. 35.

13. Contrariwise, in iii. 45 f. and xii. 9–11 "the Jews" are the common people as distinct from the authorities.

14. It is, of course, perfectly true that purely linguistically this could mean either to bring to faith or to deepen in faith. Cf. C. H. Dodd, *The Interpretation of the Fourth Gospel* (Cambridge, 1953), p. 9; C. K. Barrett, *op. cit.*, p. 114; C. F. D. Moule, *op. cit.*, p. 168.

15. K. Bornhäuser, *Das Johannesevangelium eine Missionsschrift für Israel* (Gütersloh, 1928), sees very clearly that the Gospel is an evangelistic appeal to Israel, but his failure to isolate the particular section of Judaism which John has in mind makes much of his argument very vulnerable.

16. Though cf. B. P. W. Stather Hunt, *Some Johannine Problems*, pp. 118 f.

17. Most recently J. Jeremias, *Jesus' Promise to the Nations* (Stuttgart, 1956; tr. London, 1958), pp. 37 f. and 64–66.

18. See C. K. Barrett, *op. cit.*, *ad loc.*, who, however, declines to accept what he admits "in a Jewish work this would naturally mean".

19. Its relevance was first brought to my attention by H. E. Edwards, *The Disciple who wrote these Things* (London, 1953), p. 115.

20. *Op. cit.* (London, 1956), p. 215.

21. The term was used originally of the Qumran literature by B. Reicke, *N.T.S.*, Vol. I (1954), p. 141.

13

THE KERYGMA OF THE GOSPEL ACCORDING TO JOHN

The Johannine View of Jesus in Modern Studies

Raymond E. Brown, S.S.

Raymond E. Brown, S.S. is Professor of New Testament at St. Mary's Seminary, Baltimore. He received the Ph.D. degree from Johns Hopkins University and the S.T.D. from St. Mary's Pontifical University. He has written The Gospel According to John (*1966*) for *"The Anchor Bible Commentaries", and is editor of* The Jerome Biblical Commentary. *Father Brown is also the author of* Jesus God and Man (*1967*) and New Testament Essays (*1965*). *"The Kerygma of the Gospel According to John" was first published in* Interpretation (*October 1967*) *and is reprinted by permission of the editor.*

"KERYGMA", despite the frequency of its use in modern biblical studies, remains, for this writer at least, a term with many meanings; and so it is perhaps best to state at the beginning of this paper that the kerygma of the Fourth Gospel is here understood to be its central salvific message. In uncovering this we have a unique aid, for more than any other Gospel, John (20:31) states in salvific terms the purpose for which it was written: ". . . so that you may have faith that Jesus is the Messiah, the Son of God, and that, through this faith, you may have life in his name." It is well known that the Greek manuscript evidence is divided on which form of the verb *pisteuein* should be read in this verse: the present ("you may continue to have faith") or the aorist (which *could* mean: "you may come to faith"). The former implies that the Gospel was written to confirm the faith of those who were already Christians; the latter may give support to a missionary goal for the Gospel, perhaps directed to Jews of the Diaspora. But whether directed to believers or to non-believers or to both, whether directed to Jews or to Gentiles or to both,[1] the substance of the Gospel's message is the same. It proclaims that Jesus is the Messiah, the Son of God,[2] and demands belief in him.

That Jesus is the center of John's message is confirmed by even a hasty reading of the Gospel itself. The emphasis on the Kingdom of God, so prominent in the Synoptic Gospels, has yielded in John to an emphasis on Jesus as the embodiment of life, truth, and light. No more is the parabolic language introduced by "The kingdom of God is like . . ."; rather we hear the majestic "I am. . . ." Whereas it is the Kingdom that the Synoptic Gospels describe in terms of vineyard, wheat, shepherd, and sheep, in John it is Jesus who is the vine, the bread, the shepherd, and the sheepgate. The misunderstanding that greets the parables of the Kingdom in the Synoptic Gospels greets Jesus' use of metaphors for himself and his gifts in John, for example, the misunderstanding of the living water in 4:10–15.

Thus, for John, the centrality of Jesus is assured both by the Gospel's statement of purpose and by a *prima facie* analysis of content. But what effect do critical studies have on such an understanding of the Johannine kerygma? First, does Jesus retain his centrality in the various modern theories of Johannine sacramentalism and ecclesiology? Second, how do the important modern scholars interpret John's presentation of Jesus? These are the questions to which this paper addresses itself.

Turning to the first question and beginning with sacramentalism, we find that the most diverse views[3] on John's attitude toward the sacraments still attribute a centrality to Jesus. For the Bultmannians who minimize John's references to sacraments, the reason why John shows so little sacramental interest is that he wishes to emphasize Jesus' word as the salvific factor. But even if, with more justification, one follows those who maintain that there is a sacramental interest (of varying degrees) in John, the way in which the sacraments are presented is instructive for the role given to Jesus. In the eucharistic words of 6:51–58, one of the overt sacramental passages in John, eating Jesus' flesh and drinking Jesus' blood are essential for life precisely because this eating and drinking is a form of contact with Jesus. The agent in the Eucharist is Jesus: "*I* shall raise him up on the last day" (6:54); "The man who feeds on me will have life *because of me*" (6:57). In another passage which even Bultmann admits to be overtly sacramental (19:34), both the (eucharistic) blood and the (baptismal) water flow from the side of the crucified Christ. Even more significant for John's concept of Jesus' relation to the sacraments are the covertly symbolic references to the sacraments. Because John treats the sacraments as foreshadowed in the *deeds* of Jesus' ministry (e.g. baptism in the healing of the blind man in Chapter 9) and does not mention specific institutions of the sacraments, the reader thinks of the sacraments more as the continuation of Jesus' work rather than as actions entrusted to the church. It is also informative that the references to the sacraments in Jesus' *words* are on a secondary level. In 6:35–50 the bread of life is primarily Jesus as revelation and only secondarily the Eucharist (unlike 6:51–58 which, in the judgment of many, has been added to this section). In Chapter 4 the living water is primarily a symbol of Jesus' revelation and/or of the Spirit; a reference to baptism is secondary. Such an approach prevents the sacraments from being isolated from Jesus' word; word and sacrament are complementary salvific agents. Thus, if John has a sacramental interest, the sacraments are seen as prolongations of the actions of Jesus, related to his revealing word. John's thought would militate against the sacraments being thought of as actions of a mystery religion that accomplish salvation by themselves.

Turning to ecclesiology,[4] we find scholars divided on the extent to which John appreciated the need for Christians to be united, not only directly to Jesus but also to one another in community. The *mashal* (partly parabolic, partly allegorical) of the vine and branches in 15:1–6, with its expanded application in 15:7–17, is often characterized as the Johannine equivalent of the Pauline image of the body of Christ, which Ephesians identifies with the church. Yet, while there is a stress on loving one another in 15:12, the real emphasis of the Johannine imagery is on the union of the Christian with Jesus – the branches must remain on the vine which is Jesus. There is no echo of the Pauline reference to the different functions of the members of the body. The *meshalim* of the shepherd and the sheep in John 10:1–5, with the explanations in 10:7–18, have also been thought to have ecclesiastical significance; and this is confirmed by the image of the sheepfold that runs throughout. But the primary emphasis of the symbolism is on the relation of the shepherd (Jesus) to his sheep whom he knows by name and for whom he is willing to lay down his life. Perhaps the strongest support for the idea of community in John is found in the prayer of Chapter 17 where Jesus prays "that they may be brought to completion as one" (17:23). The important parallels between the Johannine ideal of "one" (*hen*) and the Qumran ideal of the *yaḥad* ("community")[5] suggest that John found a salvific value in community. Yet the pattern of the unity that John idealizes comes from Jesus; the unity that must exist among Christians is compared to the unity of the Father and the Son. Unity is salvific because, like life itself, it comes from the Father to Jesus and from Jesus to Christians. Unless Jesus and the Father are with them, Christians can not be salvifically one among themselves: "That they all may be one, just as you, Father, in me and I in you, that they may also be [one] *in us*."[6] Thus, the ideal of community may well exist in John, but it is subordinate to and dependent on the ideal of the union of the Christian with Jesus.

The structure of the Johannine "church" is probably the most disputed area within the question of ecclesiology. If there is some church structure, does this take away from the immediacy and centrality of Jesus which John emphasizes? In the most recent discussion of the problem, Ernst Käsemann[7] admits that for John offices exist, effected by the Spirit and endowed with specific authority. But he feels that in John the unique theological importance of the Apostles has been lost.[8] The historical memory of the Apostles has not gone, but they pale into insignificance. Personally I think that our judgment here must be more qualified. There is no doubt that by using the term "disciples" to describe the Apostles during Jesus' ministry John is not simply being chronologically exact ("apostle" is seemingly a post-Resurrectional title); he is also making the Apostles the symbols of all Christians who are disciples of Jesus. Thus, when Jesus speaks to his Disciples in the Last Discourse and promises that he will return to be with them and that they will bear witness to him, he is really speaking to all believers.[9] There is a democratization of the closeness that originally only the Twelve shared with Jesus. Yet one cannot simply assume that everything said to the Twelve in John is meant to apply to all Christians. For instance, the power both to absolve and to hold men's sins is explicitly given to (ten of) the Twelve in 20:23 in a post-Resurrection scene where they have just been *sent*. (Matthew, Luke, and the Marcan Appendix all have a solemn post-Resurrection commission of the Eleven by Jesus.) There is no real evidence that such power was given to all Christians. Presumably such a power was still important for the Johannine community, and the memory that it was originally given to the Eleven is significant (although we have no data on how it passed from them to those who now hold it in the Johannine community).

Yet, although salvific functions are attributed to some within the structured community, Johannine thought emphasizes much more strongly the salvific activity of the Paraclete.[10] The thesis can be defended that the concept of the Paraclete took shape precisely against the background of the death of those who had been eye-witnesses to Jesus and as an answer to the dilemma of how to interpret Jesus' words in the face of new problems, now that the apostolic guides were dead. If in the Johannine community there are teaching offices (and this seems almost certain from I John), nevertheless the understanding of revelation and the task of bearing witness are not the exclusive privilege of any group within that community. The basic teacher of all Christians is the Paraclete who remains within the Christian and does not die out with the apostolic generation. The Paraclete's special function is to take what belongs to Jesus and to proclaim it anew in each generation (15:26; 16:14). By describing the origins and work of the Paraclete in the same language that he describes the origins and work of Jesus, the evangelist makes it clear that under this peculiar title of "Paraclete" he is thinking of the Spirit in a special way, namely, as the invisible presence of Jesus in this period when Jesus has returned to his Father. Jesus has come back to the Christian in and through the Paraclete. Thus the importance that John gives to the Paraclete is another form of the Johannine stress on Jesus as the principal agent of salvation. A structured Johannine "church" there may be, but that church must be subordinate to Jesus. The church in itself is not the source of salvation; only the Spirit of Jesus gives life.

And so we may conclude in answer to our first question that the centrality of Jesus in the Johannine kerygma is clear no matter which solution one adopts in the disputed questions of the Gospel. Even those who believe that John is interested in the sacraments and that he recognizes the function of community and of church structure must acknowledge that in John's thought these sacraments and institutions in no way replace the work of Jesus. For John, Jesus remains central because only in him and through him divine reality (*alētheia*) and life have come within the grasp of man through faith.

But now let us turn to the second question. If Jesus is central, what does John ask man to believe about Jesus? In the answer to this question the effect of the diverse modern approaches is much more apparent. We shall discuss briefly the ideas of Rudolf Bultmann, Oscar Cullmann, and Ernst Käsemann, attempting not only to show the differences and import of the respective views, but also to use each view in bringing out valid insights into the Jesus of the Johannine kerygma.

As in so many other New Testament questions, it is Bultmann who by the consistency of his existential approach has brought the problem of the Johannine understanding of Jesus into clear perspective. Bultmann acknowledges that John describes Jesus as the pre-existent Son of God who has appeared as man, but he thinks that such a mythological notion is not to be taken literally. "Jesus is not presented in literal seriousness as a pre-existent divine being who came in human form to reveal unprecedented secrets."[11] Rather, according to Bultmann, John uses pre-existence to stress that Jesus' *word* did not arise from human experience but came from beyond. In John there is no christological instruction nor any teaching about the metaphysical quality of Jesus' person – what is important is that Jesus brings the words of God. The Johannine Jesus reveals nothing but that he is the Revealer; and even that must be understood in existential terms: It is he who in his own person brings that for which man yearns. Thus, by faith in Jesus the Christian receives the affirmation and fulfillment of his longing for life but comes to know nothing of Jesus other than the fact that Jesus makes salvation from God possible (only the *Dass*, not the *Was*).

Such demythologizing of the Johannine picture of Jesus has encountered opposition among scholars. We can well understand this

H

if we remember that Bultmann is not claiming that he himself has demythologized the Johannine Jesus but that this was John's idea! While we shall give below two opposing views that supply necessary correctives, we should emphasize that in the starkness of his position Bultmann has captured one aspect of the Johannine kerygma, that is, the decision to which John calls the believer. The Johannine portrait of Jesus may depict more about Jesus himself than Bultmann can see, but it really does depict Jesus as the fulfillment of man's desire to whom man cannot remain indifferent. Because Jesus is the light, a man must either open his eyes and see or turn away into darkness (3:19–21). There is a proto-existentialist strain in John, and Bultmann has offered a healthy corrective to purely mystical and speculative approaches to the Johannine Jesus.

Yet if Bultmann does justice to the challenge in the Johannine discourses and to the element of decision demanded by the words of Jesus, he does not seem to do justice to the theological implications of the context in which John has set these words.[12] John presents Jesus as the new Tabernacle and the new Temple, as the one who replaces the waters of Jewish purifications and the locus of Jewish worship. Systematically in Chapters 5–10 John has Jesus acting on the occasion of great Jewish feasts and replacing the significance of the themes that were prominent in these feasts. All this is meant to tell the reader something about Jesus himself in relation to Israel, not simply that he is the Revealer without a revelation. Moreover, if one rejects Bultmann's theory of an Ecclesiastical Redactor[13] and recognizes that there are implicit sacramental references throughout John, then John is relating to Jesus the subsequent post-Resurrection existence of the Christian community with its sacramental life. He is presenting Jesus in some relation to church history, not merely as the Revealer without a revelation.

It is Cullmann who has insisted most strenuously on this broader aspect of the Johannine picture of Jesus.[14] He agrees with Bultmann that John places the Christian before Jesus in the position of decision but stresses that the decision is founded on and related to salvation history. By the fact that he has written in a Gospel format that professes to recall the historical life of Jesus, the evangelist makes the career of Jesus the center of God's salvific process. According to Cullmann's interpretation of John's thought, in accepting Jesus one accepts both the before and the after of the salvific process, that is, what God has done in Israel and what God has done in the church. John's picturing Jesus as pre-existent is not simply a mythological way of describing the origin of his teaching. It is a necessary part of the portrait, for if Jesus unifies salvation history, he must have existed from its beginning. Nor is the Johannine interest in a futuristic eschatology[15] (which Bultmann denies) accidental, for if Jesus unifies salvation history, then through the Paraclete he must be at work in the era of the church.

If Cullmann does justice to many elements in the Fourth Gospel that Bultmann's existential approach neglects, one may still wonder whether the picture Cullmann paints of the Johannine Jesus Jesus as "the center of time" is not more Lucan than Johannine. John does present Jesus as related to Israel and to the church, but he reinterprets this relationship in both directions. In reference to the past, the institutions of Israel are not so much fulfilled as they are replaced. John would not deny that these institutions had significance before Jesus came,[16] but only Jesus is from above.[17] Abraham, Moses, and Isaiah were important, not primarily because they advanced God's plan of salvation in their own times, but because they saw Jesus and spoke of him (5:46; 8:56; 12:41). A sense of the continuity of Old Testament history leading to Jesus is not prominent in John. In reference to the future, the uniqueness of Jesus and the importance of the individual's relation to him dominate in John over any emphasis on continuity from Jesus to ecclesiastical structure. As we mentioned above, the Paraclete is the most important bond of union between Jesus and later Christians, and the Johannine Paraclete is not really an ecclesiastical figure.[18] But, we may ask, does not tradition in John supply a sense of continuity? Certainly one of the great gains in Johannine studies is that now many scholars admit that the Fourth Gospel does contain independent historical tradition (this is illustrated in the works of C. H. Dodd). And, of course, the Gospel itself claims that it is based on eyewitnesss tradition (19:35; see also 21:24; I John 1:1-3). Yet in no other Gospel has the tradition of Jesus' deeds and words been so thoroughly reinterpreted, and there is in John an air of sovereign assurance that through such reinterpretation the real Jesus is truly speaking to men. Indeed, John's Gospel is an example of the Paraclete's taking what belongs to Jesus and explaining it to men. Thus, the sense of continuity based on eyewitness tradition is matched (factually if unconsciously) by the discontinuity of new insights into that tradition supplied by men guided by the Paraclete – the apostolic and the prophetic functions are both at work.

Cullmann insists that salvation history implies discontinuity as well as continuity. Perhaps, if sufficient emphasis is placed on discontinuity, one could say that John presents Jesus in the context of salvation history. But personally I would wonder whether use of this terminology in reference to the Johannine view of Jesus brings out sufficiently the difference between John's approach and that of Luke and Matthew. There is, moreover, as we shall see immediately below, an element of Johannine Christology that is not accounted for in terms of salvation history.

Käsemann, while also reacting to Bultmann, is almost at the opposite extreme from Cullmann in highlighting the uniqueness of John.[19] From a study of the Last Discourse and the prayer of Chapter 17 he maintains that John was proposing a real Christology. In portraying Jesus as the pre-existent, John has reinterpreted the historical career of Jesus to mean that God actually walked upon this earth. The faith that John demands of the Christian is not simply a *fides qua creditur* but an incipient *fides quae creditur*; it is a faith that involves the acceptance of dogma, namely, the one basic christological dogma of the unity of Jesus with the Father.[20] Käsemann's words are like a gauntlet thrown down before the whole Bultmannian position:

> Unlike other New Testament usage, the mythology employed in the Fourth Gospel has no longer the sole function of proclaiming the salvation history and worldwide dimensions of the christological events. It is rather the beginning of dogmatic reflection in the strict sense of the word and opens up the way to the christology of the later Church. The question of the nature of Christ is now thematically discussed, still in the framework of soteriology, of course, but with an importance and isolation that can no longer be accounted for in terms of exclusively soteriological interest. Now the internal relation of the Revealer to God as His Son is just as emphasized as the Revealer's relation to the world.[21]

Although I might like to modify the absoluteness of Käsemann's affirmations, I believe that he is right in insisting that Johannine faith has a dogmatic content and that John was very much interested not only in the *Dass* but also in the *Was*. How can Bultmann's contention that John is not really interested in who Jesus is do justice to 20:31 which insists explicitly that men must believe who Jesus is (Messiah, Son of God) in order to have life in his name? The inclusion of the clause, "that you may have life in his name", shows that John's outlook on the question of Jesus' identity is not purely ontological; nevertheless John insists that faith, in order to be saving faith, must involve the affirmation that Jesus is the Son of God.[22]

Käsemann is also right in insisting that John does not simply portray Jesus in the context of salvation history.[23] That an element of Johannine faith touches on the relation of Jesus to salvation history is implied in the demand that men believe in Jesus as the Messiah. But the Johannine portrait of Jesus as the Son of God moves out of the realm of history and has incipiently ontological implications about the inner life of God.[24]

In summarizing the answer to our second question, then, we may say that while one cannot reconcile Bultmann, Cullmann, and Käsemann in their views on the portrait that John paints of Jesus, each one of these scholars has brought out important elements in that portrait. No one of the three portraits is totally satisfactory; but by using one to tone down the other, we can come to a rather good appreciation of the Jesus that John presents to his readers for their belief. If we return to the Gospel's own statement of its purpose, we find (admittedly by way of oversimplification) that Cullmann does the most justice to John's demand for belief in Jesus as the Messiah. Käsemann does the most justice to John's demand for belief in Jesus as the Son of God. Bultmann does the most justice to the quality of the Johannine Jesus that calls forth a decision of faith, "that you may have life in his name".

But, before we close, we must call attention to an aspect of Käsemann's study that is very important in evaluating this Johannine kerygma[25] about Jesus. If the Johannine portrait of Jesus is many-splendored, it has very definite limitations. Precisely because so much of the Fourth Gospel was written in an atmosphere of polemic, the Gospel has a tendency to be one-sided. In particular, the Gospel's picture of the ministry, dominated by the divinity of Jesus, does not do full justice to Jesus' humanity. Such a statement may at first seem questionable since this is the Gospel that begins with an insistence that the Word became flesh. Yet Käsemann has a point (exaggerated to be sure) when he asks: "Does this statement really mean more than that he descended into the earthly realm and there became accessible to men?"[26] At any rate one must judge the practical meaning of 1:14 in the light of John's picture of Jesus during the ministry; and many of the attitudes that John attributes to Jesus are hard to fit in with the estimation of him as "truly man . . . like unto us in everything except sin" (Chalcedon).[27] For instance, the Johannine Jesus knows the thoughts of all men (2:25), he has all power from the Father so that he can lay down his life and take it up again (10:17–18). Such a Jesus scarcely agrees with the description offered by Hebrews 4:15: "One tested in every way as we are (but without sin)," for ignorance and the inability to predict death are two very human tests. And certainly the Synoptic Jesus, prostrate in the dust of Gethsemane, trembling in fear of death, is more subject to the human condition than John's Jesus.[28] In the Fourth Gospel Thomas does not confess Jesus as Lord and God until after the Resurrection; but that confession could really have been made at any moment in the Johannine account of the ministry by one who had eyes to see. (Actually in the first chapter of the Gospel (1:49) Nathanael confesses Jesus as the Son of God.) The Resurrection may take the veils from the Disciples' eyes, but Jesus is not really transformed – the risen Jesus has walked through the land during his ministry.

Despite the centrality that it gives to Jesus and the richness of its portrait of Jesus, the Johannine kerygma needs to be supplemented. With Käsemann, we agree that the church did not make a mistake in taking the Fourth Gospel into the canon, but it would have made a mistake if it had not placed the Gospel According to Mark alongside the Gospel According to John.

NOTES

1. For a discussion of the various views on the destination and purpose of the Fourth Gospel see R. E. Brown, *Gospel According to John, i–xii*, The Anchor Bible (Garden City, N.Y., Doubleday & Company, 1966), pp. lxvii–lxxix. I ask the reader's indulgence if I refer to this volume rather than repeat the argumentation and bibliography contained therein. The Scripture quotations are my translation.

2. The first of the two titles predicated of Jesus is taken fom Jewish salvation history but reinterpreted in a Christian way. The second, while possibly of Jewish background (implied as a designation of the anointed king in Ps. 2:7?), is certainly at home in the gentile world. Thus the titles do not settle the question of whether John was written for Jews or for gentiles or for both.

3. Brown, *op. cit.*, pp. cxi–cxiv.

4. *Ibid.*, pp. cv–cxi.

5. See F. M. Cross, *The Ancient Library of Qumran*, rev. edn., Anchor Books (Garden City, N.Y., Doubleday & Company, 1961), p. 209.

6. There is no echo in John that the bishop is the principle of unity, as found in the Ignatian epistles. Yet a Gospel concerned with the ministry of Jesus is probably an inadequate witness for the total situation of the Johannine community. (Personally this writer is not at all impressed by the argument that if John accepted a fully developed ecclesiology, he would not have hesitated at the anachronism of reading it back into the ministry of Jesus, any more than he hesitated at reading back a fully developed Christology into the ministry. John states explicitly that the real meaning of Jesus was not understood during the ministry; thus he shows a certain awareness of the anachronism of the Christology that he presents. If John shows some care about the historicity of his interpretation of Jesus who is the proper subject of the Gospel, we might expect even more care about his treatment of the Church which is not the proper subject of the Gospel.) If we recognize that the Johannine epistles represent the same world of thought as the Gospel does and bear a more direct witness to the state of the Johannine church, then we may recall I John 4:6: "Anyone who has knowledge of God listens to us, while anyone who does not belong to God refuses to listen to us." This attributes a type of doctrinal authority to some members of the community, and these members must inevitably serve as a visible unifying force.

7. *The Testament of Jesus* (London, SCM Press, 1969), pp. 28 ff. He does not think that such offices are endowed with privileges.

8. There are difficulties in Käsemann's argument here. He maintains that in early Christian thought Peter was the representative of the historical group of the Disciples and that this should be associated with the early tradition that Peter was the first witness of the risen Jesus. But Käsemann says that, while the latter idea still glimmers faintly behind John 20:6 ff., the Johannine narratives of the Resurrection focus not on Peter but on Mary Magdalene and on Thomas. One may ask, however, whether any of the Gospels put stress on Peter as the first witness of the risen Jesus? Luke 24:34 is the only echo of this tradition in the Gospels. Matt. 28:9, 16 mention appearances to the women and to the Eleven; Luke 24:13, 33 mention appearances to the two disciples on the road to Emmaus and to the Eleven; the Marcan Appendix adds to the Lucan list an appearance to Mary Magdalene – there is no significant difference between John and the Synoptics here. On the other hand Peter's place as the representative of the circle of the Twelve is found in Matthew, Luke, *and John* (without being related to his being the first witness to the risen Jesus). In particular it is explicit in John 6:68 and also in the stray Johannine tradition found in 21:4–19 (not composed by the writer of the body of the Gospel but Johannine nonetheless). The peculiar feature in John is not the neglect of Peter but the introduction of the Beloved Disciple. This Disciple is just as prominent in the Gospel narrative as Peter. Pictured as a friend of Peter's, the Beloved Disciple is not a rival to Peter in *ecclesiastical* significance. If Peter symbolizes the churchman to whom the flock has been entrusted (21:15–17), the Beloved Disciple symbolizes the Christian who is close to Jesus in love and in readiness to believe. None of the passages dealing with the Beloved Disciple attribute to him a role significant for church structure.

9. The Twelve are not mentioned specifically as the audience of the Last Discourse, although those mentioned by name at the supper appear in the lists of the Twelve (Judas Iscariot, Peter, Philip, Thomas, another Judas [Lucan lists], and

perhaps even the Beloved Disciple if he is John of Zebedee). Rather the audience of the Discourse is designated as "his own" (13:1), and a comparison with 1:12 f. suggests that this term refers to all those who have accepted Jesus and thus replaced the "his own" (the hostile "Jews") who did not accept him. That the evangelist meant the Last Discourse to be directed to all Christians is also suggested by a comparison of John 15:15 ("I have called you friends") with III John 15 which applies the same term to Christians in general.

10. For a full treatment, see R. E. Brown, "The Paraclete in the Fourth Gospel", *New Testament Studies*, Vol. XIII (1966–67), pp. 113–132.

11. *Theology of the New Testament*, Vol. II (New York, Charles Scribner's Sons, 1955), p. 62. See pp. 33–64, esp. pp. 62 f., 66.

12. Bultmann's source theory has profoundly influenced his understanding of Johannine theology. Precisely because he regards the speeches of Jesus as coming from the Revelatory Discourse source, while the signs come from another source and the narrative framework comes from the evangelist, he does not give sufficient emphasis to the way in which the various parts modify each other. His picture of the Revealer without revelation is the distillate of the thought of his hypothetical Revelatory Discourse source, but is it faithful to the thought of the whole Gospel? It is interesting that Cullmann centers his opposition to Bultmann's interpretation precisely on the fact that John has written in the format of a Gospel account of Jesus' life.

13. That a redactor worked on the Gospel is more than probable, but what were his motives? Was he a "Johannine Redactor", faithful to John's thought, preserving stray Johannine material, and working to bring out ideas that were implicit in John? Or was he an "Ecclesiastical Redactor", foisting on the Gospel a theology that was foreign to it in order to make it "safe" and acceptable to the church? To disprove the latter interpretation one must examine Bultmann's examples critically, e.g. the work of the redactor in 6:51–58 has clear eucharistic reference, but there is already a eucharistic undertone in 6:1–50.

14. *Salvation in History* (New York, Harper & Row, Publishers, 1967), esp. pp. 268–291.

15. A fuller exposition of Cullman's views on Johannine eschatology may be found in the dissertation of his student, Paolo Ricca, *Die Eschatologie des Vierten Evangeliums* (Zürich, Gotthelf, 1966).

16. "Salvation is from the Jews" (4:22); 1:16 f. can be taken to mean that there was *charis* in the law given to Moses but this has been replaced by the fullness of *charis* in Jesus Christ.

17. In Johannine terminology the things of the Old Testament were not "real" (*alēthinos*). The manna was not the real bread from heaven (6:32); Israel was not the real vine of Yahweh (15:1).

18. Since the Paraclete is the Holy Spirit (seen in a special role) and John relates the Spirit and baptism, logically one might assume that John would attribute to the organized church some control over the gift of the Paraclete, since in the practical order the church would determine who would be baptized. But certainly John never brings such an idea to the fore. It is the Father (or Jesus) who gives or sends the paraclete to those who love Jesus and keep his commandments.

19. It is not easy to pass judgment on his *Testament of Jesus*. Käsemann's

strength is his use of dialectic; no modern New Testament exegete has been more consistently successful than he in isolating problems by the use of sharp contrast, e.g. his studies on the diversity of New Testament theologies and on the problem of early Catholicism in the New Testament. Like Bultmann, Käsemann makes other scholars think; what he writes is always worth reading, and this book is no exception. Yet his very method means that the emergent picture is often more sharply delineated than was true of the original situation. What Käsemann sometimes gives us is what a New Testament author *should have* thought if he had been perfectly logical and had followed his ideas to the conclusions toward which they were directed. In the present instance one may wonder if John's Christian contemporaries considered him so audacious as Käsemann considers him? On p. 2, n. 2, he criticizes me for stating in the Introduction to my Anchor Bible *John* that the differences between John and the rest of the New Testament are not so sharp that John cannot be brought into the Christian mainstream. I attempt to justify this in the commentary where I constantly point to the real similarities between John and the Synoptics; but Käsemann, p. 7, rejects such an approach as exemplified in C. H. Dodd's work – contrast is the significant factor! But life is often less dialectic than the scholar's method. For example, certainly John has gone further than the other Gospels in presenting Jesus as incarnate *Sophia*, but the interpretation of Jesus in terms of a wisdom figure was already present in the "Q" tradition. Certainly John has emphasized the pre-existence of Jesus and carried this into the ministry more thoroughly than any other New Testament work; but the basic idea of pre-existence is found in the pre-Pauline hymns, and Matthew and Luke have begun in their infancy narratives to develop the implications of this for the ministry of Jesus. We cannot question either the novelty or the uniqueness of Johannine thought, but we do question whether it is a radical break with traditional Christian thought. Käsemann, pp. 25, 74 ff., maintains that the Fourth Gospel came out of a naïvely Docetist circle of Christian enthusiasm and that in bringing John into the canon the church did not recognize that she was preserving the voice of those enthusiasts whom she had later condemned as heretical. Despite Käsemann's nuances, in my opinion, he reaches this judgment only by isolating certain tendencies in Johannine thought and by making John responsible for a development of these tendencies that did not demonstrably come until later. One could do the same thing for Matthew since certain tendencies visible in Matthew could and did develop into Ebionitism. The tendencies that Käsemann sees in John are, for the most part, really there, but considerable exaggeration and exclusivity were required before they would become heretical, just as there was required an exclusive exaggeration of Pauline tendencies before Paulinism became Marcionism.

20. *Op. cit.*, p. 25. Personally I tend to wonder about the rigidity with which the distinction between two types of faith is applied in New Testament studies. Has Christian faith ever been a pure *fides qua creditur* since the Resurrection? Undoubtedly my Roman Catholic background is showing here, but I cannot help feeling that a problematic of Reformation times colors much of the discussion of New Testament faith.

21. *Ibid.*, p. 23. (The translation here is not taken from the English version of *The Testament of Jesus*, which appeared after this article was written.)

22. Even though I John 4:2 f. is stressing another aspect of faith in Jesus, it illustrates that what one believes about Jesus is quite important. In frequently referring to the Johannine epistles, I do not suggest that the Gospel can always be interpreted through the epistles or that there are not clear differences between these works. But since these works are so similar that they are attributed by scholars to the same school of thought (and even, by some, to the same writer), it seems good methodology to presume that they will be more often in agreement than in disagreement and that the burden of proof lies on those who would claim differences.

23. For Käsemann's reservations about the use of the term "salvation history" for John, see *op. cit.*, pp. 30 f.

24. Cullmann's *The Christology of the New Testament* (London, SCM Press, 1959) has been criticized because, while quite correctly emphasizing the functional aspect of Christology, it does not do full justice to the ontological elements that begin to appear in late New Testament works. On pp. 3 f. his position is nuanced: "When it is asked in the New Testament 'Who is Christ?', the question never means exclusively, or even primarily, 'What is his nature?', but first of all, 'What is his function?'" One can certainly agree with that statement, but the secondary interest in Christ's nature, for which Cullmann leaves room, seems subsequently to be lost in his treatment, especially when he claims (p. 326), "All Christology is *Heilsgeschichte*."

25. The word "kerygma" recalls the title of this paper, and some readers may reflect that the dogmatic features in John's portrait of Jesus really take us out of the area of kerygma, especially if one has a Bultmannian understanding of kerygma. As I mentioned at the beginning, I am never quite sure what kerygma means, especially when a rigid divider is placed between kerygma and dogmatic content. Obviously a purely speculative dogma about the inner life of the Trinity is not part of kerygma, but is John not kerygmatic if he insists that the Son whom God gave because he "so loved the world" was really his Son? If John demands faith in this, it is because the relationship of Father and Son tells us how much God really loved the world.

26. *Op. cit.*, p. 9.

27. Käsemann classifies John's thought as a naïve or unreflected Docetism, but one might debate whether this is a felicitous term. Käsemann is correct in maintaining that many of the statements in John that have been interpreted in an anti-Docetic manner are not necessarily so. Rather the strong anti-Docetism comes from I John. But precisely because there is an anti-Docetic polemic in one work of the Johannine school, one may wonder whether another work of that school is best classified as Docetic, even with the qualifications of "naïve" and "unreflected" (see n. 22 above). Perhaps the difficulty stems from what is meant by Docetism. If Docetism is the contention that the body of Jesus was a phantom or not an integral part of Jesus Christ (and this is what I John attacks), then I do not think John is Docetic. One need not overemphasize the kenotic import of "The Word became flesh", but at least it would seem to preclude such crude Docetism. John's portrait of Jesus is closer to a Monophysitism where the humanity is swallowed up in the divinity and dominated by the divinity than to a Docetism where there really is no humanity. But perhaps one might best avoid

either of these designations, for inevitably they suggest a situation where the weaknesses in John's Christology have hardened and become exclusive – in short, a situation that goes beyond John's own thought and might even have been repugnant to him when he saw its extremism.

28. On the question of ignorance, Mark 5:30–33 clearly implies that Jesus did not always know men's minds. Matt. 9:22 carefully corrects this implication, so that already in Matthew we do have the divinity overshadowing the humanity in the question of knowledge. Yet only John (6:6) would feel impelled to assure the reader that, if Jesus asked Philip where they were going to get bread to feed the crowd, it was not because he did not know what he was going to do.

14

THE SEARCH FOR THE THEOLOGY OF THE FOURTH EVANGELIST

James L. Price

James L. Price is Professor of Religion, Dean of Undergraduate Education, and Vice Provost at Duke University. He holds the Ph.D. degree from Cambridge University, and is the author of Interpreting the New Testament (*1961*). *"The Search for the Theology of the Fourth Evangelist" is based on his presidential address for the American Academy of Religion in 1965; it has been previously published in the* Journal of the American Academy of Religion (*March 1967*) *and is reprinted by permission.*

THE SEARCH for the theology of the Fourth Evangelist opens many doors into that complex labyrinth known as "the Johannine problem". Yet in spite of the intense explorations of researchers it cannot be said that its corridors have been fully lighted, that the end of the quest has been reached. This article calls attention to several of these darkened passages that have attracted the most interest during the last quarter century; evaluates some of the findings; and suggests how the effort of many scholars may advance our understanding.

Whatever misgivings are shared concerning the present position of "biblical theology" as a scholarly discipline, few would doubt that among the books of the New Testament the Gospel of John especially invites theological explanation. This statement does not mean only that the Gospel is capable of theological explication, or that it contains material essential to the construction of a Christian theology. John's witness to Jesus Christ is itself a theological explanation – or at least the beginning of one. The Fourth Evangelist has a theology in the proper sense of the term.[1] A fundamental assumption of modern Johannine scholarship is that a careful examination and articulation of the theology of the Fourth Gospel is required, on the basis of the historical situation and standpoint of the Evangelist. The understanding of the Fourth Evangelist must be re-exhibited in contemporary statements, so far as this is possible.

One has to say "so far as this is possible", for it must be admitted that the search has been elusive, if not inconclusive. Why has the theology of John been so strangely resistant to systematic analysis and explication? Does the answer lie in the mind of the Fourth Evangelist, in his style of thought and expression? Was he a man given to spiraling, vagrant flights of mystical speculation that escape rational synthesis? Or did the syncretistic influences of his age and place introduce into his thought that logical inconsistency and contradiction which some have found in his writing? Is the way to our understanding of John's theology blocked by a too-limited knowledge of his intellectual world and that of his first readers? Alternatively, does the solution to the problem lie – nearly hidden – in the obscure literary history of the Gospel of John? Is this canonical writing only an exiguous survival of the Evangelist's theology? Must we conclude that the Gospel is a patchwork thing, published posthumously from notes left by its original author somewhat in disarray, and that later editing distorted or obscured the Evangelist's thought?

There has been no dearth of effort among modern scholars in pursuing these questions, or in checking out the solutions found in the answers given to one or more of them, But it is obvious that the sum total of this research has been sufficiently inconclusive to discourage theological reconstruction. With the exception of Rudolf Bultmann's magisterial work, few noteworthy expositions of John's theology have been attempted. "It is true," as Rudolf Schnackenburg comments, "that several good outlines of John's thought exist, but these are hardly more than introductions. We might even wonder at the fact that christology – the central issue of John's teaching – has for a long time had no scholar ready to deal with it." One can heartily agree with this distinguished Roman Catholic scholar that it would indeed "be worth bringing into the full light of day all that in John's theology has permanent value and ever-increasing contemporary relevance".[2] One feels also a genuine sense of deprivation that this time is not yet. Perhaps there is some gain, however, in observing the signs of the present time; in identifying, if we can, some of the guidelines that have been established for this task of theological reconstruction.

I

Among the oldest doors into the Johannine labyrinth is one that invites and explores comparisons between John and the Synoptic Gospels. The earliest commentators, writes Maurice Wiles, sought the intentions of the writer of the Fourth Gospel not by reference to John 20:31, but by comparing it with the first three. "All the expositions of [John's] purpose are in effect developments of the dictum of Clement, that it is intended to be a πνευματικὸν εὐαγγέλιον (a spiritual gospel), in supplementation of the earlier ones whose concentration had been upon τὰ σωματικά (the bodily – or perhaps we may translate – the naked facts)."[3]

Nineteenth-century biblical critics, equipped with new tools for textual and source criticism, entered this same door. Less interested than were the ancient exegetes in discovering the christology of John, they explored the corridor in "quest of the historical Jesus", reading Clement's words to mean that the Synoptics were the primary sources for a life of the Nazarene. Two results followed, however: the uniqueness of the Johannine traditions of Jesus' ministry was clarified and the question of their pre-literary history raised; and the Fourth Gospel was examined as a primary source for tracing the development in the post-apostolic age of Christian apologetics among the Hellenists.

A particular turn taken by some researchers in this corridor holds interest for us. The conclusion was reached that the Fourth Evangelist had employed some materials from the earlier Gospels, not in order to support their reliability or to provide valuable additional facts about Jesus, but rather to reinterpret, correct, and improve upon the Synoptic portraits. One of these researchers, Hans Windisch, goes so far as to affirm that John's intention was not to supplement but to replace the older Gospels. John rejected them, and aimed to drive them out of circulation in the church.[4]

Biblical scholars sensitive to the revival of interest in the theology of the New Testament after the Second World War were not slow to realize the methodological implications of these developments within source criticism. Comparisons with the earlier Gospels were thought to provide essential clues not only to the discovery of the Fourth Evangelist's historical purpose but to his special theological interests. One thinks at once of the writings of Eric Titus who assumes that the comparative work of scholars (e.g. B. H. Streeter) establish the probability of John's dependence on Mark, and on Matthew and Luke as well. An understanding of "the message of the Fourth Gospel" may be gained by observing, among other things, John's "appropriation" of Synoptic materials for his special purposes.[5]

There were other scholars, however, who had followed the earlier guides into this corridor of comparative study only to reach different conclusions. Bultmann, Dodd, F. C. Grant, Menoud, Noack, Haenchen – to mention a few – became skeptical of the view that John's thought had been influenced appreciably by the Synoptic Gospels. If these scholars "do not deny outright that he was acquainted with the Synoptic tradition, they insist that he takes account of the older Gospels only to a small extent . . .; in general, they say, John goes his own way and creates a new form of the Gospel which is independent of the Synoptics".[6]

It is evident today that this issue of dependence/independence has not been settled finally. Are we therefore to conclude that the approach to John by way of the Synoptists leads only to a dead end? Probably not. One should take notice here of C. K. Barrett's illuminating commentary.[7] Yet it is now very doubtful that this door can be expected to provide a major access to the theology of the Fourth Evangelist, whatever other purposes it may serve. It is misleading to suppose that one need only identify and explain the difference between, let us say, those miracle stories in John which have near parallels in the Synoptics in order to perceive the Fourth Evangelist's theological understanding of Christ's "works" as "signs". Aside from the doubtful presuppositions of dependence and improvement, this approach abstracts, and evaluates by means of external criteria, only a fragment of John's teaching concerning "the work" of Christ.

II

Since this is a typological rather than a chronological review of the search for John's theology, no reason need be given for looking next into the doorway that may be labelled, "redaction criticism". But there is a certain logic in this sequence of exploration. It was due partly to their disappointment in the results of a comparative study of the Gospels that some researchers entered this corridor after emerging from the other. A process of editing, it was thought, might account for the superficial conformities of the text of John to the Synoptics, besides explaining several other features of the Fourth Gospel.

Bultmann's elaborate theory concerning the composition of John merits our attention, not only for its novel complexity, but also because it is typical of modern *redaktionsgeschichtlich* research. Many scholars before Bultmann had observed that the sequence of narrative and of discourse in the Fourth Gospel does not follow a straight line, that there are numerous obscure connections or disjunctions in the text. These have been explained in a variety of ways: either the Evangelist failed to assimilate disparate source materials, or his Gospel underwent a process of editing and interpolation, or it suffered an accidental displacement and/or parts of the original text have been rearranged.[8] Bultmann's analysis contains variations of all of these earlier theories.

Two principal alternatives suggested by those who first travelled this corridor in search of the theology of the Fourth Evangelist may be distinguished. On the one hand, some believed that the redactor of the Johannine source materials – the one who had stamped the whole with his style and theological perspective – was the Fourth Evangelist himself; on the other hand, some held that the Fourth Evangelist's writing was subjected to one or more extensive revisions so that a critical reduction becomes necessary before any restatement of its original theological perspective can be given.

In Bultmann's analysis these literary theories, with certain qualifications, appear as successive stages in the composition of the Gospel. His criticism of the language, style, and methods of the Evangelist enables him to separate the author's writing from the hypothetical sources he employed. Bultmann is also convinced that he can distinguish the Evangelist's theology from that which is implicit (more or less) in the latter's sources. Of special interest here is Bultmann's view that the Fourth Evangelist was a demythologist. The Evangelist's principal achievements were the transformation, into more credible conceptions of revelation, of a Christian miracle tradition, the *Semeia-Quelle*, and the Christianizing of a collection of gnostic discourses, the *Offenbarungsreden*.[9] Furthermore, Bultmann's analysis of difficulties and incongruities in the text of the Gospel enables him to locate interpolations and glosses made by later hands.

The novelty of Bultmann's redaction hypothesis consists in his claim that the same editing process resulted in a rearrangement of the order of notes left by the Fourth Evangelist; in certain additions to these notes in order to conform them to later orthodoxy; and in the composition of an appendix, Chapter 21.

As we shall soon indicate, Bultmann travels other roads in search of the theology of John. But since for Bultmann the *redaktionsgeschichtlich* corridor is a main artery, we must ask whether his guidebook observations lead onto the right track.

Bultmann's literary methods for separating the Evangelist's writing from his sources have not been uncontested. Shortly before the completion of Bultmann's commentary, Eduard Schweizer published the results of a detailed study of the literary characteristics of the Johannine books. Applying these to the Fourth Gospel, he concluded that no continuous sources could be distinguished from the Evangelist's work on a basis of diverse linguistic or stylistic data.[10] Ten years after Bultmann's commentary appeared, Ruckstuhl applied and extended Schweizer's critical methods to dispute Bultmann's separation of sources.[11] Soon after, a Scandinavian scholar, Bent Noack, published a monograph also containing a repudiation of the grounds upon which Bultmann established his hypothetical sources. "It is fair to say," writes Moody Smith, "that Ruckstuhl's elaboration of Schweizer's style-statistical method and his application of it to Bultmann's separation of sources have raised serious questions about Bultmann's procedure and results."[12]

Smith also calls attention to a basic methodological question. In view of the demonstrable stylistic unity of the Fourth Gospel, "the crucial question at issue between Ruckstuhl and Bultmann concerns the extent to which the evangelist could have imposed his own style upon the source material or imitated the stylistic characteristics of the sources". Bultmann believes that such unity as the Gospel manifests may be accounted for by supposing that the Evangelist imitated and worked over his material. While this possibility cannot be denied, it is reasonable to doubt that such editing "should have resulted in a random distribution throughout the sources of stylistic characteristics such as Ruckstuhl and Schweizer have adduced". If, indeed, the Evangelist assimilated the sources to his own style, does it not follow that the task of source criticism becomes problematic, and "any results must be regarded as highly questionable"?[13] Charles Goodwin has shown that when John uses a source we can check on, namely, the Old Testament, he accommodates everything to his own purposes.[14] If we did not have before us the texts of the Old Testament to which John alludes, it is obvious that we could not reconstruct the originals. Is it not unreasonable, therefore, to suppose that one is able to reconstruct sources otherwise unknown, at least with such assurance as Bultmann claims?

In fairness to Bultmann it must be recognized that he does not claim certainty for all his results. Yet it is evident that his assignment of passages in John to various sources is a crucial step in his exegesis. The uncertainty of his procedures and results casts doubt upon all hopes that source criticism will provide a major thoroughfare in the search for the theology of the Fourth Evangelist. Doubtless the problem of the sources will continue to have relevance to the exegesis of John. Yet, after the relative failure of Bultmann's prodigious effort, source criticism cannot any longer claim priority, as Haenchen has observed.[15]

Within the purpose and scope of this article it is not possible to discuss adequately Bultmann's "ecclesiastical redactor" hypothesis. This material is identified primarily by means of theological analysis. Contextual questions are given secondary consideration. An appeal is seldom made to stylistic criteria. Instead, Bultmann assumes that the Fourth Evangelist is both a consistent and an original thinker and that, where specific passages would seem to be incompatible with the leading ideas in the Gospel, there is reason to suspect editorial interpolation. Moreover, when these suspected passages closely correspond to the conventionally orthodox interests reflected in Christian writers of the early second century, Bultmann feels justified in denying that these views have any place in the theology of the Fourth Evangelist.

To the ecclesiastical redactor are assigned four major types of emendation: (1) ideas relating to a sacramental appropriation of the saving work of Christ; (2) passages proclaiming a futurist eschatology in terms of Jewish-Christian apocalypticism; (3) verses harmonizing John's Gospel with the Synoptics; and (4) statements laying claim to apostolic and eyewitness authority.

In order to support his intricate redaction theory, Bultmann assumes a heavy burden of proof. Having followed his exegesis of each suspected passage, the present writer concludes that most of his arguments fall short of being convincing. John's sacramental interest is far too pervasive to be eliminated by the excision of the several passages Bultmann denies to him. The problem of the juxtaposition of a realized eschatology and a futurist eschatology in the Fourth Gospel may be solved in other, more defensible ways than by Bultmann's resolution of the tension, as will be observed later. The rest of the material assigned to redaction appears neither to be consistent nor to justify the motives that are alleged for its inclusion.

A more reasonable alternative to Bultmann's theory – or to any other claiming that the Evangelist's theology has undergone significant revision – is the conclusion that the writer was himself the principal "ecclesiastical editor" of Johannine traditions. However uncertain our knowledge of the particular sources he used and of their origin, and however obscure the circumstances surrounding the composition of his Gospel, we may believe that congenial materials were incorporated.[16] The elimination from the Gospel of the several passages that may be attributed, with some confidence, to redaction by other hands affects but slightly the task of theological reconstruction.[17]

III

A third door beckoned many researchers in the early years of this century. Through it one entered the fascinating corridor of the history of religions. Blocked in their search for the identity of the

Fourth Evangelist and perplexed by the uncertain results of source criticism, scholars began a systematic exploration of the cultural *milieu* of the author. Their question was: What intellectual environment had influenced the theology of the Evangelist as well as nurtured the felt needs of his readers?[18]

Explorers in this corridor reported that alternative routes soon appeared. The first sign-post read "Judaism", the second, "Hellenism". Many scholars who probed this complex maze claimed that the second of the two routes seemed more promising since the Evangelist – according to tradition – had been situated in a center of Hellenistic Christianity. But this latter route seemed itself to open in various directions. Some found that the books of the Alexandrian Jewish philosopher Philo provided illuminating parallels; others sorted the miscellaneous materials of the Hermetic Corpus for affinities; still others looked backwards from second- and third-century references to "gnostic" views to find in John the beginning of these speculative heresiologies.

Meanwhile, the alleged Jewishness of John's Gospel – reflected in its traditions and in the apparent direction of its apologetic – led others to explore the alternative route. Hugo Odeberg ransacked extant haggadic materials that revealed a mystical piety similar to that manifested in John. He discovered that the Johannine writings pay attention to Old Testament texts of importance for Jewish Merkabah mysticism, and that the Fourth Evangelist used similar exegetical methods.[19] Other scholars were encouraged by their studies of Judaica to revive the older view that the Fourth Gospel was intended for Jews of the Diaspora.[20] The wisdom books of Hellenistic Judaism were quarried for background materials.

The pioneer work of C. H. Dodd and of Bultmann gave prescience, in quite different ways, that those who travelled paths that seemed mutually exclusive, would actually converge upon a common area and benefit from a shared discovery. Dodd placed the Gospel against the background of what he called "the higher religion of Hellenism", and found approximations to John's theology in the Hermetica and, to a lesser degree, in Philo. According to Dodd, the Fourth Gospel was intended primarily for non-Christians concerned about eternal life who might be ready to follow the Christian way were it presented to them in terms "intelligibly related to their previous religious interests and experience".[21] While Dodd reacts to a too-exclusive

stress upon an Old Testament and Jewish background to the Gospel –
a reaction in favor of a stronger Hellenistic outlook – he is ready to
admit that John's traditions may have been selected in such a way as
to provoke the reflection of Jews of the Diaspora. Dodd writes: "The
Evangelist shows himself to be deeply versed in Judaism . . . his
mind moves with equal freedom in the Jewish and in the Hellenistic
ways of thought . . . as though both were native to him, so that they
are deeply fused into a theology that is neither Jewish nor Greek,
but intelligible from both sides."[23]

As early as 1925 Bultmann was attempting to explain the phrase-
ology common to Johannine, Ignatian, and Syrian mysticism by
postulating a common origin in gnostic mythology. He claimed that
a gnostic-dualistic thought arose in Persia in pre-Christian times,
spread westward, and left deposits on the soil of Palestine and Syria.
The Odes of Solomon, as well as certain texts preserved by Mandean
and Manichean sectarians, were valued by Bultmann as sources for
recovering the gnostic mythology presupposed by John.[24]

The effort to derive John's thought from Oriental Gnosticism
seemed far afield from its presupposed Jewish or Hellenistic proven-
ance, but in Palestine the Qumran manuscripts were found. These
scrolls provided documentary evidence for what some would call "a
pre-Christian, gnosticizing Judaism". Moreover, the remarkable
discoveries at Nag Hamadi shed further light on the problem of the
relation between the Fourth Gospel and Gnosticism. These texts
offered support for the existence of an early Christianity of a gnostic
type, containing both Jewish and non-Jewish ideas.[25] However, the
discoveries at Nag Hamadi have cast doubt upon the adequacy of
Bultmann's theory that the "Gnostic Redeemer Myth" was prevalent
at the time John wrote, and upon his claim that the structure of
John's christology is patterned upon this pagan mythology.[26]

It cannot now be said that the history-of-religions research has
fully illumined the background of John's theology, although much
progress may be claimed. Several premature judgments have been
refuted by this research. No longer can John's thought be considered
"an acute Hellenization" of the Gospel that is far-removed geo-
graphically and intellectually from the Palestinian world of Jesus and
of the early church. Nor can John's theology be reduced to one
esoteric "school" and assumed to be intelligible only within a
severely limited circle of ideas. The theology of John cannot be

straight-jacketed, so to speak, into some sectarianism of the second-century world. It has been shown that John was sensitive to several currents of thought widely influential in his age, and that one must be wary of all efforts to reduce everything in the Gospel to a single, pre-existing pattern of ideas. The more thorough the comparisons between John's Gospel and the relevant literature of his time, the more impressive the evidence for the originality of its theology and of its specifically Christian content.

IV

Concluding observations are made from the vantage point of a fourth doorway into the Johannine labyrinth, a door that may be labeled "theme research". Some persons who have explored the *religionsgeschichtlich* maze have found their way here, or discovered that their corridor led into this promising passage. Concepts or themes appearing in extraneous sources, some involving recent discoveries, have seemed proximate to those in John and have appeared to shed light on the latter's meaning.

The term *Logos* with its vagrant nuances still provides for some interpreters the indispensable key to John's christology. Alternatively, others agree that in the theme of Spirit-Paraclete one discovers the leading, unifying concept.[27] Neither of these terms unlocks the secrets of John's proclamation concerning Jesus the Messiah. Yet as related themes they are mutually illuminating. Against the background of the *dabar Yahweh* of the Old Testament, enriched by the Wisdom theology of ancient Judaism, John proclaims the self-revelation of God in Creation, but more especially in Israel's history up to and including the one "on whom the Spirit descended and remained . . . Jesus the son of Joseph from Nazareth" (1:33, 45). Subsequently John affirms that the *paracletos* is God, revealing himself through Christ the crucified-exalted one. Jesus Christ baptizes with the Holy Spirit; and in union with his own he leads them "into all truth" and "declares the things that are to come" (1:33*b*; 16:13).

The imagery of the inspired or inspirited Word, made flesh in Jesus, finally enlightening and judging men who walk in darkness, focuses the distinctive *heilgeschichtilich* perspective of the Fourth Gospel. Yet it is unlikely that this cluster of themes reveals the Evangelist's special contribution. Instead, one may find reflected in them a *Gemeindetheologie*, the conceptual world of John's Christian community. This is certainly the conclusion if the view of many scholars carries conviction that the Prologue and the Paraclete passages were once independent of the Gospel, having been composed by forerunners or more probably by disciples of the Evangelist.[28]

Some scholars claim that the eschatology of the Fourth Gospel affords the open-sesame required. John's originality as an early Christian thinker is manifested in his reinterpretations of such traditional eschatological terminology as "the last day", "in that day", "eternal life", "resurrection", and "the judgment". Especially noteworthy are John's repeated phrase, "the hour is coming and now is" (4:23; 5:25), and the many references to Christ's "going" and "coming" in the farewell discourses (Chaps. 13–17). Dodd and Bultmann have skilfully explicated an element of the theology of the Evangelist called his "realized eschatology".

Within the experience of the church, and probably under the influence of pre-gnostic thought, John does offer a reinterpretation of Christian eschatology. More explicitly than elsewhere in the New Testament, prominence is given to those aspects of biblical hope which are already fulfilled in and through Jesus the Messiah (3:18; 5:24; 12:31; 16:11, etc.). Yet in the text of the Gospel there are references to what is yet to come, to what is not yet completed. For example, the old conception of the Son of Man as final judge stands beside the assertion that the judgment is a present reality. Bultmann, as noted earlier, denies this futurist eschatology to the Evangelist. But the attribution of these passages to "ecclesiastical redaction" is no more satisfactory a solution to the problem than is the supposition that the Evangelist was merely accommodating himself to a traditional language that no longer held theological significance for him. The correct solution would seem to be that the difference between John's eschatology and that of one or another of the Synoptists is one of emphasis rather than substance. As Eduard Schweizer has written, the "Evangelist did, in a new environment with its new questions, just what the original proclamation had done in Palestine. He preached Jesus Christ as the one who decided everything here and now. And because he made this proclamation so clearly and decisively, the hearer also understood that he had received in Jesus Christ not only [life in the present] but also the fulfilment in glory

which the Son has with the Father. . . . John taught a realized eschatology that is *necessarily* an eschatology that will also be realized in
the future."[29] (Cf. 14:2 f.; 17:24; also 12:44–50.)

The studies of C. F. D. Moule and of Alf Corell have significantly
illuminated this special understanding of the eschatological tension
of the early church. Moule has shown that the only "realized
eschatology" in the Fourth Gospel is on the individual level. Insofar
as there is any "coming" in the near future, essentially it is not a
world-wide manifestation but a secret, private coming to Christ's
own. Rather than replacing a futurist eschatology in a collective or
corporate sense, these intimate "comings" are only the correlative
of that future.[30]

Corell affirms that "the Johannine eschatology will remain misunderstood or a matter of doubt until we discover the 'collective',
that is, the Church in the Fourth Gospel".[31] Along with Schweizer,
and Nils Dahl, Corell has greatly assisted students of John's ecclesiology in making this important discovery.

Reflection upon the Fourth Evangelist's eschatology leads to a
consideration of his understanding of the church, and its mission,
but also, we may note, of his soteriology – the conception of Christ
as Redeemer who gives to those who believe in him "life eternal". Are
we perhaps to find in this concept of "life" or "eternal life" the
controlling theme of the Gospel? When due regard is given to the
Evangelist's own statement of purpose in 20:31, one may lean
toward an affirmative answer. Yet to speak of John as "the Gospel
of Life" is to give attention to its emphasis on the effect or consequence of Christ's coming, while neglecting its cause or purpose.
Clearly, the Fourth Gospel seeks to confirm faith, to assure believers
that they have eternal life. Eternal life, however, consists in having
knowledge of the one true God and of him whom he has "sent"
(17:3). John proclaims Jesus the Messiah to be the unique Son of
the Father, because it may be said of him that he is "sent" by God's
love into the world. Thus the authority of Jesus as the Son appears
to be a more basic theme.

This explains perhaps the Evangelist's extensive use of juridical or
forensic terminology. The idea of witness is joined to that of sending,
and the witness is to what has been seen or heard – to what is known
and is therefore true. These juridical themes are curiously interwoven with each other. None of them is capable of being explained

in isolation, yet they run together, converging towards the Person of him whose words culminate in those sovereign formulae, ἐγώ εἰμι. Perhaps it is this convergence that makes John's thought so resistant to systematic analysis yet gives coherence to all his christological statements.

John the Baptist, also "a man sent from God", bears witness to the true light, to the one who ranks before him (1:8; 3:28). But Jesus is "sent into the world to bear witness to the truth" (18:37). He bears witness – as one who has come from heaven – to what he has seen, to what no other has ever seen (3:11 f.). The works God has given the Messiah to perform also bear witness to the Messiah, as do the Scriptures. Both testify to his authority (5:13 ff.).

"Sending" therefore means that Jesus' authority is founded upon God's authority, for the Son came into the world to do the Father's will (4:34; 5:30, etc.), to do the works of God, and to say what he was commanded to say (3:34; 12:49). "Sending" therefore means also that Jesus does not seek his own glory but that of the Father (7:18), and that everyone who believes in Jesus and accepts his words – his commandment – believes, at the same time, in the Father who sent him (5:23 f.; 12:44 f.).

Yet what Jesus accomplished (19:30) is proclaimed as only a beginning. The *paracletos*, who is sent to the disciples, teaches them everything, and reminds them continually of what Jesus has said (14:26; 15:26). This Spirit-Paraclete is not only a special gift to the disciples; the Spirit will also convince "the world" of "sin, righteousness, and judgment". And this conviction takes place only through the proclamation of Jesus as the Christ. Thus, the Son continues his work of bestowing life or declaring judgment. The disciples, who act upon his authority, witness to his work and words (4:35 ff.; 15:27). So also in the Fourth Gospel the sending of the disciples is joined to the bestowal of the Spirit (20:21–23). The Evangelist declares that the glorified Son, the exalted Lord of the church, and his witnessing disciples jointly participate in the eschatological harvest, in which sower and reapers rejoice together (4:35 ff.).[32]

Théo Preiss, the French Reformed scholar, calls attention to this complex of ideas, designated by him as "the jurical mysticism" of John's theology. Nils Dahl and others have found in this terminology the distinctive formulation of the Evangelist's Christian theology. But no simple pattern emerges from this perspective. There is undoubtedly something elusive about the thought of the Fourth Evangelist. "In a style of grandiose monotony, it develops a few unchanging themes. Looked at closely, its poverty is extreme, like those melodies of only three of four notes. And yet on this reduced keyboard we hear a music of infinitely varied harmonies, each note evoking so many reverberations that even the most attentive ear cannot capture them all at once."[33] It is this peculiar combination of simplicity and profundity, product of the Evangelist's mind and experience rather than the complex literary history of his Gospel, that renders inadequate most – if not all – of the restatements of John's theology.

NOTES

1. G. Ebeling, "The Meaning of 'Biblical Theology'", *Journal of Theological Studies*, N.S., Vol. VI, Pt. 2 (October 1955), pp. 222 f.

2. *New Testament Theology Today* (New York, Herder & Herder, 1963), pp. 92 f., 106.

3. *The Spiritual Gospel* (Cambridge, Cambridge University Press, 1960), pp. 10 f.

4. See A, Wikenhauser, *New Testament Introduction* (New York, Herder & Herder, 1963), p. 302.

5. Titus and Colwell, *The Gospel of the Spirit* (New York, Harper & Bros., 1953). See especially, Titus, *The Message of the Fourth Gospel* (New York–Nashville, Abingdon Press, 1957), pp. 20–25.

6. Wikenhauser, *op. cit.*, p. 301.

7. *The Gospel According to John* (London, SPCK, 1955). See the summary of dependence theories in *Introduction to the New Testament*, founded by P. Feine and J. Behm, completely re-edited by W. G. Kümmel, trans. A. J. Mattill, Jr. (New York–Nashville, Abingdon Press, 1965), pp. 144 f.

8. For a clear statement of the "features of the Gospel that offer difficulty for any theory of unified authorship" and a summary of "possible solutions", see R. E. Brown, *The Gospel According to John* (The Anchor Bible, Vol. 29) (New York, Doubleday & Co., 1966), pp. xxiv ff.

9. *Ibid.*, pp. xxix f.

10. *Ego Eimi* (Göttingen, Vandenhoeck and Ruprecht, 1939).

11. E. Ruckstuhl, *Die literarische Einheit des Johannes-evangeliums* (Freiburg (Schweiz), Paulus-Verlag, 1951).

12. Smith, *The Composition and Order of the Fourth Gospel* (New Haven, Yale University Press, 1966), p. 107.

13. *Ibid.*, p. 108.

14. "How Did John Treat His Sources?", *Journal of Biblical Literature*, Vol. LXXIII (1954), pp. 61 ff.

15. As noted in Smith, *op. cit.*, pp. 114 f.

16. The stylistic objections against the source theories noted above are inapplicable when it is supposed that the edited material is introduced by the original author.

17. Note here the interesting hypothesis of R. E. Brown that two editions of the Gospel were prepared by the Evangelist and a final redaction accomplished by a disciple. This theory preserves "the substantial unity of the Gospel" while explaining "the various factors that militate against unity of authorship" (*op. cit.*, pp. xxxiv–xxxix).

18. Wikenhauser, *op. cit.*, pp. 309 ff.

19. *The Fourth Gospel* (Uppsala–Stockholm, Almquist & Wiksells, 1929). See also N. A. Dahl, "The Johannine Church and History", in *Current Issues in New Testament Interpretation*, ed. by Klassen and Snyder (New York, Harper & Bros., 1962), pp. 124 ff.

20. J. A. T. Robinson, "The Destination and Purpose of St. John's Gospel", in *Twelve New Testament Studies* (Naperville, Ill., Allenson, 1962), pp. 107 ff.

21. *The Interpretation of the Fourth Gospel* (Cambridge, Cambridge University Press, 1953), p. 9.

22. See W. Grossouw, "Three Books on the Fourth Gospel", *Novum Testamentum*, Vol. I (1956), p. 38.

23. "History and Doctrine of the Apostolic Age", *A Companion to the Bible*, ed. by T. W. Manson (Edinburgh, T. & T. Clark, 1946), pp. 411 f.

24. "Die Bedeutung der neuerschlossenen mandäischen und manichaeischen Quellen für das Verständnis des Johannesevangeliums", *Zeitschrift für die neutestamentliche Wissenschaft*, Vol. 24 (1925), pp. 100 ff. See also W. Bauer, *Das Johannesevangelium*, 2te Aufl. (Tübingen, J. C. B. Mohr (Paul Siebeck), 1925).

25. See W. G. Kümmel's *Introduction*, *op. cit.*, pp. 154 ff.

26. See R. A. Brown, *op. cit.*, pp. liv ff.

27. Cf. Titus and Colwell, *op. cit.*, chap. 3. See also H. G. Wood, "The Present Position of New Testament Theology", *New Testament Studies*, Vol. 4 (1958), pp. 162 ff.

28. E.g. R. A. Brown, *op. cit.*, pp. xxxvi ff.

29. "Orthodox Proclamation", *Interpretation*, Vol. VIII (1954), p. 395.

30. "The Individualism of the Fourth Gospel", *Novum Testamentum*, Vol. 5 (1962), pp. 171 ff.

31. *Consummatum Est: Eschatology and Church in the Gospel of St. John* (New York, The Macmillan Company, 1958), pp. 2 f.; E. Schweizer, "The Concept of the Church in St. John", *New Testament Essays*, ed. by A. J. B. Higgins (Manchester, Manchester University Press, 1959), pp. 240 ff.; N. A. Dahl, "The Johannine Church and History", *op. cit.*, pp. 124 ff.

32. Ferdinand Hahn, *Mission in the New Testament*, trans. by F. Clarke (Naperville, Ill., Allenson, 1965), pp. 157 ff.

33. "Justification in John's Thought", *Life in Christ* (Naperville, Ill., Allenson, 1952), p. 10.

Sem. 1

A Barb. Soc. In The West

B The Age of Enlightenm

C Russian State + Soc . &

Sem. 2

A - The Formation of Western Soc.

B Life + Lab . In 18th C. Eng

c Soviet State & Soc.